"Team members are the heart and soul of any organization today, and the global pandemic highlighted the need for resiliency among every team. *Unbreakable* provides information that leaders can operationalize effectively with their teams to help them face any challenge or adversity presented to them in the complex world of business. I spent twenty years in the military and several years in the corporate space; this book is an invaluable resource that acts as an operator's manual on leading and equipping others to face adversity."
—Matt Bumgarner, Strategic HR Partner, Tyson Foods

"Today's teams are working more remotely than ever before, making it more challenging for them to build the kind of resilience they need to innovate and thrive in the face of rampant volatility. Kirkman and Stoverink provide much-needed guidance for building resilience in teams whose members rarely interact in traditional face-to-face ways. *Unbreakable* provides an essential, research-informed guide for leaders who are responsible for motivating complex work teams."
—Jennifer A. Chatman, Paul J. Cortese Distinguished Professor of Management, University of California, Berkeley

"You only thought you knew what made teams resilient in the face of adversity. *Unbreakable* will make you question some of your strongest assumptions regarding how to build resilience in teams and, as a result, unchain you from the stale leadership tactics that simply fall short."
—Kirk Thompson, Chairman, J.B. Hunt Transport, Inc.

"If we've learned anything during the global pandemic, it is the importance of people and the teams in which they work to be resilient in the face of adversity. Using a blend of an evidence-based approach with lots of practical examples, *Unbreakable* provides today's leaders with the step-by-step actions they need to take to make sure their teams can collectively withstand any adversity that comes their way."
—Daniel Cable, Professor of Organizational Behavior, London Business School, author of *Alive at Work* and *Exceptional*

"The skills and competencies that get you promoted into a team leadership role are not enough to ensure your success in that role. *Unbreakable* is a must-read for all professionals that want a tried-and-true approach for making the leap from star performer to star leader."
—Erin R. Moody, Director, Partner Management, Warner Bros. Discovery

UNBREAKABLE

UNBREAKABLE

BUILDING AND LEADING

RESILIENT TEAMS

Bradley L. Kirkman

and Adam C. Stoverink

STANFORD BUSINESS BOOKS
An Imprint of Stanford University Press
Stanford, California

Stanford University Press
Stanford, California

Special discounts for bulk quantities of Stanford Business Books are available to corporations, professional associations, and other organizations. For details and discount information, contact the special sales department of Stanford University Press. Tel: (650) 725–0820, Fax: (650) 725–3457

Printed in the United States of America on acid-free, archival-quality paper

Library of Congress Cataloging-in-Publication Data

Names: Kirkman, Bradley Lane, author. | Stoverink, Adam C., author.
Title: Unbreakable : building and leading resilient teams / Bradley L. Kirkman and Adam C. Stoverink.
Description: Stanford, California : Stanford Business Books, an imprint of Stanford University Press, 2023. | Includes bibliographical references and index.
Identifiers: LCCN 2022014101 (print) | LCCN 2022014102 (ebook) | ISBN 9781503629301 (cloth) | ISBN 9781503634299 (ebook)
Subjects: LCSH: Teams in the workplace. | Organizational resilience. | Leadership.
Classification: LCC HD66 .K5755 2023 (print) | LCC HD66 (ebook) | DDC 658.4/022—dc23/eng/20220825
LC record available at https://lccn.loc.gov/2022014101
LC ebook record available at https://lccn.loc.gov/2022014102

Cover Design: Jason Anscomb
Cover Image: Shutterstock

For Allison, one of the most resilient people I have ever known.—Brad
For Heather and Alivia, whom I love with all my heart.—Adam

For all the frontline workers worldwide, who demonstrated extreme resilience during the COVID-19 pandemic and beyond, we cannot thank you enough.

CONTENTS

ACKNOWLEDGMENTS

This book would not have been possible without the influence and friendship of the many colleagues with whom we have shared our team leadership journey over the years. We are forever grateful to Murray Barrick, Brad Bell, Gilad Chen, John Cordery, Stephen Courtright, Tobias Dennerlein, Michele Gelfand, Cristina Gibson, Lucy Gilson, Ricky Griffin, John Hollenbeck, Laura Huang, Jeff Pollack, Steve Kozlowski, Kevin Lowe, John Mathieu, Travis Maynard, Tammy Rapp, Ben Rosen, Sara Rynes, Debra Shapiro, Payal Sharma, Paul Tesluk, Anne Tsui, Elizabeth Umphress, Daan van Knippenberg, and Matthew Waller.

We also want to give credit to a set of big thinkers whom we have long admired and who have had such a tremendous impact on our thinking and writing about teams (as this book attests). We are especially indebted to Amy Edmondson and Karl Weick, and to those who are no longer with us: Sigal Barsade and Tom Lee.

From Brad Kirkman: I also wanted to give thanks to my former PhD students, including Richard Gardner, Alex Glosenberg, Brad Harris, Kwanghyun (Harry) Kim, Ning Li, Sal Mistry, Troy Smith, Adam Stoverink (my coauthor of this book), and Maria del Carmen Triana.

From Adam Stoverink: I'm especially grateful to my parents, David and Linda Stoverink, for instilling in me a personal sense of resilience and a passion for learning; to Matt Stoverink for being a great older brother, modeling what success looks like, and putting up with my many shenanigans during our upbringing (and beyond); to Mary Beth Marrs and Daniel Turban for inspiring me to become a business professor; and to my many friends who have played a significant role in shaping me into the person I am today, including Beth Baker, Michael Cantu, Justin Diller, Emilija Djurdjevic, Bart Ellefritz, Brad Harris, Eric Huston, Joel Koopman, Jason Quinn, and George Toubekis. And a special thanks goes out to Brad Kirkman, my dissertation adviser and coauthor of this book, for lighting my way into the wonderful world of academia.

We would also like to thank two anonymous reviewers for their invaluable feedback on the book, and Steve Catalano for his excellent editorial guidance throughout the writing process. We also owe special thanks to Madison Rye for assisting with the research for this book.

RESEARCH APPROACH

The ideas for *Unbreakable* are a culmination of over forty years of combined research, consulting, and teaching. What we present here is very evidence based. We have been fortunate enough to work with thousands of extraordinary team leaders and members in hundreds of companies on five different continents. We include our own joint research, research with our many wonderful colleagues, as well as research that we thought important to share but in which we were not direct participants. Our research approach consisted of many different techniques, including qualitative observations and interviews, quantitative survey analyses, field studies, and laboratory experiments. The team leaders and teams we studied come from a wide variety of industries, including (but not limited to) software development and other high-tech firms, manufacturing, insurance, governmental agencies, energy, telecommunications, home improvement, biotechnology, and aluminum production.

UNBREAKABLE

CHAPTER 1

TRAGEDY AT MANN GULCH

Fire. Everywhere.[1]

On August 5, 1949, high above Montana's Helena National Forest, sixteen smokejumpers readied themselves in their C-47 airplane, parachutes strapped tightly, waiting for the signal to jump. They were called to battle a raging wildfire in an area known as Mann Gulch. As the plane circled overhead, R. Wagner "Wag" Dodge, the crew foreman, and Earl Cooley, the spotter, lay side by side near the door, communicating quietly through their headphones and peering through binoculars for a safe place to jump.

The assistant spotter proceeded to drop a bright-orange "drift chute." From the distance and direction that the wind blew the chute, he could determine how far ahead of the fire he should instruct the smokejumpers to exit the plane. A landing zone was identified on the side of the gulch not yet engulfed by flames. The men were packed tightly together as they stood up and moved toward the door of the plane. A twelve-foot-long static line connected the smokejumpers' parachutes to the plane, so that when each man fell twelve feet, the line automatically opened the parachute. As the foreman customarily did, Dodge leaped out of the airplane first. The drop to the ground took only about a minute. After Dodge, the fourteen other smokejumpers (one of the original sixteen men who was supposed to jump became sick due to the strong turbulence, returned to base with the pilot, and immediately resigned from the smokejumpers) exited the plane and rocketed down to the ground within a half mile of the rapidly expanding fire.

The landing was rough. Most of the men were dragged by their chutes over sharp rocks, but miraculously, almost all escaped serious injury. Only Dodge cut his elbow, and despite that the cut went all way to the bone, there was little blood and it was easily bandaged. Once on the ground, they met up with James Harrison, who worked as a fireguard in the nearby Meriwether Canyon campground and had been fighting the fire alone for about four hours. Harrison knew firsthand the excitement and trepidation that the smokejumpers felt, as he had just retired as a smokejumper himself the year before, in large part because he knew the risks associated with the job and because he wanted to please his mother, who told him it was too dangerous. With the addition of Harrison, the fire crew had a sixteenth man back and was complete and ready to do battle.

The first order of business was to gather up all the cargo that was being dropped from the plane in separate parachutes after the men landed and would likely be scattered across an area of several hundred square yards. But just as they set out to collect their belongings, the crew heard a booming crash about a quarter mile down the canyon from their landing area. They soon discovered that the parachute for their radio had failed to deploy, and the sound they heard was said radio smashing into the ground. Better the radio than a person, the men must have thought. They would have known in that moment the tough reality that they were cut off completely from the outside world and could rely only upon one another as they set out to fight the Mann Gulch fire.

Once they retrieved the cargo, the fire crew headed down into the gulch in the direction of the Missouri River. From the air, it was clear that the fire (which was later determined to have started when lightning struck a dead tree) was located on the ridge between Mann Gulch and Meriwether Canyon and was burning partway down the Mann Gulch side but not yet into Meriwether. Without much warning, and as is often the case with Western wildfires, a sudden shift in the wind caused the fire to expand rapidly, which had the unfortunate effect of cutting off the crew's planned route. Although the men didn't know it at the time, later reports suggested that what was a fifty- to sixty-acre fire when the crew arrived had expanded to over three thousand acres in little more than ten minutes. This meant a massive and somewhat unforeseen intensity in the heat and smoke that accompanied the fire. And to make matters worse for the crew, the heat from the fire was dangerously amplified by the scorching ambient temperature of ninety-seven degrees, the result of an oppressive heat wave that had produced the hottest day on record for the Helena area to that date.

After Dodge and Harrison returned from a reconnaissance mission at the front of the fire, Dodge barked out instructions to William Hellman, his squad leader and second-in-command, to take the rest of the crew to the northern side of the gulch and then lead them down the canyon to the river. He also instructed Hellman not to take the crew down to the very bottom of the gulch but to have them "follow the contour" on the other side of the slope, ostensibly so they could keep an eye on the main body of the fire and thus remain safe. Unfortunately, in the heat and the smoke, the crew got separated by a wide distance and became confused. They ended up in two groups over five hundred feet apart and could not see one another, which had the effect of obscuring from each group whether the other was in front or behind. One of the problems with Hellman leading at this point was that the foreman (in this case, Dodge) was typically at the front of the crew leading the team, with the second-in-command at the back. But the roles were reversed, at least for Hellman.

Dodge decided that the conditions were worsening, and so he and Harrison made their way back toward Hellman and the crew. Once they reached them, Dodge retook the lead and began guiding the crew toward the river. Dodge led the crew for about five minutes down the gulch, and even though he was starting to get very worried, he didn't think he should create panic by sharing his concerns. Instead, his focus was on moving his crew to safety.

Suddenly, Dodge saw something terrifying. The fire had actually crossed Mann Gulch and was racing up the ridge straight for his men. Two of the crew members, Walter Rumsey and Robert Sallee, reported not seeing it, which meant that none of the crew likely saw it either. With only a 150- to 200-yard head start on the fire coming for them, Dodge reversed direction and started going back up the canyon away from the river, aiming for the top of the ridge. Many in the crew did not understand this abrupt about-face, as they did not see what Dodge had seen. Dodge loudly ordered the men to immediately drop the tools they were carrying so that they could start to run—and fast. At that point, the fire was only a hundred yards behind them. In the chaos that ensued, Dodge noted that, although some of the men quickly rid themselves of their packs and tools, others refused to do so. One of the men, David Navon, had even stopped to take pictures of the fire, perhaps contributing to a sense of complacency or a feeling that all was well, given that someone was taking time to photograph the approaching fire.

But all was not well. A look of dread came over the crew members as they realized that the fire was fast closing in on them. Dodge concluded that his men were not going to make the remaining two hundred yards up to the ridge in time to escape. Up ahead, Dodge rushed to build a small "escape fire." The object of such a fire is to burn an area that an approaching fire would move around. Dodge kept yelling at his men, "This way! This way!" to get them to run toward this safe area, sure in the knowledge that this move would save everyone from imminent danger. It is believed that some of the men were so far away that they never heard Dodge's commands. Those who were close enough to hear were confused by his actions, as setting a fire intentionally is normally done to create a backfire, or a fire line designed to cut off an advancing fire, which wouldn't have been done in this case because there was not enough time. Sallee recalls thinking that Dodge must have gone nuts, as he questioned why the foreman would run ahead of his crew only to actually light a new fire in front of the fire he had ordered his men to try to escape! This was something no one had ever seen in the history of the Forest Service. None of these men could fathom what Dodge was up to, and they decided they did not want any part of it. In fact, one of the men shouted, "To hell with that! I'm getting out of here." The men ignored Dodge's calls and made a run for it to the top of the ridge. Running to a ridgetop was a commonly accepted maneuver taught to every smokejumper because the rocks and shale cannot serve as fuel for fire, and winds often meet at the top and dissipate. At this point, however, Dodge figured the men had only about thirty seconds before the fire overtook them. He knew the ridge was too far to reach in that short time.

In the confusion and the swirling smoke and fire, the separation between the men grew. A small group of men jumped out in front, somewhat close to Dodge's escape fire. The rest of the men were several paces behind and spread out in a line that measured approximately a hundred yards. Rumsey, Sallee, and a third man, Eldon Diettert, were in the lead group and ran as fast as they could toward the safety of the ridge. As they neared the top, they realized they weren't going to make it. Suddenly, they saw a "reef" between them and the ridge. A reef is an exposed piece of ancient ocean bottom that serves as a barrier and keeps the ridge from eroding. The men knew that if they were to survive, they would have to find an opening in that reef. In a fortunate stroke of serendipity, the smoke lifted just enough to spot a breach and then again to help guide their way. Sallee was first through the crevice and immediately felt the temperature drop a bit. Rumsey was next through the opening. Sadly, Diettert didn't make it. He died on his nineteenth birthday. Sallee recalled that no one could have made it out alive if they had left Dodge even just a few seconds after they did.

Rumsey and Sallee reasoned that Dodge must have been setting a buffer fire to slow the main fire down, but again, the timing of such a maneuver was confusing. Besides, Dodge was setting this new fire only two hundred yards from the top of the ridge, which they thought he should have been able to reach had he been running. From the reef, Rumsey and Sallee were shocked as they recalled seeing Dodge lying face down in the hot ash created by his escape fire, his mouth covered with a handkerchief he wetted with water from his canteen, waiting for the main fire to move around him. Dodge later recalled that when the roaring fire went over him, he felt his body lift off the ground several times. A short while later, Rumsey and Sallee saw the outline of Dodge slowly appear through the billowing smoke, exhausted but alive. Rumsey and Sallee then attempted to look for other survivors, but the intense heat cut short their efforts, and they returned wordless and despondent back to Dodge.

Thirteen smokejumpers died at Mann Gulch that day. During the recovery mission, Harrison's wristwatch was found with its hands melted at exactly 5:56 p.m., which was believed to be the time at which the flames overtook the crew. The events above are eloquently described in greater detail in Norman Maclean's phenomenal work of nonfiction, *Young Men and Fire* (Maclean also wrote *A River Runs through It*, which was made into a Hollywood film directed by Robert Redford).

The Mann Gulch disaster highlights the crucial role that resilience plays in a team's success and the forces that make a team *unbreakable*. For the team of smokejumpers, resilience could have saved their lives that day.

Regardless of whether your teams face life-or-death scenarios, they are sure to face adversity in some form. In today's volatile, uncertain, complex, and ambiguous (often abbreviated *VUCA*) business environments, all teams do. How well your team responds to that adversity will depend on its resilience.

WHAT IS RESILIENCE, AND WHY IS IT SO IMPORTANT FOR TODAY'S TEAMS?

In our work with many teams and organizations over the years, we have developed a definition of team resilience, which is a team's capacity to bounce back from a setback that results in a loss of valuable team processes.[2] Let's take each of the three parts—capacity, bounce back, setback—of that definition in turn. A setback occurs when critical team processes start to deteriorate. By team processes, we're referring to what are generally known as "action" processes, because they take place when teams are attempting to complete their tasks or when they are, in essence, "in action." These are the activities that are directly tied to successfully reaching goals, and so not surprisingly, when these processes start to break down, team performance takes a hit. That hit is a setback.

There are three important action processes every team must perform to accomplish its goals. First, a team must have effective coordination processes. These are activities that enable a team to orchestrate the sequencing and timing of its activities. For firefighter crews like those battling the Mann Gulch fire, coordination is absolutely essential. All team members must know their own roles and how they fit with all the other members' roles. Of course, not everyone will be assigned to pumping stations, just like not everyone will be the primary lead on the hoses used to extinguish fires. Moreover, timing is everything when fighting a fire, as the Mann Gulch example sadly showed. How the crew members sequence everything they do ultimately determines how successful they will be in putting out fires, literally and figuratively.

The second key team process is monitoring, which refers to team members' keeping an eye on one another, tracking and communicating progress toward goals, making all team members aware of what needs to be done, and, importantly, assessing team resources and external conditions related to achieving key goals. Imagine trying to fight a fire without monitoring. It would be impossible! Crew members on the fire engine would need to make sure that there was adequate water available for the size of a particular fire. Firefighters hosing down the fire would need to frequently radio back to the fire engine to update fellow members on the status of the fire. In the case of a wildfire, environmental conditions like heat and humidity would need to be constantly gauged against current resources available to the crew. Again, without effective monitoring processes, firefighter teams would have a very limited ability to do their jobs effectively.

Finally, the third key team process is backing up behavior, or coaching, assisting, and helping (perhaps even replacing) teammates, as necessary. Let's continue with our firefighter example. Exhaustion is likely to overtake those firefighters who have to extend themselves to fight large fires. As a result, backing up behavior is critical, as teammates will need to jump in to relieve fellow members who require rest, water, or food to maintain their strength and endurance. A team's backing up of behavior is possible only if effective monitoring practices are in place. For teammates to know when to step in and back one another up, they must be on the lookout for signs that someone needs help. In other words, teammates should always "have one another's backs." Even if teammates are not directly replacing fellow members, they may still play a backup role as coaches, encouraging their fellow teammates and, when appropriate, urging them to dig deeper and persevere. Serving as a positive motivational force can go a long way in terms of

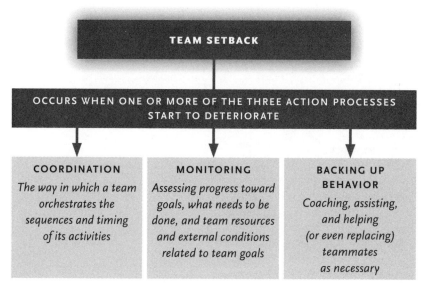

FIGURE 1.1. The Nature of a Team Setback

supporting and reinforcing fellow team members' performance, especially during trying times. If any or all of these three team processes (coordinating, monitoring, and backing up) deteriorate, a team is said to have suffered a setback. Since action processes are those that are directly linked to team goals, deterioration of action processes means that progress toward goals has slowed, or even stopped completely. Figure 1.1 summarizes the nature of a team setback.

Returning to the definition of team resilience, for a team to demonstrate resilience, it must *bounce back* from the setback. A team bounces back when its members work together to return to its pre-adversity performance level, or possibly even beyond. In fact, many teams grow stronger and even more resilient because of a setback. These teams take the time to assess what happened, take an inventory of lessons learned, and execute changes designed to better equip them for future setbacks. In bouncing back, the hope is that teams can create virtuous (positive) rather than vicious (negative) dynamic cycles of learning and performance, which are critical for today's teams working in volatile circumstances.[3] Some great examples of this include the intense revamping of firefighter training and an increased reliance on the science of fire behavior that the US Forest Service undertook after Mann Gulch in order to improve future performance. Figure 1.2 shows the nature of a team's bouncing back. Again, the hope is that after overcoming adversity and bouncing back from a

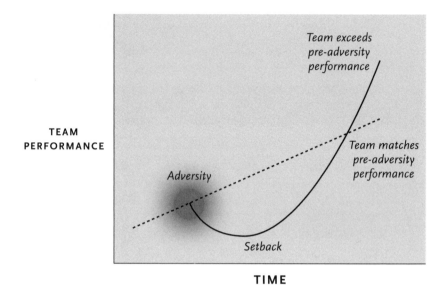

TEAM
PERFORMANCE

TIME

FIGURE 1.2. The Nature of a Team's Bouncing Back

setback, teams will eventually be able to exceed the performance level they had before adversity struck.

The third and final component of our team resilience definition is *capacity*. Team capacities are typically referred to as team emergent states. These are dynamic properties of teams that "emerge" as teammates interact with and relate to one another. Note that we use the term capacity purposefully because it suggests a team's potential to achieve its goals after a setback. In other words, a team can be resilient without having an actual setback, because resilience is the capacity to address adversity, not necessarily actually addressing it. For firefighter teams, the extensive training and development that they receive serve to build up the resources so important for resilience in the event of adversity. Even if a firefighter team suffers a setback when battling a fire, it's not an indication that the team lacks resilience. In fact, by definition, for a team to demonstrate resilience, it must first suffer a setback. After all, how can a team demonstrate that it's unbreakable if nothing has tried to break it? If a team consistently achieves its goals without experiencing any setbacks, then it's not demonstrating resilience; it's demonstrating team performance. Again, a team cannot bounce back if there's no deficit from which to bounce. In other words, a team need not suffer a setback to *be* resilient; however, a setback must happen for a team to *demonstrate* its resilience.

Think of resilience the way you might think of power in organizations. A person or team doesn't have to actually exert its power over others to be powerful. To be powerful, that person or team must simply have the capacity to influence others should it ever need to. The same applies to team resilience. A team need not bounce back from a setback to be resilient. It simply must have the capacity to do so. In that sense, team resilience is a type of reservoir that a team can draw from in times of need.

HOW ARE RESILIENT TEAMS DIFFERENT FROM
TEAMS OPERATING IN STABLE ENVIRONMENTS?

One question we get asked a lot when we discuss our work on team resilience is this: Isn't team resilience just a fancy name for team performance? Or, framed another way, are there any key differences between resilient teams and high-performing teams? In answering these questions, we always begin by returning to the definition of team resilience, which is a team's capacity to bounce back from a setback. It's the ability to take a hit, suffer a loss, and return to a normal level of functioning or, hopefully, an even higher level than before. Simply put, resilient teams are unbreakable. Sure, they bend from time to time as adversity weighs on their team processes. But they snap back. Resilient teams *never* break.

So, how do resilient teams differ from high-performing teams? Bouncing back after a setback means more than just performing at a high level. There are many high-performing teams that excel in calm waters but sink at first sight of a storm. Those teams are not resilient. So, what distinguishes a resilient team from a high-performing team that performs well only in stable environments? Over the past two decades of working with thousands of teams from hundreds of companies, we've found that when adversity strikes, resilient teams do three specific things exceptionally well. They are skilled at making sense of situations, they coalesce, and they persist.

Sensemaking is a form of problem solving that's unique to adverse situations, as there is no need to make sense of a calm situation in which everything is going smoothly. However, when disruptions occur in our routines and our lived experience is different from what we expected, we must pause to take stock of the situation, interpret what's happening around us, and develop a response plan. This is exactly what resilient teams do. Before acting, they take the time to make sense of a situation, generate a solution to a problem, and form a strategy for overcoming it.

Think about the erosion of sensemaking among the firefighters at Mann Gulch. Although there were several key instances, perhaps the most notable was the inability of the men to make sense of Dodge's escape fire. The men were incredulous that Dodge was building such a fire, and they interpreted his actions to mean he was lighting a backfire, normally used to cut off an advancing fire. However, the men knew this would be impossible given the time they had to deal with the advancing fire. And so they could not make sense of what Dodge was doing, which made them ignore his commands to come toward him. In fact, it was probably the loss of sensemaking that caused the men to panic, which ultimately cost them their lives.

Dr. Karl Weick, professor emeritus of organizational behavior and psychology at the University of Michigan's Ross Business School, was actually the first person to analyze the events of the Mann Gulch disaster using a sensemaking lens, and he did so with the purpose of discussing what makes organizations more or less resilient.[4] His work was the inspiration for our reanalysis of Mann Gulch from a team resilience perspective. Weick discussed the fact that when the smokejumpers arrived at Mann Gulch, they had expected to engage with what firefighters referred to as a "10:00 fire." This type of fire is labeled this way because it means that it can be largely contained and isolated by 10:00 a.m. the next morning. Even the spotters on the airplane that brought the crew to the fire openly characterized it this way. So the firefighters brought this "mental framing" to their challenge, which led to a whole host of sensemaking mistakes in addition to Dodge's escape fire.

Weick referred to other sensemaking errors, including lack of clarity about who was in charge of the crew when Hellman was at the front for a time; Navon's snapping photos of the advancing, menacing fire, which caused a disconnect between his actions and what the firefighters saw with their own eyes; Dodge's reversal of direction, first toward what appeared to be the safety of the river and then in the exact opposite direction back up the ridge, as the rest of the firefighters likely did not see the fire jump the gulch in front of them; Dodge's instructions to drop their tools creating a loss of identity for them as firefighters (they may have asked themselves, "How can I fight this fire without my tools?"); and Dodge's confusing orders juxtaposed to the instinctual urge to flee a fire that was imminently bearing down upon them.

Sensemaking requires that teams work closely together and engage in effective information processing, communication, and decision making. This highlights the importance of *coalescing*, the second element that differentiates resilient from high-performing teams. Coalescing is the act of team members uniting in the face of adversity. Unfortunately, research tells us that coalescing is not the norm. Rather, when adversity strikes, individual team members have a natural tendency to shift their focus to their own self-interest at the expense of their team.[5] This results in a breakdown of team processes, as the team splinters and struggles to coordinate in a cohesive manner. Unlike their brittle counterparts, members of resilient teams bond together despite the forces of adversity working to tear them apart.

For the Mann Gulch firefighters, clearly the stress of the moment caused the team to fracture. Getting separated in the confusion and smoke certainly did not help. When one of the men reacted to the confusion by shouting, "To hell with that! I'm getting out of here," it was a perfect example of people suddenly putting their own self-interest first above the best interests of their team. Although one could argue this is a natural human reaction to danger (it's the *flight* in fight or flight, after all), the firefighters' extensive training should have been designed to thwart any natural inclinations in them to take an "every man for himself" mentality. Weick echoes this rationale for the lack of coalescing given their relative lack of familiarity with one another; a foreman who was not that well known to them barking out what seemed to be nonsensical commands; temperatures nearing 140 degrees with incessant noise created by the fire, raging winds, and exploding trees; and crew members all seeing different things due to their individual vantage point and the thick, billowing smoke. These challenges made coalescing particularly difficult for the Mann Gulch firefighters.

The third essential piece of the resilience puzzle is *persisting*. Adversity often takes a psychological toll on team members. It's deflating to see something your team has worked so hard to build begin to crumble before your very eyes. This can result in feelings of hopelessness and thoughts of giving up. These thoughts and feelings are contagious in a team, and they escalate as members discuss their dire circumstances. It's in these very moments that resilient teams dig deep and summon the motivation to press forward. Persisting is the manifestation of a team's grit. It's the process through which teams forge ahead through rough waters.

Mann Gulch also presented challenges to the firefighter crew's persistence. Clearly, the psychological effects of this disaster unfolding were debilitating. First, they were headed toward the river, then suddenly back in the opposite direction toward the ridge, and then finally they were told to stop well before the ridge and join Dodge in what appeared to them to be a backfire. Feelings of hopelessness surely would have taken hold, and as the author Maclean phrased it, after leaving Dodge, "they were suddenly and totally without command and suddenly without structure and suddenly free to disintegrate and free finally to be afraid."[6] Tragically, largely due to a failure of sensemaking and coalescing, there was no team left to persist in fighting the fire.

Taken together, the three resilient actions described here enable teams to bounce back from a setback. These actions differentiate resilient teams from those that perform at a high level but only in stable environments. Bouncing back requires teams to make sense of the situation and develop an effective response plan (sensemaking), come together as a single unit and coordinate their response (coalescing), and maintain the motivation to see the plan through to the end (persisting).

WHAT'S IN THE REST OF THE BOOK?

Having established a basic understanding of what resilient teams do during times of adversity, we turn next to the factors that hold teams back, preventing them from performing these resilient actions. That is the focus of chapter 2, in which we use the Mann Gulch tragedy and several other notable team failures to walk you through four common pitfalls that cripple a team's bounce-back attempts.

We then shift to the primary purpose of this book: building and leading resilient, unbreakable teams. This focus is closely related to the three actions just described and the pitfalls described in the next chapter. In fact, these actions and pitfalls serve as the foundation that will guide our resilience-building framework. To build a resilient team, leaders must focus their efforts on developing specific team qualities that enable teams to engage in the three resilient actions and avoid the resilience pitfalls. Our research has identified four such qualities, and we designate full chapters (chapters 3–6) to developing each one in your teams. In chapter 7, we walk you through an example, from start to finish, of a resilient team bouncing back from adversity. This chapter offers an overview of the entire team resilience cycle, including activities that can aid a team in minimizing adversity before it strikes, managing it while it's present, and mending what is likely to be a tired and weary team after the adversity subsides. In chapter 8, we consider the special case of how leaders can build resilience in their remote and hybrid teams in which members do not interact face-to-face much (or at all) and might even be spread out in different countries across multiple time zones. In the conclusion, we offer leaders a set of diagnostic tools for assessing their teams' level of resilience and their own leadership actions devoted to building team resilience. By the time you get to the end of the book, you will have the knowledge and the blueprint for building resilient teams that are *unbreakable*.

CHAPTER 2

THE FOUR TEAM PITFALLS OF THE MANN GULCH TRAGEDY

The tragedy at Mann Gulch provides a glimpse into team failure during times of adversity. This particular case was a catastrophe with life-or-death consequences. But regardless of whether you and your team face this level of physical danger and risk in your day-to-day work, there is a great deal we can all learn from the Mann Gulch smokejumper team. We point to four critical team pitfalls that led to the Mann Gulch tragedy and highlight the fact that these pitfalls are all too common in every type of team, regardless of industry or type of work. These pitfalls are the following: too little (or too much) team confidence, an inadequate teamwork roadmap, limited ability of a team to improvise in the moment, and a lack of psychological safety. Each pitfall impeded the smokejumper team's resilient actions, thereby limiting its capacity to bounce back. And as we'll explain, each pitfall is directly associated with the absence of one of the four critical resilient resources. Figure 2.1 shows the four team resources that help teams become more resilient in the face of adversity.

TEAM PITFALL #1—TOO LITTLE OR TOO MUCH TEAM CONFIDENCE
Individual Team Member Confidence Does Not Add Up to Collective Team Confidence

A key ingredient that helps teams overcome and recover from adversity like the one in the Mann Gulch fire is a moderately high level of overall team con-

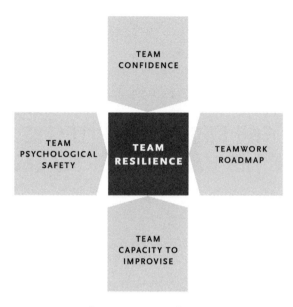

FIGURE 2.1. The Four Team Resilience Resources

fidence. Too little confidence means that team members lack a collective belief that the team will succeed in the face of adversity. Too much confidence
means that the team probably won't fully prepare for the variety of adversities
that could come their way. From the outset of the events at Mann Gulch, we
can probably assume that most (if not all) of the smokejumpers were confident in their individual abilities. After all, had they not been confident, they
would probably not have jumped out of an airplane circling a massive fire in
the first place! Each smokejumper also had experience fighting fires. Although
the team had a foreman (as they always did), firefighters in wilderness fires that
are spread out over a wide area typically like to think of themselves as their own
boss fighting their part of the fire, which leads to a sense of personal responsibility for staying alive. This sense of being in charge made sure that all individual smokejumpers were fast and confident in their own decision making.

By definition, all teams possess a certain level of interdependence, which
is the extent to which members collaborate, coordinate, and depend on one
another to get their jobs done. Smokejumper teams fighting wildfires often
possess a specific type of interdependence referred to as pooled interdependence. This means that crew members are assigned a particular part of a fire
to put out so that the entire fire shrinks as each crew member is successful;

that is, they "pool" their efforts for the greater good. As Maclean eloquently points out in his book, these smokejumpers were likely thinking that they were the best and that this wildfire would be no match for them. Some even think of firefighting as a game in order to psychologically cope with the immense challenge, and with that in mind, the smokejumpers probably thought that this particular fire (like all the others they had faced) wouldn't be much competition for them.

There were two flaws regarding team confidence that were embedded in the way the men approached the Mann Gulch fire. First, just because each individual smokejumper was supremely confident in his own abilities to tackle the fire, that doesn't mean the men necessarily felt collectively confident in the entire crew's capacity to get the job done that day. Think about a basketball team whose five members all believe they are the best individual performers in their sport. Individual confidence and bravado, however, do not mean that the five basketball players are collectively confident in their team's ability to win games. On the contrary, they might all individually believe they can be the highest scorer or the best defender, but they do not have much faith in their team's ability to be the best overall team. So, a key lesson from Mann Gulch—and we can't stress this enough—is that individual team member confidence, summed up, does not equal team confidence.

Second, because the overall team lacked a collective sense of confidence, despite each individual firefighter having supreme confidence in himself, the crew's confidence eroded very quickly when adversity struck. Making matters worse, the crew had never before worked with Dodge as a foreman. That meant they didn't have experience with the types of leadership actions Dodge might choose when the fire began to get out of control. As noted, many of the men were confused by Dodge's lighting of the escape fire. They did not follow his instructions but rather haphazardly decided to run for their lives. The other missing piece for the crew that day is that the men did not collectively have any experience fighting big fires like Mann Gulch. So their sense of confidence was probably misplaced and inappropriate as the fire quickly expanded in size and intensity. The crew members were also relatively young, so they did not have the requisite experience to make decisions needed in this type of massive "blowup." With experience comes wisdom, and it is the wisdom to recognize what you know and, more importantly, what you do not know that best characterizes an appropriate level of team confidence. Again, with too little or too much confidence, a team is likely to fail.

The combination of too much individual confidence and too little collective confidence handicapped the smokejumper team's ability to perform each of the three resilient actions: sensemaking, coalescing, and persisting. We mentioned that when adversity strikes, there is a natural tendency for team members to shift their attention toward their own self-interests and away from the interests of their team. This phenomenon is exacerbated when team members are confident in themselves but not in their team. Such a perfect storm results in a flurry of disorganized behavior as individual team members begin behaving as independent entities. This is exactly what happened at Mann Gulch, as the smokejumpers scattered rather than coming together as a single unit. At the most crucial moment, the team failed to coalesce. With the team fractured, it was unable to make sense of the situation. Rather than communicating about what was happening, they all turned and ran. No effort was made to interpret their surroundings or form a response strategy. No effort was made to listen to the guidance of their team leader. Without a solid understanding of the situation or a plan to move forward, the team simply couldn't persist. At that moment, the smokejumpers were no longer a team. They were merely a group of individuals fleeing for their own lives.

The interplay of individual and team confidence is further complicated when confidence levels vary among team members. This happened to a team of pharmacy development specialists we worked with at a major US health insurance company. The primary purpose of the team was to support the company's customer service representatives and ensure that they had all the information and tools needed to resolve customer inquiries in a timely and courteous manner. The team aided this process by investigating and troubleshooting any system issues that emerged and generating weekly training content for the reps. The team had six members, with some specializing in benefit eligibility, some in benefit coding, and others in the development of reference material.

On paper, this should have been an all-star team. All members were intelligent, highly skilled, hardworking, and more than capable of performing their roles in a manner that would exceed expectations. There was just one problem—unfortunately, a big one. Two members of the team had an excessive level of self-confidence, and this overconfidence ultimately had a disastrous impact on the rest of the team. Not only did the overconfidence of these two members cripple the team's ability to bounce back from adversity; that overconfidence *was* the adversity.

The two overly confident members, referred to by one teammate as "the two egos," were so sure of their own abilities that they believed they were the only competent people on the team. This led to them not trusting their teammates to complete any task that was even remotely important. For example, it was common for team members to take turns developing training content for delivery to the reps, with the expectation that the rest of the team would chip in with ideas and suggestions for improvement. When one of the two egos created the content, all teammate recommendations were ignored, and the content was delivered without any changes. But when any of the other teammates created the content, the two egos would rip it to shreds and completely redo all the work themselves. This, of course, resulted in the two egos taking on a disproportionate amount of the team's responsibilities, which led them to complain that they worked harder and longer than any of other their teammates and further fed their opinion that everybody else on the team was incompetent. In response to their complaints, teammates would attempt to help, but each time, their work was again ripped apart, the two egos would redo it, and the cycle perpetuated.

Their excessive self-confidence and opinion that their performance was superior to everyone else's led them to treat their teammates with condescension and incivility. For example, if someone were to ask them a question, instead of just answering or pointing them in the right direction, they would typically respond with some snarky version of "It's concerning to me that you don't already know the answer to this." They would also talk down to their teammates during team meetings (but of course only when the supervisor wasn't present) and talk negatively about them to the customer service reps they supported. Not surprisingly, this latter behavior led the reps to distrust any output presented by the other teammates.

Ultimately, the overconfidence of these "two egos" led the *team's* confidence to evaporate. Because of the constant critique of their work and the barrage of condescending comments, the self-confidence of the other team members plummeted, causing them to second-guess themselves on each task and on every thought or idea they had. As a result, the team struggled mightily. Morale was crushed; trust, nonexistent. The lack of confidence in themselves, combined with the inefficiency of having only two people handle most of the workload, forced the team to fall behind on important goals. Because the team consistently underperformed its potential, members lost all confidence in the team as a whole. This threw the team into a vicious negative performance cycle. Their belief in the team's collective incompetence lowered their output, and in turn the lowered output dropped their confidence even further, and so on. The team never bounced back. Nobody wanted any part of the toxic environment that had formed, and every single person left the team but one. In fact, turnover was so out of control that in less than thirty-six months, this five-person team lost six people (people left, were replaced, and then those people left!). It wasn't until both of the two egos finally left that the team, with all new members, was able to function in a meaningful way.

TEAM PITFALL #2—INADEQUATE TEAMWORK ROADMAP
Knowing Where the Team Is Going and Each Member's Role in Getting There

Another key ingredient for teams to overcome adversity is that members must collectively possess a clear teamwork roadmap, which refers to members' knowledge of their roles, responsibilities, and interaction patterns and their familiarity with one another's knowledge, skills, and preferences. In other words, a teamwork roadmap reflects the extent to which all team members know what their own roles and responsibilities are, and the extent to which they agree on what all other team members' roles and responsibilities are. In some instances, team members may even know how to perform one another's roles so that at any point, one person can step in for another as needed. A teamwork roadmap means that team members can collectively respond to adversity as soon as possible with little to no need for planning or discussion about who should do what in a crisis.

Our analysis of the Mann Gulch disaster revealed that the crew members did not have such a teamwork roadmap to guide their behavior when the fire blew up, mainly due to a lack of proper training. For example, the Forest Service did at least acknowledge that the dangers that could arise from unpredictable fires meant that lifesaving maneuvers the men might need to employ would depend, in part, on the extent to which they knew one another well. As a result, all crews were put through three-week training courses at the beginning of each fire season so that members could familiarize themselves with one another and their crew foreman. Unfortunately, in the case of the Mann Gulch crew, although most of the men had undergone this training, their foreman, Dodge, was not available to go through it with them, as he was put in charge of base maintenance and thus was unable to take part in the course. This had the negative effect of leaving the crew without any familiarity with their team leader. Dodge's unpredictable setting of the escape fire was made all the more surprising by the crew's lack of experience with him. Making matters worse, the separation of the team members meant that they could not reinforce their roles and responsibilities through visual contact or close communication.

Roadmaps need not spell out all details of every possible scenario. Rather, they serve as a guiding framework for teams to respond to a variety of different events, even the unforeseen. For a time, the second-in-command, Hellman, who typically held the rear position, was thrust into a leadership role in front of the men, meaning that the crew was likely unfamiliar with him or his leadership style in this forward position. And yet the teamwork roadmap should have prepared them for a scenario in which Hellman took the lead. The roadmap should also have instructed team members to immediately move toward their leader when adversity strikes so the distance between them wouldn't prohibit communication. Moreover, for those close enough to hear it, Dodge's command for the crew members to discard their tools also resulted in confusion about what each man should be doing. In other words, their specific tools helped define their roles and responsibilities, and without them, uncertainly reigned over their teamwork roadmap. As Dodge shouted instructions to join him in the escape fire area, the crew members were baffled—there was no "roadmap" at all for such a maneuver. Instead, the roadmap they were using should have prepared them for this moment, not necessarily by predicting that exact scenario but by laying out a response plan for the unexpected. The first step in that plan should have been to find the team leader and follow his instructions.

The lack of a well-established teamwork roadmap makes sensemaking much more difficult, if not impossible. In the case of the smokejumpers, they failed to even attempt to interpret the situation and generate a response plan. But even if they had, the nature of this adversity would have given them only a few seconds to do so. Without a roadmap in place to serve as a guiding framework, the time it takes to understand what's happening and what needs to happen next grows significantly. The lack of a roadmap also impedes a team's ability to coalesce. Beyond preventing the team from coming together physically, the lack of a roadmap also impaired the team's ability to coordinate individual actions, as it wasn't clear what everyone should be doing at that moment. And because team members didn't know what to do, the team couldn't move forward as a unit. In other words, the team couldn't persist.

After the Mann Gulch disaster, a task force was convened at a meeting in Washington, DC, to generate a set of practical recommendations that could serve, in part, as a firefighting teamwork roadmap. The recommendations included various strategies, such as knowing exactly what one's instructions are and following them at all times, identifying key points of one's assignment and acting in order of priority, establishing and maintaining regular communications with all crew members, quickly recognizing changing conditions and immediately revising plans to handle them, and making sure foremen know at all times where their men are and what they are doing. Such a generally agreed-upon set of guidelines ensures that teamwork roadmaps are codified and acted upon in any situation.

Teamwork roadmaps aid all types of teams in a wide variety of adversities. Take mountain climbing, for example. In May 1996, a team of climbers set out to summit Mount Everest, the world's highest peak. There were actually several teams on the mountain at the time, and they all found themselves working together as a sort of "superteam" to overcome a common adversity. The climbers reached base camp in mid-April to start preparing. This was common practice for major ascents such as Everest. The primary objective of this prep period at base camp was to acclimatize their bodies to the higher altitudes. To do so, they would move up a portion of the mountain and then return back down, and they would do this over and over, each time increasing the amount of time spent away from camp. Over the course of several weeks, the team gradually made its way up the mountain to what was known as Camp III.

On the morning of May 9, Chen Yu Nan left his tent to relieve himself. In doing so, he made two fateful errors.[1] First, he failed to clip onto the fixed ropes installed to protect climbers from the risk of long falls. Second, he failed to attach his crampons to his boots. Crampons are spikes designed to dig into the mountain ice, thereby offering climbers enough traction to move around freely without slipping. Chen quickly lost his footing and dropped eighty feet into a crevasse. He was quickly rescued by his teammates, who were all shocked that Chen appeared to have suffered no serious injuries. And yet as time passed, it became clear that something was dreadfully wrong. Chen began to feel ill and decided to head back down to base camp alone. He didn't make it far before he collapsed and was soon found by Sherpas, who carried him the rest of the way down. Sadly, he never made it back to camp alive. Chen died on the descent of what was later believed to be internal injuries caused by his fall.

The team pressed on to Camp IV, where they hunkered down and rode out a relatively mild storm. By nightfall, the storm had cleared, and at midnight they set out again. Each climber carried extra oxygen on this final push, but they knew that there was only enough to last until approximately 5:00 p.m.[2] This meant that when they summited, they wouldn't be able to stay long. They would need to turn around and descend quickly. Although no hard stop time was established, Rob Hall, one of the group leaders, recommended that everyone should turn around by 1:00 p.m. or 2:00 p.m. at the latest, even if they hadn't summitted.

The final ascent was the most treacherous, with oxygen levels dropping and the steepness of the slope increasing as the climbers neared the mountain's peak. To assist with the more challenging areas, the team had planned for the Sherpas supporting them to move ahead and install a fixed rope in advance of the group's arrival. Unfortunately, this never happened.[3] As a result, the team experienced a significant delay each time they were forced to halt their journey and wait for the ropes to be installed. This delay was compounded by the fact that several climbers were inexperienced and traveled very slowly. These delays created a series of bottlenecks on the mountain, including one at the base of the Hillary Step, a forty-foot vertical rock face considered one of the most challenging obstacles to conquering Everest. As climbers waited for those in front of them to scale the rock, the clock continued to tick.

While those in the front of the line summitted at about 1:00 p.m., many were still lined up at the foot of the Hillary Step at the 2:00 p.m. recommended turnaround time and continued to summit until approximately 4:00 p.m. Tragically, some of these climbers would never make it back. A storm slammed into the mountain as the last climbers reached the summit. By 6:00 p.m., it had grown into a ruthless blizzard that would've made walking on flat ground difficult, let alone descending the world's tallest mountain.[4] The descent proved deadly.

Nine people perished on Mount Everest between May 9 and 11, 1996. Several books and articles have been written about this tragedy, and although they view the event through a variety of unique lenses, they all point to a series of mistakes made by the team. In the moment, these mistakes may have appeared minor, but their consequences were tragic.

The 1996 Mount Everest disaster highlights the importance of establishing a clear and thorough team roadmap. For example, rather than suggesting a rough time frame (for example, 1:00 p.m. or 2:00 p.m.) for turning around, a clear roadmap would've stated unequivocally the latest time at which the team could pivot and still make it back to camp safely. Perhaps the climbers, who chose to advance well past the recommended turnaround window, would have taken a hard stop time more seriously. Or perhaps they would have ignored that as well. This possibility highlights the importance of not only establishing a roadmap but also instilling in the team how critical it is to stick to the plan. It's believed, for example, that Chen knew very well that he should not exit his tent without his crampons or without clipping onto the fixed rope, even if he intended to travel only a few steps. And, presumably, the Sherpas knew they were supposed to move ahead of the team and install the fixed ropes before everyone else arrived. Why they didn't is still somewhat of a mystery. But had all the team members followed the roadmap, they could've prevented the bottlenecks that created major delays and resulted in climbers summitting past the point of no return.

TEAM PITFALL #3—INABILITY TO IMPROVISE

Even the Best-Laid Plans Can Become Worthless as
    Conditions on the Ground Change

Another critical ingredient for a team to overcome adversity and bounce back is the collective ability of its members to improvise in the face of adversity. A team is said to be able to improvise when it can extemporaneously make something novel out of previous experiences, practices, and knowledge. As is common with most adversities, existing routines and responses are often useless when adversity turns situations upside down. As a result, teams must be able to pivot at a moment's notice and respond in ways that draw upon members' collective improvisation.

We might argue that the three-week training course offered to the Mann Gulch smokejumpers at the beginning of fire season did not adequately allow crew members to develop a deep understanding of the team's prior experiences and expertise or the type of preparation required for the crew to be creative when the fire called for an adjustment. In fact, the Forest Service did not have the budget to keep the smokejumpers around the base when there were not a lot of fires burning. This essentially meant that when things got quiet, the smokejumpers were sent out individually to work on special projects, such as trail building, which was unrelated to developing a team's collective ability to improvise. There was also a tension between training crew members to act swiftly and decisively on their own when adversity struck but also making sure crew members took orders from their foreman without any hesitation. Such a contradiction could have contributed to the men ignoring pleas from Dodge about joining him in the escape fire. By the way, a major invention that resulted from analyzing the Mann Gulch fire was to train all firefighters on how to set escape fires, as Dodge had done.

Dodge's quick improvisational thinking was made all the more remarkable by the fact that he had never initiated such an escape fire in all his previous firefighting experiences. However, for teams to be improvisational, one person's momentary spark of creativity is rarely enough. Teams need to collectively improvise so that various member ideas can be combined for even greater improvisation than that of one person. Because the dangerous conditions created a sense of disorientation among the crew members, the team struggled with sensemaking. For example, they couldn't make sense of, or even begin to think about, employing Dodge's improvisational escape fire. The crew was paralyzed and could not engage in improvisational thinking. This, of course, meant that no coordinated plan was generated, which meant no coalescing, and ultimately no persistence.

For team improvisation to occur, it would have been essential that the Mann Gulch team had a fully operational communications system for making informed decisions about the safety of the crew. Oftentimes, improvisation means a response to a sudden change of course. Communication is essential, not only to ensure that a variety of perspectives are leveraged to choose the most appropriate direction but also to make sure that the entire team is aware that the direction has changed. For teams like the Mann Gulch crew, such communication could have occurred either via face-to-face interaction or a reliable radio system. As noted, the thick smoke hastened the men's confusion and disorientation as they tried to decide how to escape the fire. Because the men were in different groups and some were spread out over a hundred yards or more, direct contact was almost impossible. Maybe this communication breakdown could have been prevented if their teamwork roadmap had informed them either to not spread out too far or to regroup immediately when adversity strikes. Maclean described what the men must have experienced when ignoring Dodge's instructions and striking out on their own, referring to it as a "great jump backwards into the sky."[5] Similar to the situation faced by the Mann Gulch smokejumpers, stories abound of teams failing to improvise during adversity or trying to improvise but doing it badly.

The need for improvisation was made abundantly clear to a team of healthcare professionals at Memorial Medical Center in the Uptown section of New Orleans, Louisiana.[6] In August 2005, the city was ravaged by Hurricane Katrina, one of the largest and most destructive storms to ever make landfall in the United States. In the wake of the storm, the medical team at Memorial faced a harrowing five days of caring for hundreds of patients despite flooding, no electricity, no running water, and overflowing toilets. Rescue helicopters and boats arrived sporadically over the course of those five days, making the evacuation process long and arduous. When those opportunities to evacuate presented themselves, the team, with little to no sleep, scrambled to mobilize as many patients as they could. They traversed dark hallways and stairwells, with indoor temperatures exceeding one hundred degrees and air that reeked of sewage and body odor. They quickly grew depleted, so depleted that at one point after the sun set, those in charge at Memorial declined an offer by the Coast Guard to evacuate more patients, stating that the helipad, which had no guardrails, would be too dangerous in the dark and that the staff was badly in need of rest anyway.

And yet it wasn't these physical demands of caring for and transporting patients in the middle of a disaster zone that presented the greatest challenge to the team. The team's greatest challenge began to emerge a few days earlier in the form of a crucial decision that would surely haunt the team for the rest of their lives, no matter how many ways they tried to justify it. Approximately two days after Katrina struck, the hospital's generators gave out. The generators were being used to power essential ventilators and life support monitors for intensive care patients. What was already an urgent situation became critical. Without breathing assistance, several patients died. Many others were in very dire straits. Several members of the team quickly hashed out a plan for triage. They created three groups of patients and assigned each group a number reflecting the order in which they would be evacuated. The healthiest patients were assigned a number 1. Many of these patients were able to walk on their own. They were given priority to evacuate first, followed by those in the 2 group, who would require more help. Those assigned a 3 were considered worst off. They were the illest, and some had even signed do-not-resuscitate orders.

Triage decisions are always challenging for medical staff. But choosing who to assign to which group, while difficult and at times even emotional, paled in comparison to the decision that followed. What happened next would ultimately bring multiple team members to tears that day and would captivate not only a city, but an entire nation, for years to come. The team made the determination that some patients in critical condition were unlikely to survive an evacuation. They were barely hanging on as it was. And one patient on the seventh floor was paralyzed and weighed almost four hundred pounds. The team thought there was no way they could transport this person down all those flights of stairs in the dark. They knew they had to improvise.

Sadly, their idea for improvisation was to euthanize the patients. Some team members made the decision to inject patients in the third group with a lethal dose of morphine and midazolam, a powerful sedative that slows breathing. Some of these patients were still quite alert when the injection was administered and were told that it would make them feel better. Not everyone on the team was involved in this decision, but several knew about it. And while it gutted them to their core, they didn't stop it.

In the aftermath of Katrina, forensic analysis found elevated drug levels in twenty-three bodies found in the abandoned hospital and determined that twenty of them were victims of homicide.[7] This story sparked widespread ethics debates and resulted in the arrest of three team members. The public ultimately sympathized with the team's situation, and a grand jury chose not to indict. "I want everyone to know that I'm not a murderer, that we are not murderers," said Dr. Anna Pou, one of the team members, on an episode of *60 Minutes*.[8]

And yet many people believe that they should have at least tried to evacuate these patients.[9] Rodney Scott, a surviving patient, later had this to say: "How can you say euthanasia is better than evacuation? If they have vital signs, get 'em out. Let God make that decision." And bioethicist Arthur Caplan commented that a decision to inject a lethal dose of drugs is "not consistent with the ethical standards of palliative care that prevail in the United States."[10] He further noted that a doctor's objective should never be the death of a patient.

Of course, it's far easier for those on the outside to say what should have happened. In the heat of the moment, however, improvisation is often extremely difficult. In the absence of a guiding framework or well-established contingency plan—for example, a comprehensive disaster preparedness and response protocol—teams are at risk of improvising down a path that could result in tragic consequences. Perhaps if the team at Memorial Medical had previously encountered a similar tragedy, even if it were simulated, they might have leveraged this experience to generate a different plan with a more positive result.

TEAM PITFALL #4—LACK OF TEAM PSYCHOLOGICAL SAFETY

Team Members Have to Be Comfortable Enough with One Another to Be Their True Selves

The final ingredient critical for a team to be able to overcome adversity is a team's level of psychological safety, or the degree to which a team's members believe they are "safe" to take interpersonal risks with their teammates. In times of adversity, a team's members must be comfortable offering their perspectives and opinions without fear of being ostracized or shut down by fellow members.

This, at times, can be quite difficult. Research has consistently shown that team members typically tend to share information that is already generally known, which is referred to as the common knowledge effect.[11] Such an effect is the result of team members wanting to "fit in" to their team and be viewed as a trusted insider. When people offer unusual or "out of the box" ideas or otherwise challenge team consensus in some way, they are taking a risk and may be viewed as a team disrupter, maverick, or outsider. So offering safe opinions and ideas that "go with the flow" is one way that team members reinforce their identity with their team.

The events of Mann Gulch demonstrate the dangers of the pressure not to speak up and offer counterintuitive ideas or suggestions. Dodge's idea to create an escape fire was rejected by his crew members, as such an idea appeared strange and foreign to the men. The fact that they were not familiar with Dodge personally likely exacerbated the situation because they had not established a psychologically safe atmosphere in which members could share unusual ideas or practices that the team could adopt. Fear is the enemy of psychological safety in teams, and the Mann Gulch crew members may have been unimaginably afraid of the approaching fire. But in the presence of such fear, it is unlikely that they spoke up and offered their ideas and suggestions. And with that fear, even when Dodge offered up an unusual idea, his team members could not effectively process or respond to it.

Psychological safety is arguably the one quality that is most critical for all three resilient team actions. The beauty of a team is that it brings together a variety of people with different experiences, expertise, and cognitive styles. This should give teams an advantage over individuals when it comes to sensemaking, as they then have a broader array of thoughts, opinions, and ideas to consider. However, for this sensemaking to occur, teammates must feel safe speaking up, even when they know that what they have to say could be uncomfortable for others to hear. Without this feeling of safety, members are likely to remain silent, which results in less information for the team to process and, ultimately, lower-quality decisions.

Psychological safety is also at the core of the coalescing process, as it is based on a foundation of mutual trust and respect. Members of teams with low psychological safety—who don't trust their teammates and don't feel respected by them—will struggle to unite in those moments when doing so is so crucial. If a team can't come together in times of adversity, it won't be able to forge ahead and persist as a unit.

The lack of psychological safety is at the heart of many teams' inability to bounce back from adversity and succeed. Low psychological safety can result in groupthink, which occurs when a team of people, out of a strong desire for harmony or conformity, makes irrational or dysfunctional decisions.[12] Examples of groupthink abound, such as the space shuttle *Challenger* explosion in 1986, in which team members had existing data suggesting that the O-rings in the solid rocket boosters would likely fail in the unusually cold weather that day in Florida but the launch was authorized anyway and team members went along with it; or the failed Bay of Pigs invasion of Cuba in 1961, in which President Kennedy's top advisers were not willing to speak up about the numerous bad decisions that were being made.

A good example of a team making a bad decision based on low psychological safety is the Volkswagen emissions scandal, commonly referred to as "Dieselgate."[13] Under major pressure from upper management to reduce nitrogen oxide emissions in its diesel engines for the US market, which constituted significant adversity to the company's profitability, a team of engineers decided to try to "trick" the emissions testing system by intentionally programming turbocharged direct-injection diesel engines to activate their emission control systems only during laboratory emissions testing. The software trick meant that, during routine regulatory testing, VW diesel engines emitted nitrogen oxide in line with US federal standards. However, after the cars successfully passed these emissions tests, they were eventually found to emit up to forty times more nitrogen oxide in real-world driving conditions.

In 2014, Volkswagen's deception was discovered by the California Air Resources Board in a commissioned study to examine emissions discrepancies between European and US vehicle models. A group of scientists from West Virginia University, using a Japanese onboard emission testing system, discovered the excess nitrogen oxide emissions during road tests on multiple VW models. Additional investigations were launched, and Volkswagen's stock price decreased by over a third. The CEO, Martin Winterkorn, resigned from his position, and other top leaders were suspended, including Heinz-Jakob Neusser, head of brand development; Ulrich Hackenberg, head of Audi's research and development; and Wolfgang Hatz, head of Porsche's research and development. In January 2017, Volkswagen pleaded guilty to criminal charges, acknowledging that a team of engineers had developed the emissions devices because, without them, the diesel engines would not pass US emissions tests. As of 2022, Volkswagen had spent over $33 billion dollars in fines, penalties, financial costs, and buybacks.

What led this team of engineers to develop a system to cheat US emissions standards, putting billions of dollars in profits and company valuation at risk in doing so? Why didn't anyone speak up and say this was a bad idea? Our analysis of the events—and others' analyses—point a finger at low psychological safety. When adversity struck in the form of new, lower emissions expectations, the team's sensemaking resulted in a decision to engage in illegal activity. Clearly, various team members knew what they were doing was illegal and unethical. But the tremendous stress thrown at the team from upper management (make the diesel engines satisfy US emissions standards or else!) created an environment of adversity for them that contributed to a serious lack of psychological safety. This meant that team members did not speak up, disagree, or stop the cheating from happening, even though it went on for months. Would they have chosen an ethical path if more team members felt safe enough to speak up? We think so. But as it was, the fear that many of these engineers on the team must have felt meant that all members colluded in this illegal effort. In this case, the team did coalesce and persist, but they did so down a path that they knew was wrong—one that ultimately led to their downfall.

If you're thinking that a lack of psychological safety may have also played a role in the Memorial Medical tragedy, you're absolutely correct. A decision was made to head down an immoral path, and although some teammates did speak up against the action, they did so quietly and without intervening in the act itself. Nobody had the courage to step in and stop it. As the adversity in teams becomes more common as a result of increasing levels of volatility, uncertainty, complexity, and ambiguity, we are sad to say that we think we will continue to see such horror stories produced by the lack of psychological safety.

CHAPTER 3

TEAM RESILIENCE RESOURCE #1

TEAM CONFIDENCE

Imagine yourself as a member of a software development team for a midsize high-tech company. Your organization recently pulled off a major software sale to a client that has not typically made purchases from your outfit in the past. The sale was considered somewhat of a coup, and everyone responsible for sales and client support was very enthusiastic about the accomplishment. Although you were not personally involved in the sale, your team has been tasked with client support to make sure the software functions properly and meets all the client's needs.

As the day of the software launch rapidly approaches, your team is confident that the design and functionality of the software are right where they should be. Although your team has never been responsible for such a complex piece of software or for supporting such a large and important client, it has had many previous successes with similar, albeit smaller, software projects and clients. As a result of these positive experiences, your team is quite confident going into the project. Everyone believes the team can handle just about any issue that might crop up. To be sure, your team is not overconfident by any stretch. All the team members recognize that the team isn't perfect and that a wide variety of problems—big and small—have come up before and could very well strike again at any moment. You would describe your team as possessing a healthy balance of confidence and caution. As a result, you've spent a great deal of time preparing for various possible situations. Such preparation has paid off in the past, as your team has always been able to handle the unforeseen glitches that come with launching a major software solution.

It's now Friday morning on the day of the launch. The software is scheduled to go live at 9:00 a.m. Just a few minutes before the launch, you and your team-mates huddle together, each with a laptop, to begin to monitor all the steps underway. At precisely 9:00 a.m., the software goes live, the client's customers begin to access the site, and you take a full breath for the first time in quite a while. This could be your team's finest hour, and for that matter, your company's.

Everything appears to be going well, but at 11:15 a.m., your team notices that traffic has slowed considerably on the client's site. This is totally unexpected: everyone thought customer traffic would accelerate following the launch as the day wore on. Then, disaster strikes. The whole site crashes, taking all those potential customer sales down with it. You wonder whether you should have taken that deep breath a couple of hours ago; maybe you jinxed it.

This crash is, by all accounts, a major blow to your team. And yet instead of deflating everyone, it actually had the complete opposite effect. The team members are noticeably more energized—you can see it in their eyes, and you can feel it in the air. You all knew something like this could happen, and so you prepared for it. You are ready. Without hesitation, you and your team members spring into action, engaging in a flurry of activities to try to remedy the problem. Sweat starts to bead on your forehead as you begin to realize that whatever the problem is, it's going to require more than a quick fix. In fact, you recognize that you can basically kiss your weekend goodbye; the entire team will need to rally in order to get the client site back up and running as soon as possible. Sacrificing a weekend (or more), however, is small potatoes compared to potentially losing this major client. You, your team, and your company did not put in thousands of hours to land this client and develop this software just to lose it all on one unfortunate crash.

Your team continues to huddle, working hard to diagnose the source of the crash. Like some sort of mission-control room for the nation's space program, you and your team confidently run down the checklist of possible reasons for the crash. You all exchange emails and documentation information with one another as you furiously search for faulty areas in the software. As the day wears on and your phone beeps to let you know it's 5:30 p.m., your team leader sug-gests it might be wise to pull an "all-nighter" to try to get fixes in place. She says she will order pizza from your team's favorite restaurant down the street. You politely suggest that if everyone is going to be here all night, coffee is probably in order as well. Although she does not code herself, she informs the team that she will stay in the office with your team until the mission is accomplished. Her willingness to stay with the team is part of why your team members are so confident in their abilities. You have a dedicated, supportive leader whom your team trusts. You laugh to yourself as you remember a former coworker on another team that had a similar experience; his team also had to work through a weekend to fix a software glitch. But his leader, rather than staying with the team in a show of support and solidarity, was seen on social media catching some sun at the beach. Talk about a deflating experience for the team. It turns out that coworker quit the company not long after that.

It's early Saturday morning now. Your team is exhausted but unwavering. Suddenly one of your teammates shouts, "I got it!" He found the source. Within seconds, the entire team is crowded around his laptop, brainstorming solutions to the problem. You settle on one. Everyone takes a nervous breath as you put the finishing touches on the fix. Your nervousness turns to relief as the client's site comes roaring back to life. The team rejoices with a thunderous outburst.

Your team responded resiliently. When adversity struck, the team coalesced, worked vigorously to make sense of the situation, and persisted until the solution was found. Instead of crumbling under intense pressure, this software development team was *unbreakable*.

The situation just described provides a good example of the first key resource that a team needs to be resilient: *team confidence*. Sometimes referred to as team potency, team confidence essentially means that a team's members collectively believe that they can complete just about any task or solve any problem that might come their way.[1] When adversity strikes and performance breaks down, it's easy for a team to lose hope, become frustrated, and even give up. But a confident team knows that a setback is temporary and that members have the knowledge, skills, and abilities to overcome any obstacle. Confidence keeps them engaged despite challenging circumstances. This engagement serves as motivational fuel that enables teams to forge ahead through adversity. It keeps a team of software developers energized all night as they search meticulously for the source of a site crash. Confidence gives teams the grit they need to dig deep, power through, and persevere.

And yet with all the advantages that confidence brings a team, it can also lead to its downfall. When confidence levels rise too high, they can turn into team hubris. Hubris, or excessive confidence, is just as dangerous as a lack of confidence. In fact, it is arguably even more dangerous. The feeling of invincibility that stems from overconfidence causes team members to let down their guard and believe that they are impervious to adversities, so there is no need to be on the lookout for threats. In other words, overconfident teams are not vigilant; they are complacent. And as one NASA astronaut so perfectly stated, "Complacency is the enemy of resilience."[2] Indeed, complacency prevents teams from detecting adversity in a timely manner, allowing even a minor setback to balloon into something that is no longer manageable. Further, overconfidence can make a team fragile. The confidence that leads a team to believe no setback will occur is likely to be crushed when one does.

Take the Enron scandal from the early 2000s as an example. At one point, Enron was the seventh-largest company in the entire United States. The former CEO and COO Jeffrey Skilling and former chairman and CEO Kenneth Lay were highly regarded as captains of industry, leading Enron to higher growth and profitability year after year. However, in cooperation with its accounting firm, the now-defunct Arthur Andersen, Enron duped regulators by using "off the books" accounting practices and incorporating dummy corporations to hide its toxic assets and large debts from investors and creditors. When all was said and done, the Enron accounting scandal cost thousands of people their jobs, not to mention billions of dollars lost in pensions and stocks. What could lead a senior management team to put their own company at risk with the livelihoods of so many at stake? And why, when keenly aware of multiple company weaknesses at Enron, would senior management team members collectively engage in massive accounting fraud, corruption, deception, and a smoke-and-mirrors campaign to cover it all up? A lot has been written over the years about what the team did and why, but one flaw sums up the downfall: the senior management team had a "culture of arrogance," or what might otherwise be described as too much team confidence.

It's not just team overconfidence that's the problem. Researchers have found that overconfidence can be socially contagious; that is, it can literally pass from team member to team member.[3] With this contagiousness, referred to as the "transmission of overconfidence," people are likely to become more overconfident when people around them are also overconfident.[4]

In one study, for example, researchers conducted a laboratory experiment in which they brought two strangers into a room, asked them to work quietly by themselves to guess what people's personalities were like solely from their photographs, and then measured how overconfident they were in their guesses.[5] The overconfidence scores of the two participants were different, as expected.

Then, they introduced the two strangers to each other and had them work together on the same task with different pictures for fifteen minutes. Despite only working together for a short period of time, when the researchers measured their overconfidence levels again, they found that they had converged. What is more remarkable is that neither partner was informed about the other's level of confidence beforehand, meaning that the convergence of overconfidence was purely based on social transmission. The key takeaway here is that too much team confidence is not good for team resilience, and once people's overconfidence in a team starts transmitting socially, it can be hard to stop.

For the reasons stated previously, too much or too little confidence can make a team brittle. The most resilient teams have a moderately high level of confidence. As mentioned in the example of the software development team, moderately high confidence offers a healthy balance of confidence and caution. Teams with this balance know they have what it takes to succeed, but they are also wise enough to recognize that they aren't infallible.

Recall from the Mann Gulch example that team confidence is not necessarily built by several confident team members. Just because individuals believe in their own abilities does not mean, necessarily, that the entire team will feel collectively confident. Again, aggregated individual team member confidence does not equal team confidence.

This truism was supported in a study of intercollegiate hockey teams in a midwestern hockey league.[6] Researchers measured both individual hockey player confidence and each hockey team's overall confidence and then tried to identify which was more important for team performance (measured by, among other things, margin of win, number of wins and losses, shots attempted, and scoring percentage) over an entire season. What would you predict was more important: the sum of individual player confidence or overall team confidence? The answer, perhaps not surprisingly, was that overall team confidence was a much better predictor of performance than the aggregated individual confidence of the team's members. Moreover, team confidence was more affected than individual confidence by previous team performance, meaning that overall team confidence is likely more malleable than individual confidence when team members are sizing up their previous performance. Importantly, team confidence and team performance feed off each other in that greater confidence leads to higher performance, which subsequently leads to greater confidence.[7]

Beyond individual studies of team confidence like the one just described, multiple meta-analyses (or new studies that reexamine all the original data from

a bunch of previous studies to create a more accurate picture of a particular phenomenon) have shown that team confidence is indeed very important for team
success.[8] Some of that research took the broader notion of team confidence we're
discussing here (again, think confidence to excel at any task) and compared it to
a narrower type of team confidence (confidence in performing a specific task).
Although general and specific team confidence are strongly related to team
performance, the relationship between more specific team confidence and actual
team performance depended on how member interdependence played out in
the team. In contrast, for general team confidence, team interdependence had
no effect on how strongly team confidence affected team performance. In other
words, broad team confidence matters for all types of teams, whether members
are highly dependent on one another to get their jobs done (more like a real
team, such as a hockey team) or whether they work relatively independently
from one another to accomplish tasks (more like a group, such as a collection of
insurance salespeople working in a particular geographic territory). Moreover,
given the seemingly limitless adversities that a team may encounter, possessing
such broad confidence in overcoming any obstacle is particularly critical for
team resilience.

Staying on the subject of hockey teams, a great example of the importance
of team confidence in overcoming adversity is the story often referred to as the
"Miracle on Ice." The 1980 Winter Olympics took place in Lake Placid, New
York. The United States had put together what many viewed as a ragtag hockey
team consisting of almost all amateur players, only four of whom had experience
participating in minor league games. In fact, averaging just twenty-one years
old, the US team was not only the youngest hockey team in the Olympics that
year, it was also the youngest team in US national team history! The team was
led by now-legendary head coach Herb Brooks, a former Olympian himself,
who played for the US hockey team during the 1968 Olympics in Grenoble,
France. Interestingly, in 1960, Brooks was cut from the Olympic team just one
week before the games commenced. The US would go on to win the gold medal
in hockey that year.

In 1980, as coach of the underdog US team, Brooks knew that the big kid on
the block was the Soviet Union team, which consisted of professional players
with decades of hockey-playing experience between them. They were so good,
in fact, that they came into the 1980 Olympics as the four-time defending
champion and were, of course, the odds-on favorite to make it five in a row.
As a warm-up to Olympic competition, the US team had agreed to play an

exhibition game against the Soviets on February 9, only a few short days before the start of the games—who thought *that* was a good idea? Not surprisingly, the Americans were blown out by the Soviets, 10–3, and the game was even worse than the lopsided score indicated. Experiencing the adversity of a blowout loss just a short time before the start of the Olympics did not put the US team in a good position to think about advancing very far. In fact, the coaches and players believed that they would never even be in a position to face the Soviet team again in the Olympics, so they focused on more realistic competition, like the Swedish and Czechoslovakian teams.

Sure enough, the Americans' first game was against the Swedish team, and the US players fought hard to end up in a 2–2 draw, scoring with twenty-seven seconds left in regulation after pulling their goalie to have an extra attacker on offense. In the next game, the Americans played even better, crushing the Czechoslovakian team by a score of 7–3. The US proceeded to rattle off three more victories—against Norway, Romania, and Canada—to remain unbeaten. Against all odds, and certainly not consistent with anyone's expectations before the games started, these results launched the US team into the Olympic medal round against—you guessed it—the mighty Soviets, on February 22, less than two weeks after their embarrassing exhibition loss to the same team.

In the first period, the teams played to a 2–2 tie. In the second period, the Soviets took a 3–2 lead. The Americans had a steep hill to climb entering the third period. In that period, the overmatched US team somehow managed to score two more goals, taking a 4–3 lead and holding on to win. Two days later, the US trailed the Finnish team 2–1 after the second period, which led Coach Brooks to exclaim right before the third period, "If you lose this game, you will all take it to your (bleeping) graves."[9] The US team then beat Finland with a final score of 4–2, winning the gold medal. The Soviets won the silver medal by beating Sweden. If you haven't watched the replay of the US-Soviet game (or at least the last few minutes of it), we highly recommend you do. In the closing seconds, you will hear the great sports announcer Al Michaels shout: "Do you believe in miracles? *Yes!*" Not surprisingly, *Sports Illustrated* named the Miracle on Ice the single greatest moment of sports history in the twentieth century.

After getting crushed in the exhibition match against the Soviets just a few short days before the Olympics, which was certainly a setback—the team couldn't seem to do anything right—how did the US team muster the confidence to be able to bounce back, "run the table," and face down the Soviets again in a medal-round game? The US team's captain, Mike Eruzione, explained it this way: "When we played them in Madison Square Garden, we just stood around and watched and didn't engage at all. The second time around, it was different, though. The way we were playing, the confidence we had, we were a different hockey team. It's funny—we never even discussed the last time we played them. It never came up. [Coach] Herb never said anything. It was almost like we had never even played them before."[10]

Heading into the medal round, the US team was undefeated after all, having just rattled off four straight victories. So the confidence was there. They knew they could win. And yet, although they may not have discussed it, everyone on the team vividly remembered the brutal exhibition loss to the Soviets. They knew they weren't invincible. As a result, the US team was confident but not too confident. This enabled them to coalesce as a team, make sense of the challenge in front of them, and persist through it.

Again, this is a perfect example of what resilient teams with an appropriate amount of confidence do—and don't do. Resilient teams don't let their setbacks destroy their confidence. They leverage those setbacks to keep themselves grounded. They continue to plan and prepare for the next game (in this case) or team activity. Even down 3–2 at the end of the second period, the US team might have bent, but it didn't break. Beyond keeping the US team's confidence in check, the earlier loss to the Soviets on February 9 may have helped the team in another way. The Soviet coach at the time, Viktor Tikhonov, was later quoted as saying that the blowout Soviet win "turned out to be a very big problem" because it caused the Soviets to perhaps be overconfident as a team and underestimate the US.[11] This is another great example of how overconfidence can be the enemy of team resilience.

FIVE WAYS LEADERS BUILD TEAM CONFIDENCE

So, it's clear that team confidence is essential for team resilience, but how can leaders build a moderately high level of healthy team confidence without a team becoming overconfident? Table 3.1 summarizes the five ways leaders build team confidence and provides examples of each technique.

Make Sure Team Goals and Processes Are Crystal Clear

One of the most important things that leaders can do to ensure that their teams are appropriately confident is to make sure their teams know where they're headed and how to get there. In other words, leaders should ensure that team goals and the processes by which team members can accomplish those goals

TABLE 3.1. Five Ways Leaders Build Team Confidence

Behaviors	Examples
1. Make sure team goals and processes are crystal clear	Explicitly describe to team members the link between their own work goals and strategies and those of the team to make sure they understand how they fit into accomplishing the team's objectives
2. Empower your team	a. Lead by example by setting high performance standards for yourself and then model expectations for team members (e.g., walk the talk) b. Encourage team members to participate in decision making and use their ideas and suggestions when making decisions or communicating to higher-level managers c. Coach team members by providing encouragement and support for team successes and wins, when appropriate, and giving developmental feedback when the team is struggling d. Share important and strategic information with your team members, when possible, to make them feel like insiders and trusted e. Display a high level of concern and caring for your team members by making sure they know you have their back and are looking out for their best interests
3. Be a transformational leader	a. Show conviction to the organizational mission and directly appeal to team members' emotions to create excitement and motivation; practice self-sacrifice and continuously place others' interests over your own b. Articulate a motivating and inspiring vision that challenges team members to use high standards, communicates confidence and optimism about reaching goals, and helps them develop a sense of meaning from the work they are doing c. Encourage team members to challenge the status quo and take risks, and support their creative pursuits. d. Pay attention to team members' needs and act as a mentor to help coach and address any concerns and demonstrate care and compassion
4. Be an ethical leader	Constantly reinforce doing the right thing, all the time, every time; reinforce that a long-term outlook should always be prioritized over short-term success; be a role model in building a company and team culture team members want to emulate; and consistently behave in a manner you expect from your team members
5. Offer hypothetical and/or sequenced mastery experiences (or practice, practice, practice)	Make sure your team gets the opportunity to practice and rehearse the actions they will take in the event of adversity

are very clear.[12] As simple as it sounds, you'd be surprised at how often we've witnessed teams in many organizations whose members just weren't entirely sure exactly what their goals were or how they were supposed to try to achieve them. The key objective in using clear goals and processes is to make sure that members understand the link between each of their own individual work goals and strategies and those of their team.

Think about it this way: if there is confusion surrounding the team's targeted destination or the path they should travel to reach that destination, how could the team possibly have a healthy amount of confidence in their ability to accomplish their goals, or anything else for that matter?

Take as an example the Black Mambas, an antipoaching team founded in 2013 by Transfrontier Africa to protect rhinos in South Africa's Greater Kruger National Park. Rhino horns can be more valuable than gold on the black market. Almost 80 percent of the world's rhino population is in South Africa, and in 2017, over one thousand rhinos were illegally poached for their horns. Remarkably, since 2013, the year the Black Mambas team was founded, rhino poaching has been down a stunning 70 percent.

The Black Mambas team is composed almost entirely of women, who are heroines to their community and inspiring and empowering for the next generation. How do these women have the confidence to do what they do? By having extremely clear goals and processes for their rhino protection efforts. For example, their goal is "to save the rhinos," period. That's it. They have one goal, and everything they do centers on that one single objective. If a decision must be made, the correct choice is always the one that will give the team the best chance of saving the rhinos. The processes they use include monitoring rhino habitats, gathering intel, and removing traps the poachers use to capture the animals. One team member, Leithah Mkhabela, summed it up this way: "Being a Black Mamba empowers you. Through our hard work, confidence, and all our achievements, we have made people from all over the world accept us."[13] Clear goals and processes like those of the Black Mambas serve not only as a guidepost for teams but also as a reminder of the team's raison d'être—their reason or purpose for existing. Taken together, they can help a team maintain a steadfast focus on the prize and offer the level of confidence needed to overcome adversity that otherwise could lead to the extinction of rhinos in South Africa.

Empower Your Team

A lever that can help your team become more confident is to use empowering leadership with your team as a whole.[14] When leaders empower their teams through more autonomy and decision-making flexibility, team confidence will steadily increase as members begin to accomplish tasks with greater levels of responsibility and authority. Indeed, a meta-analysis of the effects of empowering leadership demonstrated that it is associated with higher overall team performance, team creativity, and a team's members going above and beyond typical expectations (i.e., team members were more likely to be strong *organizational citizens*, a term used to describe employees who go above and beyond their formal job duties).[15] One study of software development teams in Turkey showed that when team members experience high levels of team empowerment, they are also likely to have more team confidence.[16] There are five critical behaviors that leaders can use to empower their teams.

First, to increase team confidence, leaders need to make sure they lead by example. Essentially, that means team leaders will need to set very high performance standards for themselves to model expectations for their team members. The old adage, never ask your team members to do something you aren't willing to do yourself, is applicable here. When team members see their leaders working as hard as, or harder than, anyone else on the team, it instills a sense of confidence that team members can also rise to any occasion. "Walking the talk" means that leaders behave consistently with the messages they send to their team. There is no way a team can have a healthy level of team confidence with a leader who is not willing to go the extra mile for them. It's just not possible.

A good example of modeling to boost team confidence comes from Smart Design, a strategic design firm based in New York City. During the COVID-19 pandemic, the company started instituting weekly Zoom "happy hours" that kicked off right at 5:00 p.m. However, some leaders realized that asking people to stay on a Zoom call for another hour or so after many of them had already spent eight (or more) hours on video calls didn't make much sense as a stress reliever or bonding experience. So Smart Design changed the time of the get-togethers to noon and rebranded them as "midday mental breaks." People didn't feel guilty about taking a break during work hours to socialize because the entire company had sanctioned it. Another contributor to increasing employee morale through midday social activities was the company's leaders having calendars visible to all "to show blocks of time spent not working in the middle of the day." In other words, Smart Design's leaders modeled the behaviors they wanted their team members to emulate, thereby increasing their confidence in doing so themselves and their team's overall level of confidence in tackling projects during a global pandemic.[17]

The second lever of empowering leadership to enhance team confidence is to not only allow but also actively encourage team members to participate in decision making. The more a leader solicits advice and ideas from team members, the more those team members will develop a healthy sense of team confidence. A simple "I trust your judgment" or "What do you think?" can go a long way. This is not just a matter of simply listening to your team's ideas; it's much more than that. Although listening is an essential part of healthy communication, to really build your team's confidence, you actually need to use the ideas and suggestions your team offers. This could mean that, even if you disagree with a particular idea or are not completely convinced about its viability, you are still willing to share it as part of a larger decision-making process. When teams can see that leaders are taking their ideas seriously and passing them on to others (and, of course, giving credit to those who generated them), they will have firsthand knowledge of how their ideas are being received and incorporated into company plans. In that way, members will become more confident that they are competent, valued members of their team and that they are making a real difference in their company.

Sir Richard Branson, founder of the Virgin Group, including such eponymous brands as Virgin Atlantic Airlines and Virgin Galactic (for space travel), uses a perhaps counterintuitive philosophy to run his businesses. Instead of the more common refrain "the customer is always right" (or first), he believes that employees are his company's top priority, followed by customers and then shareholders. In putting his employees first, Branson highlights the importance of allowing them to have a say in the practices and policies of his company. He personally engages in what he refers to as "walkabouts" (essentially, the classic "management by walking around," or MBWA) when he engages with frontline team members to gather their thoughts. Branson comments: "It is very easy to be out and about and not stuck behind a desk. I make a point of getting out and talking to all of our staff . . . having a notebook in my back pocket . . . listening . . . making sure that you write down the feedback that you get and very importantly mak[ing] sure you act on that feedback when you get back to base."[18] When teams see that they are being allowed to participate in decision making and that leaders are actually using their ideas, their confidence will soar.

The third key for leaders to empower teams and increase their confidence is coaching. The importance of coaching has long been recognized in organizations, but its role in building team confidence has not received as much attention. Coaching teams to higher confidence means that leaders need to provide encouragement and support for team successes and wins where appropriate. However, if a team is struggling in a particular area or with specific issues, leaders need to provide developmental feedback that helps their teams find areas of improvement. Coaching teams also requires that leaders encourage team members to solve problems together and consistently exchange information. Again, because we are talking about team confidence, not individual confidence, such encouragement and interactions will have to occur with team members collectively, more so than individually. Celebrating team success is also a key part of building team confidence, but in our experience, it's where team leaders tend to fall down the most. That is, they almost always step in when something goes wrong, but they tend to underacknowledge situations in which teams perform well. Leaders should never forget the power of positive reinforcement in celebrating team wins.

At the very beginning of the 1982–1983 NCAA college basketball season, coach Jim Valvano—"Jimmy V" to his fans—did something rather unusual with his North Carolina State University men's basketball team, the Wolfpack. On the court before the first practice, he had his team members climb up a ladder and practice cutting down the nets of the basketball goal, as a team would normally do ceremoniously after winning a national championship. He told his team that he wanted them to practice this ritual because they would be putting this net-cutting practice to use at the end of the season. He did so to help them believe that they were going to win the national championship that year. The season, though, did not go very well. The team encountered significant adversity and suffered through several losing streaks, including losing two of its last three games to end the regular season. In fact, the Wolfpack was in danger of not making the national tournament at all.

However, Coach V did not give up. He constantly reminded his team, no matter the outcome of a particular game, that they were going to win the national championship. In a somewhat surprising turn of events, North Carolina State won three straight games to take the conference tournament title, which automatically punched their ticket to the national tournament. This was the only way they could have made the tournament that year. In the national tournament, they rattled off five straight wins and found themselves in the national championship game as a seven-and-a-half-point underdog against the University of Houston Cougars. Nicknamed "Phi Slama Jama" for their prolific basketball-dunking skills, Houston featured such future NBA Hall of Fame players as Clyde "the Glide" Drexler and Hakeem Olajuwon. Coach V later famously joked that even his own mother bet against the Wolfpack: "My mother, she took Houston and gave eight points for that game. I'm telling you, I'm very disappointed."[19] In what is now ranked as one of the biggest upsets in college basketball history, North Carolina State won the game 54–52 at the very last second on a dunk shot by Lorenzo Charles. As a successful motivator, Coach V knew the power of coaching his team up to build and maintain a healthy level of team confidence, which meant that the team never stopped believing in themselves despite their string of regular-season losses. The 1983 Wolfpack basketball team was *unbreakable*. Sadly, Coach V lost a battle with cancer in 1993 at age forty-seven, but not before leaving us with his famous motivational phrase: "Don't give up: don't ever give up." That should be a lesson for all teams.

The fourth behavior critical for empowering leadership to influence team confidence is to share important and strategic information with your team. Nothing hurts a team's sense of confidence more than when a leader keeps members in the dark about significant events or current happenings in an organization. It not only sends a signal that leaders don't trust their teams; it also chips away at a team's belief that their leader really has confidence in members' ability to process and deal with sensitive information. Of course, not all information can be shared all the time, given confidentiality or privacy concerns. However, to the extent possible, making team members feel like insiders is a sure way to help build a team's overall sense of confidence.

Dustin Moskovitz, a former founder and chief technology officer of Facebook, and Justin Rosenstein, a former software engineer at Google, officially launched their collaboration software start-up Asana in 2011. Their humble goal: "To empower every group on earth to have clarity, accountability, and transparency in their daily work." Transparency at Asana means that the company is not afraid to share important and strategic information with its teams. They affectionately refer to this philosophy as "transparency 'til it hurts." According to Rosenstein, "For us, transparency is providing as much information as [an employee] needs to act in the best interest of their team, the company, and its mission as a whole." One important way that Asana shares such information transparently is to take exhaustive minutes from board meetings and weekly executive meetings and post them for every team to read. Rosenstein continued, "We think it's really critical for everyone to understand [and] to know what the high order bits are and what is top of mind for leadership."[20] This transparency ensures that teams feel included and that they know how critical they are to Asana's success. Moreover, when teams are making collective decisions about, for example, products, services, or marketing, they understand how their decisions fit within Asana's overall goals, and they're confident that they have the information necessary to make high-quality decisions that support those goals. In short, sharing information transparently strengthens team confidence.

Finally, the fifth empowering leadership behavior critical for helping a team to be more confident is displaying a high level of care and concern for team members. This sounds touchy-feely, of course, but when team members know that leaders have their back and are looking out for their best interests, they feel more confident in their own abilities and in the type of support they need to perform at very high levels. Think about times in your past when you felt as though your leader didn't care about your team's experiences or downplayed something significant that was happening to your team. Besides not being happy with that leader, you probably didn't feel very confident about your team's chances for success in that company either. When leaders openly express support and care for their teams, members tend to feel more collectively confident in their team's ability to get the job done.

In a harrowing example of leaders showing care and concern for their team, during the 2021 Union of European Football Associations Champions League Soccer Tournament, Denmark's Christian Eriksen suddenly collapsed while dribbling the ball in a match against Finland. The captain of Denmark's team, Simon Kjaer, sprang into action. Kjaer quickly realized that this was no ordinary soccer injury and was the first to reach his teammate. After realizing that Eriksen had lost consciousness, he first made sure to clear his airway and began to perform CPR until paramedics could reach Eriksen, whose heart had, in fact, stopped beating. He then shouted to his team members to form a privacy wall around Eriksen to keep the incident from becoming a spectacle for the television cameras. Finally, he personally comforted Eriksen's understandably distraught wife, which demonstrated a very high level of concern and caring for his team member and family. Fortunately, Eriksen was discharged from a Copenhagen hospital six days after suffering what turned out to be a cardiac arrest on the soccer field. During his hospital stay, he had surgery to implant a cardioverter defibrillator to regulate his heartbeat. Imagine the level of team confidence instilled by having such a courageous and dedicated team leader who always has your back (and your heart). Remarkably, 229 days after suffering cardiac arrest on the field, Eriksen made his triumphant return to competitive soccer, playing for Brentford in the English Premier League against Newcastle United on February 26, 2022.

Transform Your Team

It's possible that no leadership style has received as much attention over the past half century as transformational leadership. Transformational leadership inspires team members to enact positive change in their organization by first transforming themselves. As companies today are constantly trying to adapt and pivot to rapidly changing business environments, transformational leadership is perhaps more important for teams now than ever before. If transformational leadership is about helping team members develop themselves and engage in change-oriented practices in a company, then it should be fairly obvious why this leadership style is linked to team confidence.[21] Transformational leaders constantly build up and reinforce team confidence, and they do so via four major leadership behaviors.

First, to build up team confidence using transformational leadership, leaders need to be sound role models. Transformational leaders enjoy the trust, admiration, and respect of their teams. This is because they place a strong emphasis on self-sacrifice. They speak about the importance of transcending above and beyond self-interest to prioritize the interests of others. But they do more than speak about it. They also live it. They practice self-sacrifice, continuously placing others' interests over their own. In doing so, they make it crystal clear that they are out not to benefit themselves but to make the world a better place by living out the mission of the company and by helping their team members be the best they can be. This selflessness develops deep trust in teams, and reporting to a trustworthy leader inspires a great deal of confidence.

Marc Benioff, chairman and CEO of Salesforce, is a great example of a leader who regularly exhibits self-sacrifice. Salesforce is one of cloud computing's pioneers that has grown to be worth over $100 billion, building a profitable model around "software as service." Benioff is also one of the world's leading philanthropists. As an example of his generosity, in 2010, Marc and his wife, Lynne, donated $110 million to construct a children's hospital in Mission Bay, California. But you don't need to donate millions of dollars to be a transformational leader. You simply need to demonstrate self-sacrifice by putting the interests of others over your own.

A more realistic practice might be what Benioff does when someone is first hired at Salesforce. He insists that the new team members spend an afternoon doing some type of volunteer or service work, often in places such as homeless shelters, hospitals, or public schools. This sends a clear signal that there are more important things in life than the work being performed in the office, that sacrificing one's time and effort to help others is the true meaning of life. And by making this powerful statement on every employee's first day, he's building an entire culture of self-sacrifice. Benioff says: "I want a company where people are excited to come to work every day, where they feel good when they get here, where it doesn't take from them, but it's giving to them, it's giving to others. Why do people want to be here? It's not that we have more amenities than everybody else. We have less. We don't have a cafeteria. But we have a stronger purpose and stronger mission."[22] Note the references to mission and helping others. Integrating altruism and selflessness into the company's culture in this way inspires trust, and trust builds confidence in teams.

Second, team confidence can be increased when a transformational leader articulates a motivating and inspiring vision about where the company (or more directly, where the team) is going in the future. Specifically, a vision that builds team confidence is typically focused on challenging team members to use high standards, communicating confidence and optimism about teams reaching their goals, and helping team members develop a sense of meaningfulness from the work they are doing. A great transformational leader not only articulates where a team is going but also helps teams identify the ways and means they can use to get there. In that sense, such leaders help teams chart their course and provide resources for successfully navigating that course, ultimately boosting team confidence by illuminating the path forward. Moreover, when articulating a compelling vision, it's important to know that it's not only about what is said but how it's said. Transformational leaders draw on charismatic leadership tactics, such as reframing the vision to resonate with people.[23] It's no secret that when it comes to inspiring people to act, the delivery of a vision is perhaps more important than the vision itself! This delivery often includes analogies, metaphors, and stories that bring the vision to life.

In examining the link between a motivating and inspiring vision and team confidence and success, the consultants Nathan Wiita and Orla Leonard examined how forty-nine enterprise leadership teams spent their time.[24] One of the key findings from their study is that higher-performing teams prioritize better than lower-performing teams do. In fact, the former spent 54 percent more time than the latter on "setting direction" and "crafting a vision that serves as a guiding light for decisions." Moreover, lower-performing teams spent a surprising 83 percent more time firefighting and dealing with issues at a tactical level rather than a strategic one. Team leaders should help carve out time for these more vision-oriented pursuits, as this will result in team members feeling more confident when adversity inevitably comes their way. And when communicating a compelling vision to a team, research supports that leveraging leaders' charisma is highly effective. In fact, charisma can greatly boost confidence. In a study of 133 Spanish bank branches, charismatic leadership was tied to enhanced team confidence, which ultimately made teams more innovative.[25]

Third, a transformational leader can help build team confidence by encouraging team members to challenge the status quo and take risks, and by supporting their creative pursuits. If part of a transformational leader's job is to help orient team members toward creating positive change in an organization, then that leader will have to lay the groundwork for a team to confidently think outside the box (or think that there is no box) in coming up with innovative and creative ways to accomplish team tasks. This means guiding team members to engage in critical thinking, question traditional ways of doing things, and seek out better and more innovative methods.

One way leaders can do this is to support members in taking some time each week to work on special projects outside of their formal job role. For example, 3M for decades has allowed employees to use up to 15 percent of their paid work hours to focus on personal projects. Picking up on that idea, Google initiated something called the 20% Project, which allows employees to spend 20 percent of their week focused on projects that enhance team member innovation. One such project was even credited with the creation of Gmail.[26] But keep in mind that if you encourage team members to generate innovative ideas, you need to be prepared to give those ideas a chance. We recommend adopting an open mind here and letting your team know that, barring any obvious reasons not to, you're willing to try just about any well-thought-out idea at least once. If it works, it stays. If it doesn't, you won't continue it. No harm done. This ensures that your team members understand you're serious when you encourage innovation and don't interpret your directions as mere lip service. Research has shown that people who serve as champions of their team's innovative ideas by actively and enthusiastically promoting them enhance overall team confidence and, ultimately, team performance.[27]

Finally, transformational leaders build team confidence by paying attention to team members' needs and acting as a mentor and support system to help address their concerns. This is similar to a previously discussed core component of empowering leadership—displaying care and concern for team members. Beyond demonstrating empathy, transformational leaders are also skilled at identifying the specific needs of their team members and working tirelessly to meet those needs. This phenomenon also serves as the foundation of servant leadership. An unfortunate but all-too-common misconception is that teams are there to serve the needs of leaders. In fact, this couldn't be further from the truth. Teams don't exist to serve leaders. Leaders exist to serve teams. Why? Because leaders aren't building the actual products or providing services; teams are. The job of a leader is to give members everything they need to be successful. It means spending focused time and energy identifying team members' needs and doing everything they can to meet those needs. It also means prioritizing the needs of team members over their own: self-sacrifice.

This is a rather simple but powerful way of viewing team leadership. Think about it. What if leaders went to work every day with one primary objective— identifying which team member needs are not currently being met and then problem solving until they find a way to satisfy those needs? Figuring out ways to develop teams, to empower them, to make sure they have the resources they need to succeed, to make sure the obstacles in their way are removed. First of all, that's a fun, challenging, and rewarding job for a leader. And second, imagine you're the team members. Wouldn't you love it if, instead of your bosses nagging and micromanaging you, they made a point to ask you on a regular basis, "What can I do to help you succeed today?" It would be energizing. You would likely increase your trust in those leaders, be more loyal and committed, and be more satisfied with leadership.[28] And importantly, you would be more confident in yourself and in your team, knowing there is someone in your corner who is prioritizing your team's specific needs.

Herb Kelleher, cofounder and longtime chairman and CEO of Southwest Airlines, epitomized the servant leadership mentality. He was instrumental in building and perpetuating a culture of prioritizing employee needs. Kelleher famously stated, "The business of business is people—yesterday, today, and forever." His philosophy was that if you put your team first, always prioritizing their needs, they will enjoy their jobs and work hard not because they have to but because they want to. Kelleher's advice to leaders was to "honor, respect, care for, protect, and reward your employees—regardless of title or position— and in turn they will treat each other and external customers in a warm, in a caring, and in a hospitable way. This causes external customers to return, thus bringing joy to shareholders."[29] By his logic, prioritizing the needs of your team is not only the right thing to do; it's just good business.

Put Ethics at the Center of Leadership

Although all leaders should behave ethically no matter the circumstance (some don't, of course—recall the Volkswagen and Enron scandals), ethical leadership is particularly relevant for building team confidence.[30] Ethical leadership overlaps with the first transformational leadership behavior of role modeling self-sacrifice. But ethical leadership moves beyond self-sacrifice to take a broader view of morality. At the heart of ethical leadership is the act of doing what's "right," and this manifests in two ways. First, ethical leaders are "moral persons" in that they are role models who consistently exhibit ethical behavior. Second, ethical leaders are "moral managers" in that they actively promote and support ethical behavior among team members.[31] In other words, they not only do what's right; they influence others to do what's right as well. One meta-analysis showed that ethical leadership is positively associated with a wide range of employee outcomes, such as job satisfaction, organizational commitment, job performance and engagement, and psychological well-being; and it is also associated with a number of perceptions employees have of their leaders, including trustworthiness, honesty, fairness, leader effectiveness, and satisfaction.[32]

Ethical leadership works to build team confidence in a number of ways. One, ethical leaders constantly reinforce to their team members that they can accomplish their work by doing the right thing, all the time, every time. For example, leaders can reinforce that a long-term outlook should always be prioritized over short-term success. This should reduce the temptation to cut corners for a quick win. Such reinforcement of ethical behavior among teammates means that they will develop the confidence that they have everything they need to reach their goals and achieve exemplary outcomes, and that they have a leader who will support them when they fail, as long as they do what's right. In addition, ethical leaders are role models in that they build the type of company and team culture for team members to emulate. This means that leaders should speak openly about their own dilemmas in which they chose the ethical path, even though they knew it would result in a short-term setback. In that sense, ethical leaders show the way in terms of building confidence in team members to accomplish their tasks. Finally, one can imagine the hit to team confidence when a leader is caught behaving unethically. Trust in a leader, once broken, is very difficult to repair. A single unethical act can turn into a vicious spiral, eroding team confidence in leaders and in the team itself.

Dr. Sean Martin, a professor of business administration at the University of Virginia, and his colleagues set out to test the notion that ethical leadership helps teams build team confidence and bounce back faster from adversity. In pursuing this line of inquiry, he predicted that "ethical leaders—those who model certain values and behaviors and who hold the trust of their team members . . . would be more likely to keep the teams resilient, to help them bounce back by preserving their confidence and commitment to the group. So, we decided to put this to the test."[33] Among cadets at the US Military Academy at West Point, Martin found that even when teams of cadets performed poorly during a military skills competition, the decrease in team confidence was much less for those teams that reported having an ethical leader (for example, leaders who make fair and balanced decisions and set an example of how to do things the right way in terms of ethics) versus an unethical one (in fact, the reduction in confidence was about four times higher for teams with unethical leaders). Martin and his team concluded that "having an ethical leader is incredibly important, because when a team faces failure—which it will—if the boss is unethical, people are going to want to bail from that team or from that company. If you want teams to be more resilient to failure, you need to have ethical leaders at the helm because they have a really big impact on how people feel about moving forward and staying the distance."

Offer Hypothetical and/or Sequenced Mastery Experiences

Or, simply put, practice, practice, practice. A final way that leaders can build team confidence is by making sure their teams can consistently engage in hypothetical and/or sequenced mastery experiences, which is a fancy way of saying teams should practice and rehearse the actions that they would take in the event of adversity. When team members feel prepared to face various hypothetical setbacks and adversities, they will be much more confident in their ability to handle *actual* adversity. This is the reason firefighter teams engage in mock fire drills when they have downtime from fighting actual fires, or that airline pilots have to fulfill a certain number of hours in flight simulators to maintain their license to fly.

A great example of the power of rehearsal and practice comes from pit crews in Formula 1 auto racing, which has an international following, high television ratings, and alluring cash prizes for the fastest cars. One of the most important elements in winning a Formula 1 race is the speed with which the pit crews service the cars during pit stops and get them back on the track. Team McLaren, one of the world's premier Formula 1 teams, had been struggling with a series of blunders and mistakes by their pit crews, costing them multiple races.[34] McLaren's slow and mistake-prone pit crews led to the hiring of Stafford Murray, the leader of a team of thirty-five performance analysts and biomechanists at the English Institute of Sports Science. Murray had worked with all types of teams, including British Olympic teams. One of McLaren's goals was to reduce the average four-and-a-half-second pit stop to around two and a half seconds. In tackling that goal, Murray had the pit crews practice servicing the race cars over and over again. During each rehearsal, Murray's team of analysts examined and then reexamined every action the pit crews took, including many that someone without pit crew experience would've never even considered. Their mission was to uncover what actions led to superior crew performance in terms of speedier pit stops. What they found was fascinating. It turns out that what separated the best teams from the average ones was what they focused their eyes on during each pit stop.

After providing feedback, Murray again had the pit crews rehearse, each time making sure they focused their gaze on exactly the right things at the right time. They were practicing together like a "team of elite athletes." The result? After repeated rehearsals, at the 2012 German Grand Prix in Hockenheim, Germany, McLaren's pit crew broke the world record at the time for the fastest pit stop in history, at 2.31 seconds. Having teams engage in hypothetical mastery experiences, which allows them to practice in a relatively low-stakes environment, can increase team confidence. Then, when adversity strikes—and it often does in Formula 1 racing—resilient teams can make the right decisions to reach higher levels of confidence and performance.

CHAPTER 4

TEAM RESILIENCE RESOURCE #2
TEAMWORK ROADMAPS

An unfortunate statistic you may not be aware of is that US health-care workers report more workplace violence incidents than any other type of professional. In fact, a survey from the American Nurses Association conducted in 2018 reported that over 60 percent of nurses had experienced either physical or verbal abuse at work, or both.[1] Of course, when nurses or any hospital professionals believe that their workplace is unsafe and potentially dangerous, a whole host of negative outcomes can occur, including increased stress, burnout, absenteeism, and exiting of the profession altogether. In response to such trends, most hospitals now make use of behavioral response teams to deal with patients that exhibit the potential for violent and unpredictable behavior.[2]

Imagine you are an advanced practice registered psychiatric nurse serving as a member of a behavioral response team in a large university hospital. Your role on the team is to provide clinical assessments of patients who may be showing signs of psychiatric distress. At 8:15 a.m. on a Tuesday, shortly after arriving for your shift, your cell phone buzzes. It's a behavioral response team code call from the hospital's emergency operator system. The operator says that a patient in the emergency room is growing increasingly agitated, combative, and unwilling to follow staff instructions. As you head toward the elevator , you join three other members of your behavioral response team who have also received the code call, including a psychiatric clinical nurse and two members of the hospital's protective services (essentially, hospital security). A response code has also been sent to two other behavioral response team members, the patient's primary care physician and nurse.

As you enter the emergency room, the alerting nurse in charge of the unit (in this case, the head emergency room nurse who made the initial call) hustles your team into a side office. When a behavioral response team call goes out, if possible, it's customary for the team to engage in a "preintervention huddle" to quickly develop a plan of action. The emergency room nurse leads the conversation and informs the team that an elderly patient has been verbally threatening hospital staff and twice has tried to walk out of his room and leave the hospital. The patient had been injured in a fall at his daughter's home around 4:30 that morning and was brought to the hospital to be examined for a head injury and possible broken arm. After receiving an X -ray and determining a small fracture of the radius in his left arm, the patient was given a pain reliever and was waiting on a consultation to determine whether he had experienced a concussion.

Because the patient is somewhat disoriented, your role as the advanced practice registered nurse in psychiatry puts you in charge of the situation. Without any discussion, the team looks to you for direction. You recommend that the primary care physician accompany you to the patient's room to reassure the patient and begin to figure out whether his disorientation is related to a concussion or perhaps an underlying condition, such as dementia. You can see from the patient's chart that there has been no formal diagnosis of these conditions, but the patient's daughter had reported some recent odd behavior at home. You tell the two security officers to remain close but out of sight. You enter the patient's room with a pleasant smile on your face. As you position yourself at the foot of the patient's bed, the physician hangs back near the door. The patient appears calm and approachable. But just as you open your mouth to speak, he becomes noticeably agitated and shouts, "What's she doing here?" His eyes are fixed on the physician. Believing he is likely experiencing some form of "white-coat syndrome"—which refers to the anxiety and spikes in blood pressure that happen for some patients simply from being in the presence of doctors—you cast a knowing glance toward the physician, who immediately leaves the room without saying a word. She is replaced by another member of the team, the psychiatric clinical nurse specialist.

As you and your teammate begin to talk calmly and soothingly to the patient, it becomes clear that he is very afraid. As your conversation continues, he admits that he has been forgetful lately and has been having difficulty keeping his room in his daughter's house organized. That was the reason for the fall that morning. On the way to the bathroom, he tripped on his bathrobe, which he had dropped on the floor rather than hanging it up where he always did. His daughter had happened to hear the fall, which is how he ended up in the hospital. After drawing on your training, asking key questions, and using active listening, you hear the patient admit that he was trying to leave the hospital because he was afraid that his daughter wanted him to be moved to a nursing home because of his recent memory issues. He thought that if he could get out of the hospital, he might be able to find his way back to his daughter's house on his own. He also says he thought the physician in the room was going to start the process of sending him away, which explains the agitation toward the doctor. You throw another knowing glance at your teammate, who leaves the room and returns with the patient's daughter. She tears up as she hears about her father's fears of being "sent away" from her and his grandkids, and she quickly reassures him that she has no intention of sending him anywhere. As she and her father embrace, you exit the room with your teammate to meet up with the rest of your behavioral intervention team members.

Once in the side room again, your team huddles up to conduct a quick after-action review. In that review, you commend your teammates for responding quickly and effectively to this emergency situation. You are especially proud of the way your team members communicated, wordlessly with only eye contact, when action was needed. When the patient began to act agitated and tried to leave the hospital, your behavioral response team had a plan for handling the situation. In fact, your entire team had participated in the hospital's behavioral response team training program several months ago, which involved several days of classroom training followed by a series of realistic training simulations. The training involved practical strategies for preventing and de-escalating aggressive behavior, how to conduct an environmental risk assessment, learning an algorithm that specified common events along with potential interventions, and code documentation. You were also trained in various methods of team communication, which contributed to your team's ability to say a lot to one another without using words. The simulations actually included one very similar to the one your team just handled—an elderly patient who becomes agitated and increasingly aggressive. Because your team had rehearsed using these various simulations, you were able to act and make decisions smoothly and effectively. You thank your lucky stars that you had such a clear and effective teamwork roadmap to handle this adversity and hopefully any future such events, which are inevitable in your line of work. Because of this roadmap, instead of crumbling under the pressure of adversity, this behavioral response team was *unbreakable.*

As this example demonstrates, another key resource that teams need to be resilient is a teamwork roadmap, which is also referred to as a team mental model of teamwork.[3] A teamwork roadmap is a team's understanding of what to do and who is responsible for doing it. It captures the extent to which all team members know their own roles, responsibilities, and job requirements and are familiar with every other team member's roles, responsibilities, and job requirements. It also captures the extent to which team members know, if possible, how to perform one another's duties. When team members have a clear understanding of who is responsible for what and can work interchangeably if needed, that team has a well-functioning teamwork roadmap. A teamwork roadmap is particularly critical when adversity strikes and a team needs to harness its resilience. A teamwork roadmap allows team members to work collaboratively and seamlessly, despite the challenging conditions surrounding them. In the absence of such a roadmap, teams are likely to experience confusion and uncertainty, ultimately freezing their activity until their leader can assign duties to each person. For teams charged with rapid response, like the behavioral intervention team just described, or first-responder teams such as firefighters, emergency medical technicians, and the like, a healthy teamwork roadmap is indispensable to the ability to act quickly, overcome adversity, and save lives. However, a teamwork roadmap is important for *any* team, particularly ones that value being resilient.

Evidence suggests that for teamwork roadmaps to lead to higher team performance, members need to agree among themselves on the content of their teamwork roadmaps, or *roadmap similarity*, and the roadmaps need to accurately capture elements of teamwork needed to successfully complete tasks, known as *roadmap accuracy.*[4] For example, one study showed that roadmap similarity and accuracy promoted various healthy team action processes, including coordination, cooperation, and communication, which were in turn related to effective team performance.[5] Similar to our earlier example, teamwork roadmaps have often been studied in the health-care industry. This research has consistently demonstrated that poor teamwork roadmaps lead to greater errors in caregiving, mainly because of communication problems brought about by a lack of shared understanding among team members regarding their roles, tasks, and objectives.[6] Unfortunately, the problem is particularly acute for communication failures between nurses and physicians.[7] If the psychiatric nurse in our example had not been able to convey to the physician that the team might have been dealing with a form of white-coat syndrome, the patient would have likely become even more agitated and possibly been a greater danger to himself or others.

Beyond these individual studies, a comprehensive meta-analysis of teamwork roadmaps found that they strongly predict healthy team processes and team performance.[8] Although similar and accurate teamwork roadmaps are helpful to teams in just about every situation, they are especially critical in crisis situations, when there is often little to no time to sit down and discuss roles or when communication channels have broken down and such discussions aren't even possible. It's times like these that team members can simply refer to their roadmap to determine their next steps.

A great example of the importance of teamwork roadmaps in helping a team overcome adversity is the event commonly referred to as the Miracle on the Hudson.[9] On a cold afternoon on January 15, 2009, Captain Chesley "Sully" Sullenberger and his copilot, First Officer Jeffrey Skiles, departed New York's LaGuardia Airport on US Airways Flight 1549 en route to Charlotte, North Carolina. The team of five was rounded out with three flight attendants, Sheila Dale, Donna Dent, and Doreen Welsh. They were accompanied by 150 passengers. Skiles was in control of the plane's departure. Shortly after takeoff, and as the pilots began their routine ascent in their Airbus A320 under perfect flying conditions, Captain Sully remarked to Skiles, "What a beautiful view of the Hudson today," an eerie foreshadowing, perhaps, of the events about to unfold.

Less than three minutes after takeoff, adversity struck. At just under three thousand feet of altitude, a flock of Canada geese, each weighing ten to twelve pounds, collided with the plane. The pilots reported their view being filled with large birds (like a Hitchcock film, Sully later acknowledged), and the passengers and crew heard several loud bangs and saw flames shooting from the engines. Then, there was a chilling silence, followed by the odor of fuel. Sully and Skiles quickly realized that both engines had shut down. Sully took control from Skiles as Skiles began working the plane's checklist for an engine restart. After the engines went out, the plane continued to climb for about another twenty seconds, followed by a descent of 1,650 feet. Sully made a mayday call to ground control, stating that the plane lost thrust on both engines, and told air traffic controllers he wanted to return to LaGuardia. The LaGuardia tower told Sully to return to the airport and issued an order to stop all departures. Sully quickly realized he couldn't make it to LaGuardia and simply replied, "Unable."

Sully then inquired about the possibility of landing at Teterboro airport in New Jersey. Air traffic controllers responded that Sully could land at Teterboro's Runway 1. Sully issued a curt yes but almost immediately realized making it to Teterboro was no longer an option. He radioed, "We can't do it . . . We're gonna be in the Hudson." Sully issued the order over the cabin's communication system to "brace for impact" as the plane continued its descent toward the Hudson River. About ninety seconds later, Sully used an "unpowered ditching" maneuver to glide the plane into the river. The flight attendants described the ditching as a "hard landing" with "one impact, no bounce, and then gradual deceleration." Sully unlocked the cockpit door and ordered everyone to evacuate, waited for the last person to exit, and then walked up and down the cabin aisle twice to make sure all passengers had safely made it out. With the help of the US Coast Guard, two New York Waterway ferries, as well as other smaller boats, all passengers and the crew were safely rescued from the cold waters of the Hudson River. Many of the passengers suffered minor injuries, with one flight attendant, Doreen Welsh, suffering a deep laceration on her leg. Other passengers were treated for hypothermia. With the exception of one passenger who now wears glasses as a result of eye damage from exposure to jet fuel, there were no serious injuries or loss of life. A true miracle indeed.

The successful ditching of the US Airways Flight on the Hudson River that day would not have been possible if the crew of five did not have a teamwork roadmap to follow in the event of adversity. In many interviews over the years, Captain Sully, while not using the words *teamwork roadmap* explicitly, credits the ability of his crew to take action, often without having to formally communicate using words, for saving the passengers and crew that day.[10] In working with First Officer Skiles, Sully commented:

> In a situation where the time pressure and the workload were so intense, we didn't have time even to talk about what had happened or what we should do about it. He and I were able to collaborate wordlessly by knowing intuitively in this developing crisis what we should do to help the other based on our own long experience. He was silently cheering me on as I made each decision but ready to intervene to check my performance if he thought I was making an error. And then, finally, as we were approaching the water, again Jeff collaborated with me wordlessly. He knew that the

final critical maneuver was for me to try to judge, visually looking at this featureless water terrain ahead where depth perception's inherently difficult, the height at which to begin raising the nose to begin the landing. As we hit, we hit hard. But, the deceleration, while rapid, was uniform. Based upon the forces that Jeff and I felt in the cockpit as we slowed to the stop, it was obvious that the airplane was intact, it was stable, it was floating, people were probably still ok at that point. And, in the most amazing coincidence, Jeff and I turned to each other at that moment, at the same time, using the same words, and said, "Well, that wasn't as bad as I thought."[11]

Talk about a teamwork roadmap!

In communicating with the three flight attendants making up the rest of his team, Sully also recalled:

Fortunately, we have the advantage of having a very well-defined and very concise aviation vocabulary in which there are certain single words that are rich with meaning. "Brace" is such a word. It signals to the cabin crew, the flight attendants, that an emergency landing is imminent and that they should help the passengers avoid injury during the landing so they'll be able to evacuate by shouting their commands to the passengers. In the spur of the moment, I chose another word. So, I knew it was going to be a hard landing, I just didn't know how hard because Jeff and I had never practiced this before. So, I chose the word "Impact" to give them that vivid image. I said, "This is the Captain, brace for impact." And, immediately, even through that armored cockpit door, I could hear the two flight attendants in the front—Donna and Sheila—and I'm sure Doreen in the back was doing the same, begin shouting their commands in unison to the passengers, "Brace, Brace, Brace, Heads Down, Stay Down!" Hearing those words that day encouraged me, it comforted me, to know that by saying the few words I had but choosing the right words, I had literally gotten my crew on the same page. And that if I could find a way to deliver this aircraft to the surface intact, it would float long enough for the flight attendants to evacuate the passengers.[12]

As this famous example of team resilience shows, having a teamwork roadmap that is accurate and understood by all team members can literally mean the difference between life and death—and the difference between brittle and unbreakable teams. In the face of unimaginable adversity, the ability to communicate either wordlessly (with First Officer Skiles) or in a few choice words conveyed with great meaning (to the three flight attendants) enabled the team members to transition seamlessly from "business as usual" to crisis mode without having to waste time getting on the same page. The Miracle on the Hudson reminds us of a quote from our colleagues, Janis Cannon-Bowers and Eduardo Salas, who are both pioneers in the research on teamwork roadmaps: "When we observe expert, high-performance teams in action, it is clear they can often coordinate their behavior without the need to communicate."[13] Preparation, training, and a clear understanding of roles and responsibilities are critical to developing a teamwork roadmap.

FIVE WAYS LEADERS BUILD TEAMWORK ROADMAPS

There are five ways leaders can work to build healthy and accurate teamwork roadmaps to help ensure their teams are unbreakable. Table 4.1 summarizes the five ways leaders can build teamwork roadmaps and provides examples of each.

Hold Regular Team Meetings

The first thing all leaders of resilient teams need to do to build teamwork roadmaps is to hold regular team meetings so that all team members understand the contextual information they need to be resilient in unfamiliar territory.[14] This might seem obvious to some, but we have seen many situations when leaders mean well and think about having regular team meetings, but then work and life get in the way, and inertia kicks in. Or when they do have meetings, they are focused on firefighting rather than building effective teamwork roadmaps. Although one-on-one meetings between team leaders and individual team members are valuable for accomplishing tasks and building relationships, regular meetings with the entire team offer members the opportunity to hear what everyone else is working on. Team meetings are critical for understanding each person's role and how all roles fit together—in other words, team meetings contribute directly to teamwork roadmaps.

There are countless ways to structure a team meeting, and leaders can experiment until they land on a structure that works best for their particular teams. However, as a general recommendation, we encourage leaders to give everyone on the team a chance to report out on two items: a project update and any challenges they're facing that the team may be able to help with. With respect to the project update, team members shouldn't list every little thing they're

TABLE 4.1. Five Ways Leaders Build Teamwork Roadmaps

Behaviors	Examples
1. Hold regular team meetings	Make sure that all team members understand the contextual information they need to be resilient in unfamiliar territory and each person's role and how all roles fit together; focus on quality, not quantity of meetings; keep an eye out for quieter team members and encourage their input; communicate about adversities both current and future
2. Use team interaction training	Focus on training members on how they should work together as a team, not on task-based skills; specify developing new strategies, adjusting the way members coordinate, changing the way members communicate, and reassigning new roles "on the fly"
	Include training on three specific functions:
	a. Orientation, or raising awareness of the possible constraints impeding team resilience
	b. Mapping, or helping teams learn the action-outcome contingencies relevant for a wide variety of tasks
	c. Cross-training, or, to the extent possible, making sure members are trained to fulfill other members' roles so the team has backup and ability to replace key members at critical points in time
3. Use shared leadership	Ensure that all members of a team take on various leadership responsibilities at different times and for various tasks
4. Lead with a growth mindset	Make learning, growth, and development a core theme in messaging; encourage team members to try new things, to take risks, and to challenge the status quo; invite team members to ask questions not only of the leader but of one another; lead by example and discuss with teams each time they try something new and uncomfortable, or attempt to improve in an area where they have traditionally struggled; recognize team members who engage in learning behaviors and leverage those successes to encourage others to do the same
5. Simulate hypothetical adversities to prepare teams	Block off time in meetings to discuss a hypothetical scenario and ask each team member to report on what they would do if such an event occurred at that exact moment; give teams the opportunity to work collaboratively to overcome a variety of challenges

working on. Rather, this is an opportunity to highlight a project or two that is relevant to the entire team. Not everyone will have an update in every meeting, and that's OK. And not everyone will be facing significant challenges—and that's not only OK; it's ideal!

Of course, you'll need to keep an eye out for team members who never seem to have anything to say. In our experience, this is pretty rare, but it does happen. You'll want to raise this issue in your one-on-ones with those individuals to uncover any potential underlying issues that may be causing their silence. The point here is that leaders should be sure to give everyone airtime in team meetings, as doing so is essential to building an accurate teamwork roadmap. And reporting out is not only about the roadmap. When team members listen to one another, learn what everyone is working on, and engage in collaborative problem solving, they not only understand who's doing what and how their own individual roles fit into the big picture, but they also strengthen their team social bonds, which facilitates coalescing when adversity strikes.

Team meetings also offer an opportunity for leaders to communicate to their team about adversities—current and future. Research has identified communication as one of the most critical responsibilities of leaders.[15] And it's particularly important in the context of team resilience. This is because leader communication plays a vital role in a team's sensemaking activities. When times get tough and the team is facing an uncertain or unfamiliar challenge, members tend to turn to their leader for guidance. It's at that moment that leader communication is most essential. Regular team briefings enable leaders to discuss adversity and walk teams through possible responses. This ensures that team members have a shared understanding of what to do when certain contingencies arise and, importantly, which actions should be prioritized. Skilled leaders won't suck up all the air in the room when delivering these briefings, though. They know that these are excellent opportunities to leverage different perspectives on their team through a process known as guided reflexivity. Reflexivity is essentially a point of reflection, during which team members consider how they could modify their activities and goals to better align with the current or anticipated environment. Research suggests that when leaders guide their teams through the reflexivity process, teams generate more similar teamwork roadmaps.[16] According to this evidence, leaders can guide an effective reflexivity session by asking their teams to reflect on how things are currently going, discuss possible strategies to improve their performance, and formulate a plan for executing those strategies.

We hope by now you can see the many benefits that can emerge from a well-run team meeting. But we would be remiss if we failed to highlight that it is the *quality* of the meetings that is important, much more so than their length. In fact, some of the best meetings are quick. Brief team meetings have long been a part of the Agile project methodology, which essentially involves managing a project by breaking it up into several phases, and are typically called stand-up meetings because often they are held while members are actually standing to help ensure a quick check-in rather than a longer discussion. So, what's important here is to have an efficient number of meetings, as the Agile approach emphasizes, but to make each meeting rich in terms of information exchange and teamwork roadmap building.

When the COVID-19 crisis started and increased multiple business risks to the Shapiro Negotiations Institute, its managing partner Andres Lares and the leadership team established some guiding principles for communicating with their employees to make sure there was an effective teamwork roadmap to deal with it. First, they decided to communicate more often than usual, meeting with their entire team every Monday but also one-on-one with a core group of managers twice a week. One of the most fundamental elements of crisis leadership is that it is impossible to overcommunicate. Lares emphasized how important it is not only to meet regularly with team members but also to lead with compassion and to be completely transparent in those meetings, even if the news to be shared isn't positive. "At a time when people are feeling uncertain and it's hard to see light at the end of the tunnel, it's important to feel that what you hear from leadership is the truth," Lares said. "We want to make sure we're always clear and give our management team a level of ownership and responsibility to move the company in the direction we believe we need to go." Second, he and his team made sure that all the other team leaders ran their meetings with compassion and transparency and felt comfortable discussing adversity and setting direction for overcoming it. Finally, he and his leadership team worked hard to make sure everyone felt a "degree of unity across the entire company, something that is essential in times of crisis."[17] They focused on reassuring and comforting their teams during meetings to send a strong and consistent message: we're all in this together. In other words, the leaders at Shapiro Negotiations Institute used communication and frequent team meetings to bring the company together, and in doing so, they helped teams coalesce at a highly critical time.

Use Team Interaction Training

A second key lever for team leaders to build effective teamwork roadmaps is team interaction training, especially early in a team's lifespan. Team interaction training is not focused on task-based skills, such as how to do a job or perform a team task. Rather, it focuses on how members should work together as a team. Such training is particularly critical when a team faces unfamiliar or dynamic business environments, which of course makes team resilience of utmost importance. For example, in highly novel environments, just working harder or putting in more effort is not likely to help a team be resilient. Rather, teams in unfamiliar territory need to develop new strategies, adjust the way members coordinate, change how members communicate, and reassign new roles on the fly. Such training is also different from having a team simply rehearse a set of preexisting routines (which, admittedly, in certain situations, can also be helpful). When a team is facing a great amount of uncertainty, team interaction training will need to involve teaching members how to approach, diagnose, and execute strategies when responding to unanticipated types of adversity.

Key questions to address include: How will your team communicate when adversity strikes? How will they integrate their work efforts? How will they exchange products or resources? How will they back one another up when help is needed? Who will take ownership of certain high-priority actions, and who will provide support? Who will be responsible for monitoring systems, resources, workflows, and environmental conditions? These questions can all be answered in thoughtfully designed team interaction training. For example, leaders could benefit from running their teams through simulated adversities that force them to reassess how best to work in a concerted manner.

For team interaction training to pay off, there are three specific functions that team members should be exposed to when attempting to build up their teamwork roadmaps. First, team members should get training on "orientation functions," or raising awareness of the possible constraints impeding team resilience. Leaders should openly discuss the potential barriers their teams could face in terms of having enough resilience to survive and thrive amid adversity. Importantly, this is not the time for sugarcoating, as leaders need to be direct and honest about the various aspects of a team's environment that could short circuit members' abilities to stay resilient. Team members will respond more positively to the extent that they truly believe their leaders are watching out for them by laying out the various situational contingencies that could hurt their

general counsel and a corporate secretary at a publicly traded company. She asked the association to help her company create a crisis management plan to present to her board of directors for approval. Carol listed out various potential crises and divided them into four categories: corporate and financial, operational, nonoperational, and aftershock. As the team worked through different hypothetical crisis situations, they identified areas where the company was lacking. For example, they recommended adding a human resource employee who solely focused on the company's employees and their families throughout a crisis. They then tested their plans with a crisis simulation. One of their competitors had recently experienced a financial crisis, so they took that scenario and adapted it to their company. They tested the scenario at a management retreat with the CEO and his team, during which they envisioned events that would stress the company and the crisis management plan. In conducting this scenario-based training, they found that most of the issues involved communication; that is, when to communicate, who should communicate and to whom, and how much. After they worked through all possible scenarios, they came up with the best one and took it to the board to adopt a formal plan. Such an approach demonstrates the power of helping teams learn the action-outcome contingencies so critical for developing healthy teamwork roadmaps.

Third, to the extent possible, team members should be cross-trained in different roles so that if one or two team members cannot perform specific duties for the team, the team will have backup and the ability to replace a key team member at critical times. A number of studies have shown the value of cross-training team members on team performance. For example, in two experimental studies using computer simulations, researchers found that cross-training had a positive effect on the extent to which team members developed shared roadmaps related to how teammates were supposed to interact as a team.[22] These teamwork roadmaps were, in turn, associated with greater team coordination and the quality and quantity of team member backing-up behaviors, which were in turn related to higher team performance. Importantly, the study found that merely having team members model the various roles in their teams was just as effective in members' developing shared teamwork roadmaps as having team members actually experience the various roles firsthand. This again shows the power of training and rehearsing for developing effective teamwork roadmaps.

Tim Brown, a former CEO of IDEO, very creatively described the importance of cross-training for increased adaptability and resilience. He portrayed two types of employees, one he referred to as a letter *I* and the other as a *T*.

The *I*-shaped employees are those who have deep expertise in their particular area but are limited in terms of their ability to coordinate and collaborate across different disciplines. In contrast, *T*-shaped employees also have depth of expertise in a field but enough understanding of other disciplines to work across multiple areas, which allows them to see the bigger picture and be more adaptable and resilient. In describing what he meant when using the analogy of the letter *T*, he said:

> The vertical stroke of the "T" is a depth of skill that allows them to con-
> tribute to the creative process. That can be from any number of differ-
> ent fields: an industrial designer, an architect, a social scientist, a business
> specialist, or a mechanical engineer. The horizontal stroke of the "T" is
> the disposition for collaboration across disciplines. It is composed of two
> things. First, empathy. It's important because it allows people to imagine
> the problem from another perspective—to stand in somebody else's shoes.
> Second, they tend to get very enthusiastic about other people's disciplines,
> to the point that they may actually start to practice them. T-shaped people
> have both depth and breadth in their skills.[23]

Some have even suggested that people can be pi shaped (π), which means that they have in-depth expertise in two different areas, but they can also cut across different disciplines.[24] Whatever letter or analogy you use, the bottom line is that cross-training of team members can help build stronger and more accurate teamwork roadmaps that contribute to a high level of resilience in teams.

Share Your Leadership

The third way for leaders to build up teamwork roadmaps is to employ shared leadership, which means that all members of a team take on various leadership responsibilities at different times and for various tasks.[25] We know from research with physicians in Spain that shared leadership in teams is associated with greater team resilience.[26] Shared leadership is a collective influence process in which team members share power and constantly switch between leader and follower roles. They interact closely, influence one another, and work collaboratively to make team decisions. It stands to reason that the more team members actively engage in this type of dynamic leadership behavior, the deeper their understanding of their fellow team members' various roles and responsibilities. As such, when members share leadership responsibilities, they are more likely to develop teamwork roadmaps that are both similar and accurate. Shared leadership also promotes synchronization of team members' efforts, strategies, and responsibilities. In other words, it should lead to greater team coalescing when adversity strikes.

W. L. Gore Associates, the Newark, Delaware–based company that produces Gore-Tex and several other products, has been employing shared leadership effectively for years.[27] Gore has about nine thousand employees and a strict rule that there are no more than 150 people in each office.[28] When a new project or situation arises in the company, rather than formally assigning a leader to it, the person with the most knowledge on the issue assumes leadership. Gore refers to this type of leadership as "natural leadership" because leadership credibility is not gained through formal authority or hierarchy. Rather, leaders are viewed as credible to the extent that they demonstrate the knowledge, skills, and abilities that move a business objective forward successfully over time. The company does employ a team of higher-level leaders, called mentors, responsible for the company's overall well-being, but they still have no formal authority over projects. Shared leadership at Gore relies heavily on direct lines of communication, which can lead to much faster responses during times of great change or crisis. With such a shared leadership structure, teamwork roadmaps can be developed quickly. Most importantly, this leadership approach means, again, that there is a higher likelihood that roadmaps will be similar and accurate.

Lead with a Growth Mindset

A fourth way that leaders can enhance teamwork roadmaps is to instill a growth mindset in the team. *Growth mindset*, a term coined by Dr. Carol Dweck, a professor of psychology at Stanford University, is a belief that, with a little effort (or sometimes a lot), one can learn to be good at anything.[29] This is based on the fundamental understanding that our knowledge and abilities are malleable and can be altered by our actions. Compare this to a fixed mindset, which is a belief that we're either good at something or we're not, and this won't change. In other words, some people are born with certain gifts, and if you're not one of them, then you're just out of luck. The fixed mindset, unfortunately, is the more common of the two, and it goes without saying that it is the more harmful one. The fixed mindset decreases motivation. It leads to complacency. It causes people to avoid taking risks or stepping out of their comfort zones. It limits learning. In other words, the fixed mindset stunts growth.

The growth mindset, as you might expect, promotes growth. It drives people toward continuous improvement and motivates them to take an occasional leap of faith. It pushes people to take on new challenges, as President John F. Kennedy famously stated, "not because they are easy, but because they are hard."[30] The growth mindset enhances learning. It's not difficult to see how such a mindset among team members can strengthen a teamwork roadmap. Leaders should make learning, growth, and development a core theme in their messaging. They should encourage team members to try new things, take risks, and challenge the status quo. Emphasis should be placed not only on individual learning and growth but also on team learning and growth. Team members should be invited to ask questions, not only of the leader but of one another. They should be encouraged to observe, monitor, and learn from one another. As team members learn more about everyone else's roles and about how each role fits into the big picture, the roadmap becomes more detailed, and the team grows stronger. Leaders should also lead by example, discussing with the team each time they try something new and uncomfortable or when they attempt to improve in an area where they have traditionally struggled. They should also recognize and celebrate team members who engage in these learning behaviors and leverage those successes to encourage others to do the same. These leadership actions all contribute to a culture of growth in teams, in which the pursuit of learning becomes the norm and leads to future learning behavior.

Dr. Danielle King runs the Working Resilience Research Laboratory at Rice University in Houston, Texas, which is devoted to understanding what makes employees and teams more resilient. In one study of the interactions of forty-eight teams in five Canadian start-up companies, King and her colleague Dr. Kyle Brykman, a professor at the University of Windsor in Ontario, Canada, examined the role of leaders in helping to build and sustain resilient teams.[31] In examining several of the behaviors associated with a growth mindset, King and Brykman found that teams were more resilient if their leaders encouraged team members to take risks, make suggestions on their own, and learn from the process. In addition, leaders who created team environments characterized by open communication and language that emphasized openness and development were key to team learning and team resilience. All these attributes bring members onto the same page with regard to their teamwork behaviors. King notes: "Knowing that you have a leader who is focused on learning, and not just on performance outcomes, is critical. It's also important for them to be intentional about communicating this regularly to employees, as it can make all the difference in building more resilient teams. Leaders need to verbally reward a learning mindset. For example, when a boss responds to an employee who makes an on-the-job error by saying, 'Great, now you can learn from this experience,' rather than berating them for making a mistake, it makes a big difference."[32] This is the essence of leading with a growth mindset, which has a big impact on developing accurate and similar teamwork roadmaps.

Simulate Hypothetical Adversities to Prepare Teams

Finally, team leaders can strengthen teamwork roadmaps during times of relative calm by crafting hypothetical adversities for the team to overcome. Leaders can do this by blocking off time in team meetings to discuss a hypothetical scenario and asking each team member to report on what they would do if such an event occurred at that exact moment. Or leaders can choose a more immersive method, simulating a hypothetical scenario by turning up the heat for the team, so to speak, and challenging them to respond. Such hypothetical training prepares teams by providing them with experience in responding to specific adversities. Thus, leaders should be strategic in the types of adversities they present to their teams, predicting, to the extent possible, the challenges that their teams are likely to face in the future. However, perhaps even more important than selecting the right adversities is giving teams opportunities to work collaboratively to overcome a variety of challenges. Even if they never experience a given hypothetical, the practice will enable team members to learn a great deal about one another (and themselves!) with respect to how they think and act when adversity strikes. With each experience, another critical piece of the teamwork roadmap falls into place.

The MARS-500 mission simulation was conducted between 2007 and 2011 in a joint collaboration between Russia, the European Space Agency, and China.[33] The purpose of this collaboration was to simulate a long-duration flight from Earth to Mars and back to study the effects of psychosocial isolation in preparation for a future spaceflight to Mars. The simulation took place at the Russian Academy of Sciences Institute of Biomedical Problems in Moscow. It involved three phases, the last of which was a 520-day crewed mission, with three members from Russia and one each from France, Italy, and China. The realistic facility was designed to simulate an Earth-Mars shuttle spacecraft, an ascent-descent craft, and the Martian surface. The volunteers had cross-functional expertise in engineering, medicine, biology, and human spaceflight. The simulation captured very realistic aspects of a Mars flight, including long-term weightlessness, the effectiveness of resource management, and the effects of isolation in a hermetically sealed environment. Communication systems were even designed with a thirteen-minute delay to simulate actual communication between Earth and the spacecraft. Such a hypothetical but believable scenario is exactly the type of training that can be used to build teamwork roadmaps and bolster team resilience. Clearly, a voyage to Mars will require an extremely high level of team resilience among astronauts. We can't wait for this to become a reality.

One final point as we conclude our discussion of teamwork roadmaps: research suggests that roadmaps are influenced by team composition. For example, the smaller the team, the easier it is for members to align on their roadmap.[34] Likewise, teams with more collective experience in their work tend to enjoy better teamwork roadmaps, as do teams with fewer membership changes and teams whose members work in close physical proximity.[35] This points to the importance of leaders being careful when selecting members to join (or leave) a team. Although clearly more difficult to do today than ever before, if possible, leaders should try to maintain stable team membership by keeping members together as long as possible. They should ensure that their teams possess an adequate level of work experience—teams composed of all new employees will struggle mightily to develop their roadmaps. They should be intentional and strategic about how many people are added to a team so that it doesn't grow too large. And finally, leaders should be cognizant, especially in a business environment that is trending more toward remote and hybrid every day, that face-to-face contact matters when a team is working hard to develop a teamwork roadmap that is similar and accurate.

CHAPTER 5

TEAM RESILIENCE RESOURCE #3

TEAM CAPACITY TO IMPROVISE

Imagine you're the leader of a new product development team working for a "green" consumer goods manufacturer. For the past several months, you and your team have been working on a spray disinfectant designed to attach itself to airborne virus particles and kill them upon contact. Of course, there are other competitor products already on the market in this category that are designed to kill germs and viruses. However, many of these products work only on surfaces and contain harsh chemicals that are not designated as acceptable by Green Seal, an independent, nonprofit organization that certifies products and services that meet credible and transparent science-based environmental standards. The goal of Green Seal, which is consistent with your company's vision, is to ensure tangible reductions in the whole environmental footprint.

In working on this new product, your team follows the generally accepted product development stage model common for creating new products in your industry. In the first stage, your team engages in a customer needs and discovery effort, which involves focus groups and surveys to gauge the need for such a product. One of the most important things you learn in the focus groups was that consumers want a product that they can use when traveling and staying in hotels and home-sharing properties, such as Airbnbs and VRBOs. In the past, most consumers relied on the cleaning services provided by their accommodations staff or property owners to ensure that rooms were clean and virus- and germ-free upon arrival. However, after the devastation caused by COVID-19 and continuing issues with other viruses, such as the flu and even the common cold, consumers are increasingly taking it upon themselves to be a second "line of defense" when traveling for work or leisure. In fact, throughout the COVID-19 pandemic, you heard many stories of consumers trying to "fumigate" their hotel rooms upon entry and wiping down all surfaces, just in case any potential viruses remained after standard cleaning. But there were also many complaints from consumers about the safety of frequently using such products in large amounts, particularly in closed-door settings, and the potential impact of these chemicals on people and the environment. Using the data collected in the focus groups, your team decides to pitch an idea to your company's leadership team to create a safe, green, and refreshing spray that consumers could use when traveling (in smaller sizes) or at home (in larger sizes).

After identifying a strong consumer need for such a product, your team enters the second stage of product development, which entails designing a solution to meet this particular consumer need. During this stage, you work with an expanded cross-functional team, including sales and marketing professionals, product designers, chemists, and packaging specialists. For several months, your team develops various formulas that are tested, retested, and discarded. Some sprays remain wet too long, some are not powerful enough to kill 99.9% of viruses, and some give off an unpleasant odor that consumers are sure to dislike. Finally, with additional prototyping and trial and error, your team lands upon just the right chemical compound that will produce a fast-drying, environmentally safe, and great-smelling product.

It is time to move to the third stage: initiate manufacturing of the spray while simultaneously working on bottle design, packaging, and marketing materials. You have a great feeling about this product, and you know the timing of its release could not be better. Consumers are demanding such a product, and they want it right now.

And then . . . adversity strikes. After millions of gallons of your new spray had already been produced in three manufacturing plants around the country, you get a call from one of the chemists who had been involved from the very beginning of product design. After a bit of awkward silence, he says he has some "bad news." It turns out that although the product had passed all the human safety tests, a red flag was discovered: under certain circumstances, the spray could be hazardous for many breeds of dogs and cats. In fact, if one ingredient of your spray came into contact with a commonly owned household cleaning product, it could spell disaster for people's pets. So, what now? Your company has spent millions of dollars on the product. To shut it all down would cost a fortune. You decide to call an all-hands meeting of your cross-functional team, warning your team members that there is no telling how long they will have to meet. Bring water, bring food, bring a pillow, you say. Your team needs to summon its inner grit to persist through this crisis.

As the meeting begins, you're a little afraid that someone might start the "blame game" and point fingers in an attempt to assign responsibility for this huge mistake. However, that's not what happens at all. Much to your surprise, rather than splintering, your team begins coalescing. One of the marketing reps leads the way: "There's no sense in looking backward. That won't help our current situation. The only thing we should be doing now is brainstorming solutions to this problem." Another team member agrees and immediately kicks off the sensemaking process by suggesting that the company could simply move ahead with the product but market it only to people without pets. Another team member objects, saying that her market research had shown that there has been a huge increase in pet adoptions that started during the early stages of the COVID-19 pandemic (in fact, for a time, many animal shelters were completely empty). As a result, more people have pets at home, and, importantly, there has been a 57 percent increase in people traveling with their pets and staying with them in hotels and home-sharing properties. In fact, many hotels pivoted during this time and adopted pet-friendly policies. So the marketing opportunities for a cleaning spray that is not safe around pets was a no go.

Someone else questions whether the team is falling for the sunk-cost trap, given that so much of the chemical spray has already been produced. He suggests that perhaps the company should just "cut its losses." "What else can we do at this point?" he asks rhetorically.

A manufacturing specialist on the team reminds everyone that although millions of gallons have already been produced, none have been packaged yet. So time remains for other potential solutions (literally and figuratively).

One of the chemical engineers speaks up and says maybe the team is thinking about this all wrong. The room falls silent as everyone waits with anticipation to hear where she's going with this. She says that instead of thinking about the formulation as being something the company needs to abandon entirely, what if the answer lies in "adding something" to the existing solution. Eyebrows raise as two of the other chemists in the room ask to look at the report detailing the problem with pets. After half an hour, the two chemists start writing on a whiteboard what looks like gibberish to most of the other team members.

To the other chemists in the room, however, these chemical formulas are their natural language. Various ideas are discussed, debated, and discarded. There doesn't seem to be a single additive that could turn this existing formulation into a pet-friendly product.

Finally, one chemical engineer suggests combining two additives and then introducing this combined solution into the existing product. More furious scribbling of equations occurs. Someone else in the room objects, saying the two ingredients that are needed are too expensive, and one is in short supply. Another chemical engineer agrees but offers a cheaper and more readily available substitute ingredient that, when combined with the other ingredient, could be a potential solution. After a few minutes of stunned silence, the head of chemical manufacturing stands up: "Damn, this could actually work."

A few days later after this meeting, you travel with your team to one of the manufacturing locations to watch a demo of the new solution being added to the original formulation. The engineers insist that the new ingredients didn't change the integrity of the original product, alter the drying time, or change the pleasing smell at all. And the best news of all—the new formulation is perfectly safe for all pets. Unlike the previous product, there is no risk of the solution negatively interacting with a common household cleaning product. You can't believe your (and your team's) luck.

But this wasn't luck at all. It wouldn't have been possible if not for your team's ability to collectively improvise when challenged with a debilitating setback. You reflect on the similarities between the way your team attacked this problem and the way your drama coach held improv workshops back in high school. No one really knew what the end result would be when you started, but everyone retained an open mind, trusted one another, and constantly built on one another's creative ideas. You had to admit that improv works, even in a stressful business environment.

As this example shows, another fundamental resource that contributes to a team's resilience is its capacity to improvise. Improvisation is the act of making something new and novel out of previous experiences, practices, and knowledge. As the consumer product example showed, the team didn't have to develop something entirely new to solve the problem. In fact, the engineers ended up using existing ingredients to simply alter what they had already created. The solution didn't come easily, however, as much trial and error were involved. Ingredients were tried and discarded. Notably, one ingredient did not do the trick. Two existing ingredients were ultimately combined into something novel to solve the problem. That's the magic of team improvisation. When times got tough, your team collectively and iteratively discussed and exchanged ideas until a workable solution could be reached. Instead of folding under the weight of the pressure and costing their company millions, this cross-functional consumer products team was *unbreakable.*

The evidence examining improvisation in teams at work is small but growing. One study found that improvisational theater principles of "practice," "collaboration," "agree, accept, and add," "be present in the moment," and "draw on reincorporation and ready-mades" are applicable to enhancing improvisation in work teams.[1] Importantly, the study also found that team improvisation did not enhance team innovation unless team members had appropriate expertise, high-quality teamwork, a team culture of experimentation, and real-time information and communication (note that our consumer products team had all four of these qualities, enabling them to innovate, develop a new formula, and overcome adversity). Moreover, the study showed that the incidence and quality of team improvisation can be enhanced through training, so this is a team attribute that truly can be learned over time.

Another study showed that team improvisation has a better chance at increasing team performance when teams have empowering leaders, even when teams are limited in their abilities and resources. However, team improvisation was not as likely to enhance team performance when team members felt overloaded with too many responsibilities.[2]

Other studies have also demonstrated the power of team improvisation for improved team functioning and performance when adversity strikes. For example, in a study of teams operating in thirteen industries, those teams that designed and executed their strategies simultaneously, what the authors referred to as *improvised adaptation,* performed better in the face of adversity.[3] Similarly, in a study of new product development teams that frequently encounter bumps in the road, team improvisation enhanced new product success. Importantly, teams were more improvisational to the extent that they practiced "unlearning," or changing a team's beliefs, norms, values, procedures, and routines for getting work done.[4] A study of virtual new product development teams found that team improvisation helped improve team performance, but teams that were geographically dispersed had more difficulty translating their improvisation into performance. On these teams, real-time interaction and access to teammate knowledge and expertise were limited, making improvisation significantly more difficult (we discuss the unique challenges of building team resilience and generating improvisation in remote and hybrid teams in chapter 8).[5]

Finally, in a comprehensive examination of almost nine hundred project professionals in seventeen industries in seventy-six different countries, researchers found that in projects that demanded extreme changes (those in which 90 percent or more of their requirements changed), teams engaged in 41 percent more improvisation practices than in projects that were stable (those with less than 10 percent changes).[6] More importantly, they found that companies can work to enhance team improvisation by building cultures that promote change; making sure teams meet frequently, keep their size relatively small, and have empowering leaders; and providing management practices and tools that promote improvisation, such as those working in Agile project environments. To date, there has not been enough research on team improvisation to conduct a meta-analysis, but these results linking team improvisation and team performance in turbulent and adverse environments are very promising.

On June 23, 2018, tragedy struck a boys' soccer team (the Wild Boars, as they were known) in Thailand.[7] After a successful soccer practice, twelve boys and their coach, Ekkapol "Ake" Chantawong, rode their bicycles across rice paddies and up hills into a forest that had been recently deluged with rain. They were headed to the Tham Luang cave, a favorite destination for the team. The boys and their coach explored the cave as a team-building exercise and would often initiate new members by writing their names on the cave walls deep inside. Exploring these caves in June was not without risk, however. During the rainy season, the cave can flood almost twenty feet, so it was advisable to explore the caves only during the drier period between November and April.

It wasn't long after they entered the cave that Coach Ake and the boys realized they were in trouble. The cave was filling up with rainwater so fast that when the team tried to exit the cave, they were cut off and had to head deeper in to escape the rising waters. The team eventually made it to a small rocky outcropping about two and a half miles from the cave opening. Coach Ake, a former monk, helped calm the boys by using meditation techniques, which also helped them regulate their breathing to save air. Although they had no food, they were able to drink water that dripped down from the walls of the cave.

On the outside, friends and family began to worry when the boys didn't return home and couldn't be reached by cell phone. Parents quickly descended on the cave, where they found their boys' bicycles, backpacks, and soccer shoes near the entrance. As word of the boys trapped in the cave spread, Thai authorities called for help. Arriving relatively quickly were the Royal Thai Navy SEALs, the Thai national police, and various rescue teams. Unfortunately, most of the potential rescuers had little experience with cave diving. And the rain continued to fall, making the water level in the cave even higher and more daunting. As team members began to improvise potential solutions, attempts were made to pump water out of the cave. Unfortunately, this process was just too slow. Some of the engineers estimated that it could take up to four months to remove enough water for the boys to walk out. Engineers even tried using heavy equipment to drill passageways into the side of the mountain to find cracks that perhaps the boys could use to escape, a risky maneuver that also proved futile.

On June 28, international rescuers began to arrive, including US Air Force rescue specialists and cave divers from Australia, Belgium, Great Britain, Scandinavia, and other countries. A few days later, on July 2, two British divers, fighting tough currents, murky water, and complete darkness, found an air pocket and, just beyond, the Wild Boars soccer team. The whole scene was captured by the divers' cameras and broadcast to the world. Shortly thereafter, a military medic and several Thai Navy SEAL divers would join the boys and their coach and not leave their side for the duration. At this point, they had been trapped in the cave for nine days.

Tragically, on July 6, one of the divers lost his life. Saman Gunan, thirty-eight years old, was a former Thai Navy SEAL diver who had volunteered to help with the rescue that day. His oxygen ran out while trying to get new air tanks to the boys, and his diving partner was unable to resuscitate him. As the boys' parents got word of Gunan's death, they wondered how their boys would ever make it out when even a trained Navy SEAL did not.

As time ran low and the threat of more flooding ran high, the rescue team continued to improvise new plans for evacuation. Elon Musk offered a small submarine that could be used to transport the boys to safety—a creative solution that was ultimately ruled infeasible. One team member suggested training the boys to dive so that they could make it through the flooded caves successfully. This was also a creative solution, but with Gunan's death still haunting them, it was viewed as a "last resort."

After several more ideas were considered and then ruled out, the team finally agreed on a plan. And on July 7, somewhat serendipitously, the pounding rains that had hindered the rescue for the past two weeks came to a sudden halt. According to Thai officials, the cave was typically completely flooded by July 10. The team knew it was right then or never. The effort required over one hundred Thai and foreign divers. Once the divers made it back to the boys, each boy received a full-face air mask to make sure he could breathe. They were then attached to one diver, with another diver helping to guide them. An oxygen tank was strapped to the front of each boy, and a handle was attached to their backs (so that the divers could literally maneuver each boy through the many obstacles on their way out). The boys were given enough medication to render them semiconscious, in order to help prevent panic during their journey. Once they made it through this first part of the rescue and into a larger chamber, each boy was secured onto a stretcher, which was then carried out by a team of five men. During parts of the rescue, the stretchers were attached to a pulley system to make it up several steep slopes in the cave. Air tanks had to be constantly replaced throughout the extraction, and rescuers brought the boys out in three batches over three days because they needed that much time to continually replace oxygen tanks. On July 10, the very day that Thai officials surmised that the caves would be completely flooded, the last boy was successfully rescued. The remaining rescue team members were still inside the cave but managed to get out just as a key pump stopped working and floodwaters rushed into the cave.

The rescue of the Wild Boars clearly shows the lifesaving powers of team improvisation. The team drew its membership from across the globe and yet coalesced as a single unit. They worked collaboratively to make sense of the situation. All team members were involved in idea generation and feasibility analysis. Ideas were discussed, debated, discarded, and reconsidered. In the end, none of the three main ideas initially generated for the rescue was used. The final result was a combination of professional divers guiding the boys out using an elaborate and creative system of oxygen tanks, handles on each boy, and a system of pulleys. Against all odds and torrential rainfall, the team persisted for more than two weeks until the last boy was rescued and the final diver emerged triumphantly from the cave. This story lives on as a testament of team improvisation and, of course, human ingenuity and caring.

TWO WAYS LEADERS BUILD TEAM IMPROVISATION

There are two main levers leaders can use to build organizational teams' improvisational capabilities, and we summarize them in table 5.1.

Build Up a Team's Transactive Memory

Transactive memory is a term used to describe team members' awareness of one another's expertise, experiences, and skills. In other words, it captures not only

TABLE 5.1. Two Ways Leaders Build Team Improvisation

Behaviors	Examples
1. Build up a team's transactive memory	Help team members to understand who knows what in a team so they know who to call on at just the right time with just the right knowledge
	Work to develop the four dimensions of transactive memory:
	a. Appropriate knowledge stock, or that your team has the right combination of member knowledge by being intentional about who is on the team and making sure that all critical knowledge and skill categories are accounted for
	b. Diversified knowledge stock, or that a team's expertise is diverse and highly specialized to create a team with complementary knowledge
	c. Consensus about knowledge stock, or that all team members agree about who knows what on the team so that they can call on the right member when adversity strikes
	d. Accuracy about knowledge stock, or that all team members can correctly identify who knows what on their team to gain a collective understanding
2. Increase team creativity	Get team members talking so that they exchange and integrate different information and perspectives, or enhance team information elaboration; use relational self-affirmation
	Make sure that team members' information and perspectives being shared are unique to them, or encourage perspective taking by composing teams with a high level of thought diversity, which involves selecting members with different backgrounds, demographics, personalities, experiences, and different ways of viewing the world
	Make sure team members are comfortable listening to, and understanding in a nonjudgmental way, the thoughts motivations, and emotions of fellow members, as well as why they feel that way, or engage in perspective taking by:
	a. Consistently modeling this behavior to create a climate of perspective taking in teams
	b. Encourage pro-diversity beliefs by communicating your own beliefs about diversity and showing members how their diversity contributes to team goals
	c. Create a team's superordinate identity by using a set of focused rewards to reinforce members' identification with the overall team
	d. Make sure members brainstorm for longer durations than they would otherwise because creativity actually gets better over time (avoid the creative cliff illusion, by which people believe their creativity gets worse over time)

who knows what on the team but also, importantly, the extent to which team members *know* who knows what. Transactive memory complements a team's teamwork roadmap, which we covered in detail in chapter 4. Together, transactive memories and teamwork roadmaps make up what is known as team cognition, which describes how knowledge and skills are organized throughout a team. Recall that teamwork roadmaps represent the knowledge and skills that are shared by all team members. Transactive memory, in contrast, represents knowledge and skills that are divided throughout a team. This distribution of expertise enables each team member to focus their attention on a particular specialty. And the awareness of who knows what guides each member as to where to turn to access others' specialized expertise, thereby enhancing the ability to gather just the right information at just the right time. A meta-analysis showed that teams with more developed transactive memory perform better than those with a less developed one in terms of being more productive, more creative, and staying together as a unit longer (something known as team viability).[8]

Why does transactive memory matter for team improvisation? The logic is that if everyone on a team knows who has what particular expertise, then when the time comes for a team to improvise and create something novel out of existing information or resources, team members will know who the go-to person on the team is for specific knowledge.[9] In fact, a study of teams in two large companies in South Korea showed that transactive memory increases the level of knowledge sharing that occurs in teams, which in turn ultimately enhanced team performance because team members with well-developed transactive memory systems were more likely to apply their newly shared knowledge.[10]

You can think about team improvisation using the metaphor of an improvisational jazz quartet. Each musician is aware of the tendencies, style, and musical capabilities of every other musician. So when one person decides to riff in an unexpected direction, the other musicians have a pretty good understanding of where the music might head and can therefore join in somewhat effortlessly. Their familiarity with one another's styles and tendencies promotes trust. And this trust is essential for the quartet to move in unison, as it enables the other musicians to follow one another's lead. Even if they don't personally agree with the particular direction of the music, their familiarity with one another gives them confidence that even the most extreme divergence will end up sounding beautiful.

Wynton Marsalis, the great jazz trumpet player and musical director, describes jazz improvisation this way:

The thing about playing jazz is that they're not going to play the exact harmonies. The harmonic progression is always changing. So, you have to be able to hear and use your reflexes to respond to whatever changes. As a matter of fact, we call harmonies "changes." So, you have to be able to respond to whatever changes are taking place. And, that's where improvisation comes in. That's where it's most like the democratic process. Because you can't actually separate yourself from people that you might not like or want to be around. You have to deal with them, you have to be prepared to address changes. And, the type of style that you address a change with determines your success. Not whether you're successful in imposing your will, because if Eric [Reed] is playing the piano, I can't stop the song and make him play the harmony I want him to play. That song is going on. So, all I can do is address in some way what he's played.[11]

A team's transactive memory makes this improvisation possible. Everybody has their own expertise and style, and importantly, everyone knows everyone else's tendencies. This understanding allows the quartet to shift directions in unison without stopping the show to ask what someone else is doing. So how do leaders make sure that their teams have an adequate transactive memory to allow their teams to improvise effectively like jazz musicians? One perhaps obvious recommendation is to train team members together as much as possible, something we mentioned in chapter 4 that helps create teamwork roadmaps. The same advice applies here as well.

Evidence also suggests that leaders should focus on four distinct dimensions when trying to build up a team's transactive memory.[12] First, leaders should ensure that their teams have the right knowledge stock. In other words, does the team have the right combination of member skills, expertise, and experiences? After all, if the right skill set and knowledge are not effectively represented on a team, when adversity strikes, it will be virtually impossible for a team to improvise and overcome that setback. To build a solid knowledge stock, leaders should be intentional when selecting people to join their teams, ensuring that all critical knowledge and skill categories are accounted for. Moreover, throughout a team's life cycle, leaders should actively search for deficiencies that exist and fill those gaps either by adding new team members with relevant expertise or by training and developing existing members. Think about the last adverse event your team faced. Was there a piece missing? Could the team have benefited from additional knowledge or skills? If so, start working today to fill those gaps so that you're better equipped for the next challenge.

Second, in addition to ensuring the appropriate stock of knowledge, leaders should work to ensure that this knowledge is spread somewhat evenly throughout a team. This means a team's expertise should be diverse and highly specialized. A diversified knowledge stock enables team members to each focus on a specialized area, thereby developing a deeper understanding of that topic than could a single team member who is relied upon for expertise in multiple areas. For this reason, leaders should seek out members with complementary knowledge so that each member brings something to a team that can be combined, integrated, and converted into improvisational outcomes. Such a rich and diverse set of knowledge and experience among team members is key to resilient responses because it offers a robust inventory of potential actions to choose from when adversity strikes.

Third, once team leaders are satisfied that their team has the appropriate combination and diversity of skills, expertise, and experience, they then must ensure that there is a high degree of consensus among team members as to who knows what on the team. That is, team members should agree about who has what specialized expertise. After all, if no one can agree about who knows what, when it comes time to improvise, the team will be hampered in its ability to call on the right team member or members who have specific capabilities or ideas. So consensus is critical to ensure that when adversity strikes, team members are not fumbling around trying to figure out who to turn to for direction.

Finally, leaders should make sure that there is a high level of accuracy in their teams. That is, have all team members correctly identified who knows what on their team? This is not the same thing as reaching consensus about who knows what. After all, there could be a high level of agreement about who knows what on a team, but members could be wrong if they mistakenly think particular members know certain things but they actually don't. So, consensus and accuracy are different, but they go hand in hand. You want to make sure everyone on the team agrees about who knows what and that the collective understanding is correct.

Leaders can help develop consensus and accuracy by sending clear signals to the team about where to turn for certain information. For instance, directing team members to a teammate who has experience or information relevant to a challenge they're facing helps shape the team's transactive memory, as does being intentional in who they call on for certain topics in team meetings. For example, a simple question, such as, "Allison, you're the expert in this area—what do you think?" can go a long way to develop both the consensus and the accuracy of where certain expertise lies within the team.

Increase Team Creativity

Transactive memory is also critical for another ingredient of improvisation: *team creativity*. After all, improvisation is inherently tied to the ability to create and innovate. It stands to reason that the more diverse a team's transactive memory, the more perspectives it can draw from during the sensemaking process to generate creative solutions to the challenge in front of it. Thus, the broader a team's transactive memory, the more creative potential it has. And creativity opens the door to improvisation.

A study by LinkedIn ranked creativity as the single most in-demand soft skill.[13] For teams, research shows a consistent positive relationship between team creativity and organizational performance.[14] Although some people mistakenly believe that creativity is something most of us are born with, the vast majority of evidence suggests that people, and teams, can learn to be more creative with the right training and development.[15]

This, of course, is where team leaders come in. Leaders have a variety of proven techniques to choose from when building up their team's creativity. Perhaps the simplest is to just get members talking. For teams to reach their peak creativity, they need to spend dedicated time exchanging and integrating different information and perspectives. This activity is commonly referred to as team information elaboration, which is "the core team process driving team creativity and innovation."[16] Team information elaboration is so important for team creativity because it serves as the mechanism through which individual team members' collection of knowledge coalesces and emerges as team-level knowledge. In the absence of such information exchange, critical knowledge remains siloed, thereby preventing one of the greatest benefits of a team—a variety of different perspectives to improve decision quality. Information elaboration activates a synergistic process through which team members share their thoughts and build on one another's ideas to form a more comprehensive picture of the current situation.

Information elaboration is complicated by the fact that team members naturally shy away from sharing information with one another and are more likely to repeat existing information that fellow team members already know. This is because team members often perceive that sharing unique information puts them at risk of being ostracized for not falling in line with the rest of the team. So, in an attempt to enhance their acceptance in the team, they choose agreement and redundancy over going against the grain.[17]

How can leaders overcome their teams' natural tendencies to only discuss existing information? Dr. Francesca Gino, of Harvard University, set out to answer this question in several studies examining what she and her colleagues called relational self-affirmation. This involves asking friends, family, or co-workers in team members' personal networks to write narratives about various positive contributions the individual has made to different contexts.[18] They then gave individuals their narratives and asked them to identify the strengths that the writers highlighted. Importantly, they found that when team members were made aware of their strengths, they were more likely to share their unique information and qualities with their teams, thereby enhancing information elaboration and team performance. This is an innovative and powerful way to enhance team information elaboration, in order to unleash creativity, and ultimately team improvisation.

A second way to enhance creativity is to ensure that the information and perspectives being shared are actually unique. One of the best times to shape this team attribute is at the very outset of team formation. When choosing people to join a team, leaders should intentionally select team members who have different styles of thinking and problem solving. This may mean selecting people with different backgrounds, demographics, personalities, experiences, or different ways of viewing the world. As you might expect, creativity is extremely limited in teams with members who all think alike, where echo chambers lead to redundancy and wasted time. For information elaboration to translate into creative output, the information and perspectives being shared must be unique.

In 2005, the German pension system underwent a major restructuring, which had downstream effects on national tax and finance laws. These changes had major implications for financial institutions across the country. One financial consulting company was particularly affected. Its sales teams, charged with selling insurance and other financial offerings, were forced to pull one of its most popular products from the market. This was a major shock to the teams. Improvisation was critical, and teams scrambled to identify new ways to meet their sales goals. Which teams weathered the storm the best? The teams with more diversity. Researchers examining these teams found that as team diversity increased, the severity of the setback following the legislative changes decreased. This was because the more diverse teams were better equipped to pivot, as they had a more robust variety of knowledge and perspectives, which could be integrated via information elaboration and leveraged to identify a new creative path forward. Ultimately, this research showed that team diversity could serve as a buffer, protecting teams from the ill effects of adversity.[19]

However, just composing a team with thought diversity is not enough. Evidence also shows that for this diversity to translate into creative output, team members must be comfortable with perspective taking.[20] Thus, a third way for leaders to enhance creativity is to ensure that members are open to listening to, and understanding in a nonjudgmental way, the thoughts, motivations, and feelings of fellow members. Perspective taking, often described as stepping into someone else's shoes or seeing the world through someone else's eyes, has many benefits for teams, including greater coordination, less relationship conflict, better communication, more constructive evaluations of others' suggestions, and fuller integration of perspectives and ideas.[21] Thus, it behooves leaders to make sure team members understand the importance of perspective taking in their teams and to practice doing so on a regular basis. Research has shown that there are various levers that can be pulled to ensure that teams have a healthy level of perspective taking, which is so critical for team creativity.[22] A key way to ensure that this happens is for leaders to consistently model this behavior themselves, showing team members how to respectfully listen and consider the views of others, thereby contributing to a climate of perspective taking in their teams.

A second way that leaders can enhance perspective taking in their teams is to encourage pro-diversity beliefs.[23] When team members have pro-diversity beliefs, it means that they believe in the value of diversity. That is, they believe that diversity enhances their team's performance. One study showed that members of diverse teams identified more strongly with their team only when members had a strong belief in the value of diversity.[24] In fact, when members had lower beliefs in the value of diversity, the opposite occurred, and they failed to identify with their diverse teams. Leaders can instill pro-diversity beliefs in their teams by communicating their own belief in the value of diversity and making sure team members understand exactly how their diversity helps them accomplish their goals. Diversity training programs might include modules on the power of diversity in determining the performance of teams and show existing and compelling evidence linking pro-diversity organizational policies to organizational creativity and innovation.[25]

In 2020, Satya Nadella of Microsoft was named the top-rated CEO for encouraging diversity.[26] Microsoft's top executive since 2014, Nadella has spoken out consistently on various diversity issues, such as bias in artificial intelligence, women leaders in tech, corporate initiatives on climate change, and racial and gender diversity at Microsoft. Putting his money where his mouth is, he also began tying executive compensation to diversity metrics, and he has worked to include a senior leader's ability to build a diverse team as part of the promotion system at Microsoft. Certainly, building up and supporting pro-diversity beliefs require a great deal of effort and potential culture changes, but by doing so, leaders boost the propensity of their teams to engage in perspective taking, which translates into higher team creativity and ultimately more improvisation when adversity strikes.

A third way leaders can enhance team creativity is to use a set of focused and targeted rewards to reinforce team members' identification with their overall team, sometimes referred to as a superordinate identity.[27] An overall team identity helps convert a "we vs. they" mentality, which can sometimes exist in diverse teams, to simply a "we" mentality. If this "we" mentality doesn't exist, members of diverse teams are likely to let their biases get in the way of seeing things through the eyes of their teammates, thereby preventing them from engaging in the type of perspective taking so critical to team creativity. Using team-based rewards—those driven by accomplishments of a whole team—in addition to individual rewards is an established way to create a team's superordinate identity. Although many studies have demonstrated the power of incentivizing an overall team, most companies even today still rely almost exclusively on individual incentives.[28] The problem with this strategy is that people tend to do what they get rewarded for, and individual rewards can work against a team having a healthy superordinate identity.[29]

If you are even a casual fan of college football, you have probably noticed the small stickers often placed on players' helmets, but you may have wondered why they're there. In the late 1960s, the coaches of the Ohio State University Buckeyes football team started the tradition of rewarding individual players with small stickers for their helmets that looked like buckeye leaves. Such a tradition was continued until 2001, when a new coach, Jim Tressel, was hired to turn around the program, which had slipped into mediocrity. He decided that, instead of giving stickers for individual excellence after each game, he would give the entire offense a sticker if the team scored more than twenty-four points, and every player on the team received a sticker after a win. Responding in a "we" over "me" mentality, the team won the national championship the following year and has been a perennial title contender ever since. The lesson: never underestimate the power of team rewards for building a superordinate team identity.

Finally, to boost team creativity, leaders can take steps to enhance the quality of their team's brainstorming sessions. Brainstorming has long been considered a critical component of the creative process.[30] And there are some well-established rules that can improve the effectiveness of this important activity. Tim Brown, the former CEO of IDEO, is credited with coining the term *design thinking*, an iterative process that leans heavily on brainstorming to help teams generate creative solutions to problems. IDEO is known across the globe for its creative prowess, and its team members are particularly skilled at brainstorming. We highly recommend checking out one of their recorded brainstorming sessions, posted online for the world to see. These sessions are fast paced and highly entertaining. IDEO doesn't have a lot of rules for brainstorming, but the few that it does have are incredibly important—so important, in fact, that they're painted on the walls of their meeting rooms.[31]

IDEO's Seven Rules of Brainstorming

1. Defer Judgment—every idea is accepted, and judging is prohibited.

2. Encourage Wild Ideas—the wilder and crazier, the better; it's much easier to take an exciting infeasible idea and pare it down to something doable than to take a boring idea and make it exciting.

3. Build on the Ideas of Others—avoid the word *but*; replace it with the word *and*, which is also known as *plussing* (one person makes a suggestion, and another builds on that idea by saying, "Yes, that's great . . . *and* we could also . . ."). Steve Jobs was also famous for encouraging plussing in his teams during his time at the helm of Disney's Pixar Animation Studios.

4. Stay Focused on the Topic—although wild ideas are encouraged, make sure they don't veer off track.

5. One Conversation at a Time—avoid side conversations; make sure everyone in the team is involved in the same discussion; when someone is speaking, everyone should be listening, because you can't build on ideas that you don't hear.

6. Be Visual—engage the logical and creative sides of your brain; grab some sticky notes and colored markers and sketch out some of your ideas, then stick them to the wall to inspire others' creativity.

7. Go for Quantity—aim for lots of ideas; quality is less important; the

more ideas that are raised, the more likely that one of them will be great; even if you don't think it's a good idea, say it anyway; it may inspire someone else to build on it.[32]

Related to that last rule, research shows that groups of individuals brainstorming on their own tend to produce more ideas than teams working together.[33] Leaders should therefore ask team members to spend a few minutes jotting down ideas independently before coming together and sharing those ideas as a single unit. Leaders should also encourage their teams to brainstorm for longer durations than they might otherwise do. Evidence suggests that while persistence in idea generation is a key driver of creative output, people severely underestimate how creative they could be if they were to keep brainstorming.[34] This is because we tend to believe that our creative ideas get significantly worse as time goes by. But this just isn't true. It's a phenomenon known as the creative cliff illusion, a fallacy that causes people to end the creative process too soon.[35]

The reality is that our creativity actually gets better, or at least stays the same, as time passes. Leaders should inform their teams of this illusion and of the research that shows the critical role persistence plays in boosting creativity. Ultimately, leaders should ensure that their teams push beyond the point at which they feel their creativity is beginning to wane. It is often after this point that the best ideas are generated. All this said, leaders must also recognize that when adversity strikes, teams typically need to react with a sense of urgency, as research shows that faster response times tend to result in better outcomes.[36] For this reason, some situations call for teams to improvise on the fly. It's therefore incumbent on leaders to understand the nature of the adversity in order to manage the tension between the need to respond quickly and the need to identify an optimal solution. Leaders should play a key role in the timing of the response, pushing their teams to continue ideating when time allows and pulling the plug when it's time to settle on a path forward.

To this point, we've highlighted the vital role that improvisation plays in team resilience. Resilient teams simply must possess the capacity to improvise. But should teams always improvise during adversity? That is, should they default to generating a creative new solution and changing course each and every time they hit rough waters? Our natural response to adversity tends to be "when the going gets tough, let's try a different direction." But accumulating evidence actually tells us we would be wise to pump the brakes and consider the possibility that we may already be on the optimal path and that, although we've hit a bump in the road, the best strategy may be to stay the course rather than deviate from it.[37]

Our own research supports this notion.[38] We conducted an experiment using a virtual cooking simulation, in which participants worked together as teams of chefs in a simulated hamburger restaurant. It was a high-energy, fast-paced activity. Just like in a real restaurant, customers placed their orders for the team to fill, and the requests varied—some customers wanted plain burgers, some wanted lettuce, some wanted tomatoes, and some wanted a combination. Teams of three completed ten four-minute rounds of the simulation. The challenge in each round was for team members to fill as many orders as they could before the time expired. Members divided up tasks such as chopping vegetables, preparing and cooking the meat, plating the meal, and washing dishes. Coordination and communication among team members were essential.

Following the sixth round—right at the point that the team was starting to gel and hit its peak performance—adversity struck. To simulate a team membership change, we pulled one of the three team members and replaced them with a new participant who had no experience with the simulation or with the other team members. The two veterans in the team were challenged to train their new teammate not only on how to perform the task but also on the team processes, norms, and procedures they had established over the previous six rounds. And they had to do all this in the heat of the moment while customer orders were piling up. As designed, this proved to be quite difficult, and performance in the seventh round plummeted, signifying a severe team setback.

Halfway through that seventh round, when the team was noticeably frustrated, we paused the simulation and asked them to take a few minutes to reflect on how things were going, reevaluate their strategy, and devise a performance plan for the remaining rounds. At that point, half the teams were encouraged to consider responding to this adversity by improvising—generating a new, better way to work together. The other half were given the same instructions, but they were told to also consider persisting or staying the course—improving inefficiencies in their current strategy instead of generating a completely new one. All teams then completed the remaining rounds of the simulation using their chosen strategy.

The results were fascinating. For some teams, considering improvisation as the only viable option enabled them to bounce back from their setback faster. But for others, it had no significant impact, and in many cases, it actually hurt their performance. A deeper dive into the data illuminated what was contributing to these very different outcomes. It turns out that, before the adverse event, teams that reported higher levels of team confidence (recall the importance of team confidence from chapter 3) performed better when they considered both improvisation *and* persistence as possible response options, whereas teams that reported lower levels of team confidence tended to perform better when they considered only changing course.

These findings suggest that leaders should continue to encourage their teams to improvise, especially those teams that show signs that they aren't too sure of themselves and their current strategy. But we caution leaders who may tend to overemphasize the importance of changing course when times get tough. Our research shows that team improvisation does have its limits. If you have a team that appears quite confident in its ability to work together through thick and thin, make sure team members spend time considering improvisation and persistence as viable response options. Sometimes, all a team needs to do to overcome adversity is to dig deep, stay the course, and forge ahead on its current trajectory. It's the wisdom to know which path is optimal in which situation that makes all the difference for team resilience.

CHAPTER 6

TEAM RESILIENCE RESOURCE #4

TEAM PSYCHOLOGICAL SAFETY

Have you ever been in a team meeting with more senior colleagues and, as those colleagues began talking, you realized that you had information highly relevant to the conversation? It was a bit controversial, so you worried about how the others would receive it and just kept it to yourself. Sound familiar?

Imagine you're a junior business analyst on a consulting team working with a client to try to figure out why its profitability has dropped over the past year. Your team has seven members in total, including one firm partner (who sold the client your company's services and maintains high-level team oversight), one engagement manager (the day-to-day leader of the consulting team), and five (including you) associates and business analysts who conduct interviews with the client, carry out research, and analyze the waves of data that come in every week.

The client has been a demanding one. Each week, a member of the client team has been pressuring the firm partner on your team to deliver at least some preliminary findings and analyses on why profitability is suffering. You certainly understand the client's point of view. The company is very large and family owned, with many livelihoods at stake. It's truly personal for the family owners. Although the partner has tried repeatedly to buy your team sufficient time to conduct a thorough review and analysis of the company's business, the pressure is on to deliver some results and soon.

The partner calls a meeting with your entire team first thing on a Monday morning. She says that the client has demanded a meeting later this week so that the consulting team can present at least some preliminary analyses. Although you're the most junior member on the team, you have this nagging feeling that your team is not ready. You have some preliminary guesses as to why the profitability issues are happening, but you just don't feel ready to draw any firm conclusions quite yet. You wonder whether you should speak up now or just "go with the flow." You feel that with a couple of more weeks, your team could actually use the additional data coming in to offer your client a more evidence-based assessment of the issue. In fact, you have been crunching some numbers over the past day or so, and with just a little more time, you think you could generate something promising. Just then, the partner, a very seasoned consulting team member with a long record of success, suggests that your team should just "go with whatever it has," and she'll set up the meeting. You decide to continue your analyses anyway, hoping you might be able to offer something more concrete before the client meeting.

On Friday morning at 9:00, your entire team meets with the client team virtually. The engagement manager leads the meeting and begins to lay out the preliminary findings for the profitability drop. But catching you a bit by surprise, the engagement manager offers only a single possible reason your consulting team believes the client company is losing money. This is a surprise to you because just two days earlier in yet another planning meeting, your team had agreed to present several preliminary explanations rather than going with just one. In fact, you all recognized that you did not have the data to confidently present a single conclusion at this point in time. So the plan was to present four potential reasons and get additional feedback from the client before moving forward. Making matters worse, in the meeting the partner readily agrees with the engagement manager and tells the client that she supports the team's conclusions of the one explanation. Your major concern is that the results of your additional data analysis do not actually support the single explanation that was just given. You begin to have that sinking feeling you get when you know something that no one else seems to recognize (like in a bad horror film). That's OK, you say to yourself, let's just get through this client meeting, and then you can offer your additional analyses to your team afterward in private.

Of course, as is typically the case, that is the exact moment disaster strikes. The lead member of the client team speaks up and strongly expresses his displeasure with the work of the team so far. He says he doesn't see any reason that the consulting team had to offer that conclusion about the profitability decline.

His voice rises as he talks about how much money the family is spending on the team's services. He goes on, saying that your efforts are falling far below his and the family's expectations. The other members of the client team, again mostly family members, nod in agreement. The lead member then says it is probably time to pull the plug on this engagement. Your mind races as the team's partner tries desperately to hold onto this business by throwing out some additional ideas. There is a lot of money at stake with this client, not to mention the fact that your company has been building up its portfolio of family business clients and is just starting to gain some traction. If word were to get out about this disaster, a big segment of future family business clients could vanish.

An internal debate is raging in your mind. Should you speak up, or shouldn't you? On the one hand, you weren't certain that your results had actually uncovered the problem. And even if you were, as the most junior member of the team, was it really your place to say something? On the other hand, your team members, including the partner and engagement manager, always encouraged all team members to speak their mind. In fact, you remember the partner once saying: "If you know something our team needs to hear, don't hold back. Never let our team fail because you're afraid to say something. We hired you for a reason, and we trust you." With those words echoing in your mind and the voice telling you to "say something" getting louder and louder, you ask the partner if you can "jump in" to the conversation. Without missing a beat, the partner lets you have the floor. Nervously at first, but building up confidence as you go, you begin to explain the additional analyses you had been conducting and the two potential reasons you are homing in on that could be the culprit for the profitability loss. You can see several members of the client team begin nodding their heads in approval. You wrap up your discussion in just a few minutes (it seems like hours, though), and the lead on the client team suggests that the rest of the consulting team follow your lead, continue to collect and analyze the data you've been working on, and set up another meeting the following week. The partner ends the call with a few pleasantries, and all eyes turn to you.

You hold your breath for what again seems like a long time until the partner says, "You see, everyone, that's why I always tell you to speak up if you know something that might help our team." Addressing you directly, she says: "You just saved this client engagement and probably earned us continuing business in the family sector. I want you to lead this next phase of data collection and analysis. Let's get back to work, team." You smile at your team, but all you can utter is a simple "thanks." No additional comments are needed. You had the respect of your team going into this meeting, but this has certainly increased their confidence in you. As you walk down the hall from the conference room to your office, you reflect on how grateful you are to have a leader and a team that has made you feel comfortable enough to speak your mind when it counts. Otherwise, you probably would've just kept your mouth shut and gone down on a sinking ship.

The fourth and final resource that enhances team resilience is *psychological safety*, which is the degree to which team members feel safe in taking interpersonal risks.[1] Examples of interpersonal risks include offering an opinion that may not be popular with the other team members, challenging fellow team members' ideas when you see flaws, or introducing something new or novel that no one on the team has seen or heard before. Psychological safety is a belief shared by teammates that everyone has the freedom to speak up and take risks without fear of being shut down, ridiculed, or otherwise embarrassed.

As the consulting team example just showed, the person who had the most valuable information in the client meeting was the most junior member. In many cases like these, the junior person chooses to remain silent rather than offer up new or novel information in a team setting, not to mention in a high-stakes client meeting. There would typically be too much fear to step out on a limb like that, particularly when the most senior member of the team—the consulting company partner—clearly had a phenomenal track record with previous clients and was the person who sold your company's services to the client and built the entire relationship. However, the junior person felt a strong degree of psychological safety and was therefore able to be a part of the conversation and offer up relevant and valuable information. Without a feeling of safety, this team would almost certainly have crumbled under the pressure. As it was, though, when adversity struck and the client was ready to end the entire relationship, the high sense of psychological safety enabled the team to bounce back and live to fight another day. Rather than unraveling in the moment, this consulting team was *unbreakable*.

In our own research during the months leading up to the COVID-19 pandemic, we started examining interpersonal risks within teams.[2] We believed that the more interpersonal risks team members take, the more resilient their teams would be when adversity strikes. We were particularly interested in investigating the extent to which team members revealed personal information to one another. Given the pressure in the workplace to leave your personal life at the door, so to speak, we consider this type of disclosure to be the riskiest of interpersonal risks. Our thinking was that when teammates disclose personal details to one another, they're sending signals of vulnerability. In other words, they're saying, "I trust you, and I'm willing to open myself up to you." And in teams, we know that such behaviors are contagious. When individuals make themselves vulnerable, their teammates are likely to reciprocate with their own acts of vulnerability. Through this reciprocation process, interpersonal risks and vulnerability emerge as norms, which become ingrained in a team's culture. We know from previous research that when others make themselves vulnerable to us, we tend to like them more and feel closer to them.[3] And so we expected that as teammates take interpersonal risks with one another, they signal their willingness to be vulnerable, which brings them closer together and forms a cohesive bond within the unit.

It's no surprise that cohesive teams tend to perform well. But cohesion is exponentially more critical when a team is facing adversity. This is because stressful conditions often tear teams apart. When times get tough, team members tend to shift their focus to their own survival and success, even at the expense of their team.[4] This is why it's so important to build close-knit social ties *prior* to an adverse event. When adversity strikes, cohesion activates to create a counteractive effect, holding teammates together even as adverse forces work to pull them apart. This promotes resilient performance by enabling team members to coalesce and tackle adversity as a united front.

In our study, we examined a large number of teams across industries that were performing a wide range of tasks. We started by asking team members to report how much they fully reveal themselves to their fellow team members and how much they disclose intimate, personal details to one another. Again, we consider this type of disclosure to be the riskiest of interpersonal risks in the workplace, where such openness is often shunned. We then assessed the cohesion of these teams. As expected, the more a team collectively engaged in interpersonal risks, the more cohesive it became.

Not long after collecting these data, the world shut down. COVID-19 was sweeping rapidly across the globe. Businesses locked their doors and encouraged (or required) their employees to stay home and shelter in place. Team members who had always worked right down the hall from one another were forced to collaborate despite being scattered in every direction. To say that the onset of a global pandemic is an adversity is perhaps the biggest understatement of the century. Teams scrambled to establish new routines and novel communication channels. Team members were struggling, as all of us were.

Soon after this happened, we went back to the teams we had just observed. This time we asked their leaders to rate their teams' performance following the pivot. In other words, we captured the teams' *resilient* performance. Just as we had expected, teams that engaged in more interpersonal risk taking prior to the pandemic performed more resiliently when COVID-19 struck. Results further supported our prediction that team cohesiveness explained this effect. Although team members were separated physically, cohesiveness kept them close psychologically, and this allowed them to continue collaborating as a single unit, despite the new challenges posed by the pandemic. We then corroborated these findings in a controlled laboratory environment using a bomb defusal simulation. Just like in the previous study, teams that engaged in more interpersonal risk taking performed more resiliently following an adverse shock. And again, greater team cohesiveness explained this effect. But the nature of the laboratory setting allowed us to dig a bit deeper into this relationship. It allowed us to uncover why the cohesive teams were more resilient. In line with our expectations, the cohesive teams that had taken more interpersonal risks simply worked better together under adverse circumstances. In other words, these teams more effectively performed the critical action processes we discussed in chapter 1. They coordinated better, they communicated more effectively, and they backed one another up when needed.

The two studies, when taken together, highlight the importance of psychological safety. We already knew that feeling safe to take interpersonal risks enhances team members' willingness to speak up, which then results in a more diverse set of thoughts, opinions, and ideas. This, of course, is great for sense-making. Our study offers a second mechanism through which psychological safety enhances team resilience—coalescing. When team members feel safe enough to take interpersonal risks with one another—so safe, in fact, that they're willing to make themselves vulnerable by revealing personal information—a powerful bond emerges. A team's cohesion acts as a social "adhesive" when adversity tries to tear teams apart. It holds teams together, enabling them to coalesce instead of splinter. In other words, it makes teams *unbreakable.*

The evidence for psychological safety is vast and has been growing for several decades. Research consistently shows that psychological safety promotes solid team performance, especially for those teams doing knowledge work in which creativity and innovation are important. In the foundational study on team psychological safety, Dr. Amy Edmondson, of Harvard University, who started researching the concept in the 1990s, found that psychological safety enhanced team learning, which in turn was related to team performance.[5] This means that if you want your team to learn effectively, members need to feel that it's safe to speak up and ask questions. Another study found that team conflict led to higher performance, but only in teams with greater psychological safety, meaning that disagreements between members help teams perform better only when members feel free to speak their minds.[6] In another study of virtual teams, researchers found that psychological safety can help neutralize the barriers to team innovation, which included members being spread out geographically, a heavy reliance on electronic communication technologies rather than face-to-face meetings, frequent changes in team composition, and having many team members from different countries.[7] In addition to these studies, a comprehensive meta-analysis of psychological safety's effects on teams showed that when teams are more psychologically safe, they perform better and have more information sharing, creativity, and learning, and team members are more engaged and satisfied with their work.[8] These are all major advantages for teams in today's complex business environments.

Another reason today's resilient teams benefit from psychological safety is that it contributes to what is known as the broaden-and-build model of positive emotion.[9] Dr. Barbara Fredrickson, at the University of North Carolina at Chapel Hill, has conducted extensive research on the broaden-and-build model and found that positive attributes, including those like curiosity, confidence, trust, and inspiration, help broaden the mind and build positive social, psychological, and physical resources.[10] When team members have a high level of psychological safety, they are more open minded, motivated, persistent, and—most importantly—resilient.

In further support of the importance of team psychological safety, in 2012, Google launched an initiative—affectionately known as Project Aristotle—that was designed to examine hundreds of the company's teams in an effort to figure out which team attributes were most critical to success.[11] Abeer Dubey, one of the people analytics managers leading the project, assembled a cross-functional team of researchers, including statisticians, organizational psychologists, sociologists, and engineers. Like most people charged with leading teams, Google's managers assumed that the most important factor was team composition, that is, who was (and who was not) on a team. After all, the members make the team, right? And we've already discussed the importance of having members on a team that think differently than one another. However, Google found that there was something even more important than simply getting the right people on the bus.

After struggling a bit more to try to figure out the keys to their teams' success, Google's researchers started to look more closely at team norms, or the unwritten rules that teams use to guide their member interactions and functioning. Although they concluded that norms were key to their teams' success at Google, they didn't quite know which one(s) were the *most* important. After all, if they could figure that out, then they could train their teams to adopt the healthiest norms that the most successful teams used. Although a few norms were identified as key success ingredients for teams, such as goal clarity and a culture of dependability, you can probably guess by now which norm stood head and shoulders above the rest as the single greatest key to team success. Yep, psychological safety.

Dharmendra Modha, an IBM fellow and lead researcher of the Cognitive Computing group at IBM Research–Almaden, is a world-renowned expert in the field of cognitive computing.[12] Years ago, he had been charged with putting together a team to lead a highly ambitious government-funded project that would develop a computer chip designed to emulate the human brain. Like many teams, his members were having difficulty reaching consensus in their team meetings and emails. Certain members would not speak up, and others would dominate the conversations. He knew he somehow needed to build a team climate of openness. He ended up finding an interesting idea in a management book published in 1985.

With this idea, Modha instructed his team members that whenever they were discussing ideas, brainstorming, and making decisions, they should assign one of five colors to their arguments: white to facts; black, discernment; red, emotions; green, investing in an idea; and yellow, optimism. The goal of this color-coded system was to help team members be more objective by clearly separating facts that team members were stating from their feelings about them. He found that this system actually encouraged more reticent team members to share their ideas with fellow team members and that members became much better at discussing and integrating their diverse ideas into a coherent whole. He also created several smaller teams of individuals to "test out" their ideas and use careful measurements to assess their viability. These smaller teams were allowed the freedom to explore their creative ideas without fear of failure. In fact, rather than viewing failure as a negative, he created a climate in which they were celebrated as part of the learning process. This resulted in increased risk taking and experimentation, which are essential to innovation. Although he didn't explicitly refer to his actions as building psychological safety in his teams, that's exactly what he was doing.

One company that puts psychological safety front and center for its teams is the movie studio Pixar, responsible for top-grossing animated films like *Toy Story*, *Finding Nemo*, *The Incredibles*, *Up*, and *Soul*, garnering an incredible twenty Academy Awards since 1995.[13] In her book on psychological safety, *The Fearless Organization*, Amy Edmondson argues that Pixar's success is due largely to its leaders promoting and maintaining psychological safety in its teams.[14] Recall that in chapter 5, we mentioned Steve Jobs's "plussing" technique, which he used while CEO of Pixar to encourage team members to build on one another's ideas. Beyond contributing to a team's creativity and capacity to improvise, plussing has the added benefit of helping team members feel psychologically safe to speak their minds.

In addition to Jobs, Ed Catmull, one of Pixar's founders, is widely credited with developing and promoting a culture of psychological safety throughout the entire organization. Catmull is described as curious, humble, and interested in people's ideas. He realized long ago that the creative types that worked for him were especially sensitive to criticism, as they poured their hearts and souls into each project and had difficulty separating themselves from their work. Catmull was famous for admitting early on at Pixar, "All of our movies suck."[15] But this level of candor and honesty, rather than demoralizing team members, served as a wake-up call for all of those involved in film production.

To institutionalize a culture of psychological safety, Catmull instituted what he referred to as Pixar's "Braintrust," which started in 1999. It began during the production of *Toy Story 2*, which everyone admitted was struggling to live up to the expectations set by the remarkable success of the original *Toy Story* movie. The Braintrust started with crew members, including directors and writers, getting together for lunch, watching various scenes from the film, and discussing what was going well and, more importantly, what was not. What started as an informal gathering turned into regular Braintrust meetings that were built on a few simple rules. One, feedback must be constructive and focus on the project itself, not the individuals creating it. Two, filmmakers must listen with an open mind and commit to not taking feedback personally. Three, all comments must be empathetic, as the people giving the feedback to a particular filmmaker are filmmakers on other projects. Finally, individuals must give praise and appreciation in addition to criticism, and the focus of the feedback should be on helping others achieve their vision and ambition. Importantly, the climate of psychological safety that Catmull created and espoused ensured that filmmakers and directors—who often feel vulnerable and exposed and who carry the weight of responsibility to make their film a success—have the greatest opportunity to succeed, even in the face of adversity.

TEN WAYS LEADERS INCREASE TEAM PSYCHOLOGICAL SAFETY

The accumulating evidence on psychological safety suggests that leaders have a variety of tools at their disposal to create more psychological safety in their teams so that members can overcome potential adversities and be more resilient. These tools can be broken down into two main categories: six leader behaviors and four elements of team structure.

Six Leader Behaviors to Build Team Psychological Safety

Table 6.1 summarizes six behaviors leaders can employ to build team psychological safety and provides examples of each.

Create a Team Climate of Inclusivity

Among the most important leadership behaviors for instilling a sense of psychological safety is creating a team climate of inclusivity. When you behave in an inclusive manner as a team leader, you are actively working to involve all your team members in discussion, debate, and decision making. This could involve calling on quieter members or using a rotational discussion system in which all members have a clear path to speaking up. Asking team members for their ideas early and consistently during team meetings should also help members feel comfortable expressing themselves.

In 2020, a McKinsey Global Survey was conducted to examine the key drivers of psychological safety in teams during the early part of the COVID-19 pandemic.[16] Their research showed that a healthy team climate, or one characterized by mutual respect, a general sense of caring about one another's well-being, and a high degree of input into how teams execute their tasks, was the number one driver of team psychological safety. Of course, leaders are responsible for orchestrating the climate of their teams and thus have an outsized effect on their psychological safety. Such climate setting by team leaders should be even more impactful when adversity strikes. Indeed, McKinsey found that a healthy team climate has a stronger effect on psychological safety in teams that had a greater degree of change in working remotely than in those that experienced less change during the early phases of the COVID-19 pandemic. The major problem that their work revealed, however, is that only 43 percent of survey respondents reported actually having a healthy team climate. So, although we

TABLE 6.1. Six Leader Behaviors to Build Psychological Safety

Behaviors	Examples
1. Create a climate of inclusivity	Ask for team member input early and often, be intentional about giving members the opportunity to speak
2. Be accessible and show appreciation for team members' input and ideas	Be approachable and make yourself accessible, speak and act appreciatively, make sure that team members know you are attending to and considering their ideas and suggestions consistently
3. Encourage discussion of mistakes (and lead by example)	Lead by example and discuss your own mistakes, what you learned from them, and how they helped you grow as a team member and leader; show vulnerability
4. Be a transformational leader	Challenge your team members to think differently about an issue or a problem to lay the groundwork for members to offer up new and novel ideas and try out different approaches
5. Encourage perspective taking	Promote the benefits of viewing the world through one another's eyes, understanding one another's thoughts, motivations, and feelings. Model this behavior. Put yourself in the shoes of your team members and openly validate different viewpoints.
6. Establish a solid foundation of trust	Keep your promises. Be available. Be vulnerable. Show you care. Prioritize the things that matter most to your team. Lead the way by trusting them first.

know a healthy team climate matters for psychological safety, leaders often struggle with building such a climate.

Be Accessible and Show Appreciation for Team Members' Input and Ideas

One way for leaders to contribute to a healthy team climate and enhance psychological safety is by simply making themselves accessible. As remote and hybrid work has become very common worldwide, this can take a bit of extra effort (we'll discuss this in more detail in chapter 8 with advice for building team resilience in remote and hybrid teams). However, accessibility builds trust, which should translate into members feeling safer expressing their true selves. Perhaps even more important than being accessible is responding positively to team members' input. Leader responses when team members speak up can make or break a team's psychological safety. Expressing appreciation for their thoughts can go a long way. On the other hand, if a team member who speaks up is shut down or ignored by a leader, it's safe to say that the team will lose that team member from the discussion. That individual likely won't say another word for the duration of the conversation, and they might not say anything in future conversations either. What's worse is that if this occurs in a team meeting (which it frequently does), the whole team will see the entire event unfold. And since they don't want the same thing to happen to them, they're going to keep quiet as well. So, one bad response to a team member's input can crush psychological safety in an entire team, resulting in the loss of several key voices that could have contributed to important team discussions and decisions. And not surprisingly, it's extremely difficult, if not impossible, to make sense of a situation when nobody feels safe enough to speak up. Leaders should therefore be very intentional about how they respond when team members take risks by speaking their minds. Again, a little appreciation goes a long way.

A great example of being accessible and showing appreciation for team members' input and ideas comes from Ian Seigel, CEO of ZipRecruiter, which runs a website that connects millions of job seekers to employment opportunities based on their interests and qualifications.[17] Siegel cofounded ZipRecruiter with three friends in Santa Monica, California, in 2010, and it now has over one thousand employees and continues to disrupt the recruitment industry since its inception. Siegel describes new and innovative ideas that his team members have as (version) "1.0s." He states: "1.0s are so easy to crush with a power imbalance. When people give me an idea, I have to train myself to not respond and then figure out a way to say 'yes . . . and' rather than tell them it won't work. This prevents stifling potentially great ideas, so always listen and support version 1.0s." In terms of accessibility, he claims that there are only two kinds of managers, those you work for and those you work with. He states: "I'm more of the guy you work with. I will walk the floor. I will sit down and talk to you about what you are working on. I am keenly interested." In terms of his philosophy on psychological safety, he acknowledges that ZipRecruiter provides pretty good financial and social perks, but the key driver of the company's success and its culture is "that you feel safe saying anything to anyone." Exactly.

Encourage Discussion about Mistakes (Lead by Example)

Another key leader behavior that will ensure psychological safety is encouraging discussion of mistakes constructively by doing so first—in other words, leading by example. Fundamental to psychological safety is that it creates a climate of team learning. Part of learning for individuals and teams is being able to admit and discuss mistakes openly with teammates. Chances are that different team members will make the same mistakes unless their teammates speak up and give others a chance to learn. Discussing mistakes is not easy, but the old adage that you learn more from failure than from success is consistently supported by the research on individuals, teams, and organizations.[18] However, unless team leaders chart the course first by admitting their own mistakes and what they learned from them, it is unlikely that team members will take the plunge. So being a role model on this front is important.

Dr. Amy Edmondson worked extensively with Per Hugander, head of leadership and organization development at SEB, a Swedish financial group for corporate customers, to build psychologically safe teams at the company. In a great example of modeling how to build team psychological safety, Hugander used a two-step process. First, he started with a single team and helped it practice newly learned interpersonal skills in several regularly scheduled safe meetings. Second, he instructed team members who had successfully made progress on their difficult issues to share their experiences with other teams, beginning with the teams that reported to these individuals. Edmondson and Hugander emphasized that modeling should involve sharing "stories that portray how candor, vulnerability, and perspective-taking enabled successful outcomes."[19] By modeling their own vulnerability and pairing it with success stories, others will feel more comfortable doing so themselves, and psychological safety can grow throughout a team, and even an entire company.

Be a Transformational Leader

We've previously discussed the importance of transformational leadership in building up a team's confidence and teamwork roadmaps. It turns out that transformational leadership also helps build a team's psychological safety.[20] If a transformational leader's job is to "transform" people and processes, then it's natural that team psychological safety is a mechanism for doing so. When leaders challenge their teams to think differently about an issue or a problem (a key component of transformational leadership), it gives team members a license to offer up novel ideas or experiment with new approaches. Transformational leaders also ensure that each of their team members feels respected, valued, and appreciated. As a result, members feel safer expressing their true thoughts and opinions to their leader and their teammates.

Many studies conducted all over the world have demonstrated the positive impact of transformational leadership on psychological safety. For example, one study of teams working in South Korea found that those teams whose leaders were more transformational reported having higher psychological safety, which in turn promoted higher levels of team creativity.[21] Likewise, a study of banking institutions in Ghana found that transformational leaders built more psychologically safe teams, and those teams exhibited stronger learning behavior.[22] Another study using a sample of nursing teams in Belgium demonstrated the universal nature of this phenomenon, replicating the findings from Ghana. Teams with the most transformational leaders enjoyed the highest levels of psychological safety and team learning.[23] Clearly, as evidenced by a robust collection of studies, one of the most effective ways to develop psychological safety is to be a transformational leader.

Encourage Perspective Taking

Another way leaders can boost their team's psychological safety is to make perspective taking a regular part of their day. Recall that we previously discussed the role perspective taking plays in driving team improvisation. It involves putting oneself in someone else's shoes, so to speak, and it's also a key driver of psychological safety. When team members see the world through one another's eyes, they develop a collective feeling of empathy and understanding for one another. This activates a level of comfort that spurs open, honest discussion and interpersonal risk taking.

In chapter 2, we described the Mount Everest disaster that took place in May 1996. Lives might have been saved that day if the team had a more comprehensive teamwork roadmap or even if they had better enforced the roadmap they already had. In many books and articles written about that tragedy, another common theme has emerged. The team appeared to have lacked adequate psychological safety. This void is believed to have been largely caused by an absence of perspective taking within the team. The best-selling author Jon Krakauer was on the mountain that day and miraculously survived the ordeal. In his incredible book *Into Thin Air: A Personal Account of the Mount Everest Disaster*, he describes how the inability of team members to use perspective taking caused numerous problems.[24] He noted that several of the climbers did not have time to develop positive relationships with one another, worried a lot about what the others thought about them, and were concerned about being embarrassed or rejected for expressing their views. As a result, team members could not freely exchange their opinions or question one another openly and directly.[25] The lesson here is that team members must take the time to get to know one another on a deeper level so they can see the world through one another's eyes. It's only through this process of perspective taking that teammates can truly understand, trust, and respect one another. And it's that mutual understanding, trust, and respect that forms the bedrock upon which psychological safety is built.

Establish a Solid Foundation of Trust

Last, from a leader behavior perspective, as our consulting team example demonstrated, people will be a lot more comfortable taking interpersonal risks in their teams when they have a high level of trust in their leader. The junior business analyst likely would never have jumped into the client meeting if the partner on the team had not built up a high degree of trust with him. Leaders build trust with their teammates by keeping their promises, being available, leading the way by displaying trust in their team members, and speaking and acting consistently.

Katie Burke is the chief people officer of HubSpot, a consulting firm devoted to helping companies grow their customer bases using software products for customized marketing, sales, and customer service. HubSpot, founded in 2006, was named the best place to work by Glassdoor, the best place for women to work by Comparably, and one of the best places to work for parents by *Fortune*. Burke is a big believer that the leading contributor to psychological safety is leaders who work hard to earn the trust of their team. She states: "At its core, psychological safety is about trust. Employees are more likely to share creative ideas and take risks when they trust it won't jeopardize their performance or reputation. It's one thing to tell our teams to 'fail fast, fail often,' but how leaders actually react to mistakes is what matters. That's why it's not a coincidence that psychological safety and high performance are correlated; teams with a foundation of trust are more empowered to be autonomous and challenge the status quo than those without one."[26]

Burke points to three leader behaviors that are essential to building trust. First, leaders should ask their teams directly what they need to be successful. How do they like to receive feedback, how do they want to be recognized, or when are they most productive? Asking such questions sends a signal to team members that their voices matter, and actually acting on their preferences will build solid trust. Second, and related to our discussion about leaders modeling the behaviors they want to see, Burke states that leaders need to show vulnerability themselves. She cites Brené Brown's work on leadership vulnerability as related to leader success as a good resource.[27] Burke also walks the talk by sharing her own performance review with her entire global team, pointing to areas where she could have improved and a summary of her upward feedback. Finally, she points to the one simple question that she asks at the start of meetings with her team members: how are you feeling? She encourages her team members to share emotions openly and honestly, but only in as much detail as they feel comfortable doing. Burke states: "Starting with this question in my weekly team meetings helps me understand the energy in the room (or Zoom), and hear what's bringing my direct reports joy or stress that week outside of work. Especially for caregivers and parents during the pandemic, creating space for acknowledging distractions or frustrations is critical if we truly want to make 'bringing your full self to work' a reality."

Four Structural Levers to Build Team Psychological Safety

Table 6.2 summarizes four ways leaders can use various structures in their organizations to build team psychological safety and provides examples of each.

Create Team Charters

One evidence-based structural approach to building psychological safety is creating team charters. A team charter is a written agreement about how a team will make decisions and share accountability for producing and delivering high-quality outputs that satisfy customer needs in a timely and cost-efficient manner.[28] Some team members will roll their eyes and see creating a team charter as a waste of time. To be sure, team charters don't appear out of thin air; they take time and energy to develop, which is why some leaders skip right over them.[29] However, team charters help build up team member safety in terms of their responsibility for projects, and they provide a mechanism by which they can express their true feelings and concerns when things go off track. To contribute to a team's psychological safety, we recommend that team charters explicitly state that team members are expected to share all thoughts, opinions, feelings, ideas, and information that they believe to be relevant to their team's goals, and to do so in a manner that is respectful to all those involved. This eliminates any uncertainty about whether team members should speak up, and it provides them with cover when what they have to say isn't easy. That way, team members can lean on the charter as a crutch when they're experiencing any hesitancy. For example, you could say: "I have a thought that may or may not be received favorably by the team. But since our charter stipulates that we must communicate all information that we believe to be relevant, I feel the need to share it with you all."

TABLE 6.2. Four Team Structural Levers to Build Psychological Safety

Behaviors	Examples
1. Create team charters	Develop a written agreement about how a team will make decisions and share accountability for producing and delivering high quality outputs to satisfy customer needs in a timely and cost-efficient manner
2. Create team member role clarity	Make sure that team members are clear about the roles they should play on their team
3. Ensure a high level of peer-to-peer support	Strike a balance between supportiveness and too much freedom to disagree or debate
4. Make sure team members feel supported by their organization	Make sure team members know that the company cares about their opinion and well-being, would forgive a mistake on their part, strongly considers their goals and values, and would be willing to help them if they need something

Abhijit Dasgupta, vice president and head of business technology solutions, strategy, and continuous improvement for AbbVie, the global biopharmaceutical company founded in 2013 as a spin-off of Abbott Laboratories, strongly believes in the power of team charters to build psychological safety in his global team.[30] According to Dasgupta, "The Business Technology Solutions [BTS] organization in the US is pretty big, but internationally there is sometimes only one person from BTS in a country. To make sure our colleagues feel like a part of a single organization, we've gone through a process of identifying our vision, team charter, operating model, and the behaviors we expect of each other. That brings us together." To leverage the team charter to build psychological safety, Dasgupta also encourages his team members to read *Radical Candor*, by Kim Scott.[31] The book emphasizes approaching team conversations with curiosity and a desire to help others by fostering their growth, which also helps instill psychological safety. A written team charter can be critical in laying the groundwork for radical candor because it can answer questions about what radical candor should look like in the workplace, how and when it can be used, and how to overcome others' initial discomfort with it.[32] Dasgupta adds: "We truly believe in being transparent and speaking our mind, and it doesn't matter what level of the organization you are in. The only restrictions are, you've got to stay respectful, and you've got to come to the table with an open mind."

Create Team Member Role Clarity

Related to the importance of team charters, leaders can also enhance psychological safety by creating role clarity in their teams. When members are clear about what roles are expected of them, they should feel safe speaking up when doing so is critical to performing those roles. The good news is that team charters should serve the purpose of enhancing role clarity for many teams. However, this isn't always the case, because some team tasks just won't lend themselves to a team charter, such as a very fast-paced task with a short duration. Even in teams that are well suited for charters, leaders should not rely solely on the charter to establish and maintain role clarity. Oftentimes, team members are assigned temporary roles that may not be outlined in a charter. For example, leaders often assign a devil's advocate or an inquisitor to enhance the quality of team discussions and decision making. If a person's role is created for the sole purpose of poking holes in a team's ideas or approach, then that person should feel a high degree of safety in doing so. Likewise, if certain members are assigned responsibility for quality or responsiveness, for example, those individuals will be much more likely to go out on a limb to ensure that those attributes are protected and maximized.

Dr. Kathleen O'Connor, of the London Business School, coaches teams on the power of using a devil's advocate to instill a sense of psychological safety in teams.[33] She argues that this should help teams avoid the communication trap we mentioned previously of simply repeating what is already known by team members out of fear of being ostracized or singled out when introducing novel ideas or information. O'Connor says that critical to enhancing psychological safety is creating a healthy culture of debate within a team to make it OK to be wrong. She also suggests that the devil's advocate role rotate among team members so that the same person does not get stuck in the same role and come to be viewed as the team contrarian. Rotating the role also makes it easier for members to disconnect an opinion or argument a person is making from the advocate's personality. This should also make it easier for team members to focus more on the information at hand rather than the person providing it. When members are assigned the role of speaking up and disagreeing, that should free them from worrying about being punished for dissenting and allow psychological safety to flourish.

Ensure a High Level of Peer-To-Peer Support

Another structural remedy for increasing psychological safety in teams is for leaders to ensure that their teams have strong peer-to-peer support. This requires striking a balance between supportiveness and maybe too much freedom to disagree or debate. For example, if a team's members are too supportive of one another, they may not want to upset the good feelings and harmony in their teams by disagreeing or speaking up. In that case, teams are likely to end up with groupthink, in which team members choose to go with the flow rather than go against the current. Groupthink results in a team getting trapped on a particular path, even though one or more members may have a sinking feeling that they're headed in the wrong direction. In contrast, if leaders create an environment in which members are constantly disagreeing with or criticizing one another, they may run the risk of having a team that fractures or breaks apart because members cannot ever agree on a path forward. So, the trick with peer support is finding a middle ground that works to increase psychological safety. That balance might best be described as respectful debate, and it's incumbent upon the leader to monitor this activity and put up guard rails if a team begins veering too far in one direction or the other.

Echoing the notion that psychological safety can be taken too far and can create counterproductive work environments, Shane Snow, author of *Dream Teams*, recounted a situation he had when he held a series of "culture talks" in his organization with his team.[34] He states:

> I wanted everyone to "feel comfortable" at work. I recognized our growing demographic diversity, and I wanted to make sure that the team continued to treat each other well even as they became more of a merry band of misfits than a uniformed army of soldiers. But what I learned is that the idea of making a team environment completely *comfortable* was at odds with growth and problem solving. If you stay completely comfortable at the gym, your muscles will never grow. A great leader's job is to help people combine their different ingredients and push further than they could go on their own. That's inherently uncomfortable. The job of a leader is not to protect their team from discomfort. It's to protect them from *harm*—and to help motivate them to push through the discomfort and harness it for growth.

As Snow so aptly put it, psychological safety is not designed to create a team climate opposed to discomfort. It really is all about making sure team members feel safe enough to experience discomfort and use those feelings for greater learning and team performance. You could say that psychological safety ensures that team members are "comfortable getting uncomfortable." So team leaders need to make sure they do not swing the pendulum of psychological safety too far to the side of avoiding uncomfortable discussions or situations in terms of peer-to-peer support.

Make Sure Team Members Feel Supported by Their Organization

Finally, evidence has also shown that when team members believe they are supported by their organization (and not just their leaders), they are more likely to experience team psychological safety.[35] When team members feel a high degree of organizational support, they are likely to report that their company cares about their opinion and well-being, will forgive a mistake on their part, is willing to help if team members need something, and strongly considers their goals and values.[36] Of course, many team members view their leaders as key representatives of their organizations, so it behooves leaders to communicate to team members that their company does value, respect, and care for them. However, an even better way to demonstrate organizational support is to enlist the help of some of your company's senior leaders. Team leaders should consider requesting that senior leaders send a quick note of appreciation to their team members or even drop by their offices or jump into a virtual meeting from time to time to ask how they're doing and if there's anything they need.

As evidence of the importance of organizational support, McKinsey & Company found that promoting psychological safety begins at the top of organizations.[37] When senior leaders worked to create a company culture of inclusiveness by role modeling positive, supportive leader behaviors themselves, there was a cascading effect such that team leaders throughout the company were more likely to seek out opinions that differed from their own and treat others with respect in doing so. Companies that encourage senior leaders to take steps to create supportive organizational climates also help instill psychological safety in their teams because team members will look to these senior leaders for signs and clues about what the company values. For example, promoting cultural awareness throughout the organization about the different beliefs and norms

CHAPTER 7

LEADING YOUR TEAM THROUGH A CRISIS

Imagine yourself as the vice president of client services for a small marketing firm. Your company specializes in the marine recreation industry, producing marketing strategy and content for luxury yacht and sport boat manufacturers. In your role, you lead a cross-functional project team dedicated exclusively to serving the needs of your company's largest client—a client that accounts for more than 40 percent of total revenues. Your team blends a variety of expertise, including three members responsible for creative content, one for market research and data analytics, one for information technology, one for production, and one for media. You also have a project manager responsible for generating schedules, coordinating activities, tracking progress, and ensuring that all deliverables are on time and under budget. Your team has achieved what can best be described as legendary status throughout your company and, importantly, in the eyes of your client. Your marketing campaigns have been enormously successful, garnering international attention, earning numerous advertising awards, and leading to client sales that have exceeded projections for five consecutive years. Oh, and you've never missed a deadline.

It's Tuesday morning. You sit in your office, peering out the window with a glazed look in your eyes. Your gaze locks in on some budding tulips, the first sign of an early spring, and you're wondering whether your team's unblemished streak is about to end. Your project manager, Emily, just left your office in tears.

Earlier in the morning, she received a devastating phone call. Her father fell ill, and his doctor estimates that he has only a few weeks left to live. She asked if it would be all right for her to take that time off so they could spend his last days together. Your heart sinks. "Of course," you reply. "Take as much time as you need. I am so terribly sorry to hear this."

You care deeply about your team members, and it pains you to know that one of them is suffering. You're also keenly aware of the business implications of this situation. Your team is two weeks away from your first-quarter campaign deadline, the largest and most comprehensive campaign your team has ever tackled. In addition to traditional print and digital paid media, the campaign includes a complete website redesign and a blowout launch party where the client will reveal its new product line. The event will be held on the water and will feature a lineup of chart-topping musical artists on a floating stage. Guests will park their boats in front of the stage and "raft up" by roping their vessels together and enjoying the concert and product reveal as a community.

Emily is a rock star. She's incredibly intelligent, talented, reliable, hardworking, and caring. Her teammates love her. She's developed powerful bonds with each of them. To put it simply, she's the glue that holds the team together. Losing her at this late stage, when pressure is intensified and a long list of deliverables is soon to be coming due, will be a massive blow to both the team's morale and its logistics. Although she offered to continue working remotely from the hospital, you firmly stated: "Absolutely not! There's only one thing you should be concerned with for the next few weeks, and that's being present and spending your time with your father. Don't worry about us. We'll be just fine."

But will you be just fine? There's no question that this is the worst possible time to lose your project manager. Your client's trust and confidence in your team have led to the largest marketing investment in the company's history. The campaign's success hinges on meeting the deadline. Even the smallest delay will risk missing out on ad placements in key industry magazines and at the boat show. Is your team ready for this? Can they overcome this adversity and meet the deadline without their linchpin? You're about to find out. You snap out of your daze, exit your office, and call an emergency all-hands-on-deck meeting.

Your team immediately recognizes the seriousness of your tone, drops what they're doing, and moves quickly to the conference room. Once seated, you break the news that they'll need to complete the campaign without Emily. The team is silent, hanging on your every word. This is a critical moment. You know that what you say next will determine whether they leave inspired and energized or deflated and demoralized. You take this opportunity to open up, speak from your heart, and make yourself vulnerable.[1] "I know how this news makes you feel because I feel it too," you tell them. "I feel a mixture of emotions swirling around inside me. I'm nervous. I'm anxious. I'm even a little scared. And yet, at the same time, I'm hopeful, confident, and even excited about this challenge. We're going to succeed. And not only will we succeed, but this is going to be the best campaign we've ever produced. Look, we're ready for this. We've prepared for it."

And you *had* prepared. Two years ago, when you were promoted to vice president, one of your first actions was to craft a team resilience blueprint. You were on a mission to build a resilient team. In fact, you still have the handwritten notes that mapped it all out. At the time, you dug deep into the team resilience research and learned that the best way to prepare your team for inevitable adversities is to build up four resilient resources: team confidence, a teamwork roadmap, the capacity to improvise, and psychological safety. So, at the top of the first page of your blueprint, you wrote "Building a Resilient Team" and listed those four resources followed by several action items to strengthen each one. You've worked hard over the last couple of years to follow this blueprint, and you've seen noticeable improvements in all four areas.

The second page of your team resilience blueprint was titled "Leading Teams through a Crisis." It summarized the three stages of team resilience: minimizing adversity, managing adversity, and mending after adversity. Under each stage, you listed specific actions. Figure 7.1 illustrates the team resilience blueprint.

MINIMIZING ADVERSITY

Your first stage, minimizing adversity, began long before any adversity even presented itself. You're well aware that it's never too early to prepare your team for the inevitability of unexpected challenges.

Preparing

Beyond equipping your team for adversity by building up the four resilient resources, you also worked to minimize adversity by simulating a variety of possible scenarios and working together to determine the best path forward. The logic behind this was twofold. First, the more exposure the team members can get to specific challenges they might face, the more prepared they should be when those challenges arise. Second, even if they encounter adversity that wasn't in a practice scenario, the regular routine of engaging collaboratively in

BUILDING A RESILIENT TEAM

TEAM CONFIDENCE	TEAMWORK ROADMAP
–CLEAR GOALS AND PROCESSES	–FREQUENT TEAM MEETINGS
–EMPOWER!	–INTERACTION TRAINING
–BE TRANSFORMATIONAL	–SHARED LEADERSHIP
–BE ETHICAL	–BE TRANSFORMATIONAL
–MASTERY EXPERIENCES	–HYPOTHETICAL ADVERSITIES

CAPACITY TO IMPROVISE	PSYCHOLOGICAL SAFETY
–BUILD TRANSACTIVE MEMORY	–CLIMATE OF INCLUSIVITY
–INCREASE TEAM CREATIVITY	–APPRECIATION FOR INPUT!
	–DISCUSS MISTAKES + LEARN FROM THEM
	–BE TRANSFORMATIONAL
	–ENCOURAGE PERSPECTIVE-TAKING
	–BUILD TRUST!

FIGURE 7.1. The Team Resilience Blueprint (2 parts)

problem solving during hypothetical scenarios should make them more comfortable and effective when facing a real problem in need of a solution.

These hypothetical scenarios didn't take much time out of your team's day. Every couple of weeks, you simply carved out a ten- to fifteen-minute problem-solving block at the end of your team meetings. Prior to each meeting, you identified a possible problem, on your own or by polling your team members for ideas. During the meetings, you presented the hypothetical challenges to the team and asked members how we should respond. For example: "We're experiencing an internet outage, and it will be down until tomorrow. How can we complete our project and deliver it to our client by the end of the day today?" and "We're nearing the end of a project, and we're all exhausted and losing steam. How can we regain our motivation and finish strong?"

You are comforted by the fact that you had actually practiced a scenario very similar to today's. In fact, a recurring hypothetical problem that you have presented is "Our project is due today, and Robert is out sick. How will we meet our deadline?" Each time you use this example, you change the name of the team member. You found this to be an especially meaningful exercise. One advantage of doing this in advance is that the "sick" employee is present during the conversation, something that would not be possible if you waited until that person was actually out. You've

LEADING TEAMS THROUGH A CRISIS

MINIMIZING ADVERSITY

- PREPARING
  - BUILD THE 4 RESOURCES
  - HYPOTHETICAL ADVERSITIES
- DETECTING
  - EVERYONE IS VIGILANT
- SENSEMAKING + STRATEGIZING
  - TEAM DISCUSSION
  - EMPOWER!
  - "WHAT DO YOU THINK?"
  - CO-CREATE AN ACTION PLAN

MANAGING ADVERSITY

- TEAM MORALE (MOTIVATION, CONFIDENCE, CONFLICT)
- SHARED PURPOSE
- SET MILESTONES
  - SHOW APPRECIATION!
  - CELEBRATE SMALL WINS
  - MANAGE CONFLICTS
- TEAMWORK (COORDINATE, MONITOR, BACK-UP
  - DISTRIBUTE THE ACTION PLAN
  - DAILY 15-MINUTE HUDDLES
  - BUDDY SYSTEM
  - PITCH IN!

MENDING AFTER ADVERSITY

- REFLECTING
  - TEAM DEBRIEF
  - ROSES (SUCCESSES) + THORNS (STRUGGLES)
- LEARNING
  - WHAT WILL WE DO DIFFERENTLY NEXT TIME?

found that the presence of these future "sick" employees is particularly important because they know their role the best and so always have the most to contribute to the discussion. About three months ago, it was Emily's turn. Although in that scenario she was out for only a day (not weeks), the exercise was highly informative. Emily explained to the team exactly where to find her project management files and who to go to for a variety of questions. She even walked teams through her approval checklist so that someone could step in and approve deliverables. You're confident that this exercise adequately prepared your team for today's challenge.

Detecting

One thing you learned while reading articles about team resilience is that early detection of adversity can greatly reduce the severity of its effects.[2] Of course, the sooner adversity is known to the team, the quicker it can be addressed. For example, an interpersonal conflict between two teammates that is unknown to you (or to the rest of the team) can build up and fester until it boils over and creates irreparable damage— to the team, a project, or even your client relationship. Detecting this conflict early by vigilantly tuning in to subtle cues would enable you as the leader to step in and intervene, thereby containing the adversity before it gets out of control.

You frequently encourage your team to be forever vigilant to changing circumstances, to be on the lookout for the early signs of adversity, and to inform the team immediately of any irregularities. In the current situation, Emily presented the adverse situation to you immediately, and so the detection came without effort. However, your awareness is only half of the detection process. The other half requires that the team is made aware. This means that you can't sit on the information. You must communicate the problem to your team both promptly and clearly, which is why you called the all-hands team meeting.

Sensemaking and Strategizing

"So, what does this mean for us?" you ask your team. "I recognize the vital role that Emily plays in keeping our team on track. How exactly does her absence impact our workflow and timeline? What specific difficulties will this create for each of you? And what questions do you have for me or for one another?"

This launches a lively conversation in which the team begins to make sense of the challenges before them. Each time a team member raises a concern, you jot it on the whiteboard. When the conversation dies down, you shift into problem-solving mode. "OK," you say as you point at the board. "This is what we're up against. Let's craft a strategy for overcoming each of these challenges. Let's go down the list together and chart a path forward."

As you lead this discussion, you're careful to adopt an empowering leadership style. Rather than simply stating what you think should be done for each item, you probe the team to brainstorm solutions collaboratively. You fold your thoughts into the discussion as well, but the last thing you want is for this to be a one-way conversation in which you share and they listen passively. So, at several points throughout the conversation, you repeat the same four words you've frequently used in your team meetings: "What do you think?" This is a simple but powerful question that signals to your team members that you trust them, that their voice matters, and that there is shared ownership in the challenge you're facing and in the responsibility to generate solutions to it.

As they tend to do when you empower them, your team members rise to the challenge and generate a solid list of strategic solutions. In less than an hour, your team mapped out new communication and workflow channels, divided and reallocated Emily's duties, and committed to a new schedule that will extend everyone's work hours until the project is completed. Several solutions were pulled directly from the "sick teammate" simulation you facilitated several months back. The others were pure improvisation.

MANAGING ADVERSITY

At this point, you've minimized the adversity to the extent that you possibly can. You proactively built up the team's resilient resources, prepared them with periodic simulated challenges, notified them as soon as adversity struck, and facilitated team discussions during which everyone worked collaboratively to make sense of the situation and chart a path forward. It's now time for the team to execute that strategy to overcome adversity and hit the deadline.

It's during this stage that you support the team in managing the adversity. Your objective is to give the team members everything they need to progress toward their goals despite the adverse conditions under which they are operating. You view your role as consisting of two separate but related components: managing team morale and facilitating teamwork.

Team Morale

Team morale refers to self-esteem, assurance, confidence, drive, humor, and a good outlook within a team.[3] You know that one of the most important aspects of teamwork, especially when adversity strikes, is motivating your team and ensuring that team members maintain that motivation for the long haul. You've already put quite a bit of prework into team motivation by building up one of the four resilient resources: team confidence. Research is pretty clear that confident teams are more engaged when times get tough, which spurs persistence and enables them to persevere through adversity.[4]

To get them off to a strong start, you do your best to align everyone around a common mission: "Look, I know you're all dreading what we're about to do. The next couple of weeks are going to be tough on all of us. We're shifting from 'business as usual' into crisis mode. We'll need to learn new processes, take on new responsibilities, and work longer hours than we're accustomed to. You're probably feeling upset, frustrated, maybe even angry. And that's OK. That's natural. But do me a favor. Take those negative feelings and channel them into something good. Use them as fuel toward our common mission. Part of that mission, as always, is to exceed our client's expectations. But this time, there's more at stake. One of our own is hurting. And as if she didn't already have enough to worry about at home, she's also concerned that she's letting us down. That's the last thing she needs right now. Her focus should be 100 percent on her family. So, let's show her she has nothing to worry about over here. Let's get this done for Emily."

You feel that they responded well to your pep talk, and they appear energized and committed to doing what it takes. But a lot of time will pass between now and the deadline. Momentum will wane, and it's your responsibility to build it back up. Fortunately, you have a couple of additional motivational levers to pull. First, you adopt a "milestone" approach. You roll the conference room whiteboard out to a common space where you know the team will see it several times a day. On the board, you break down the project tasks into five milestones. Over the next two weeks, as each milestone is reached, you throw a mini-celebration, complete with snacks, treats, and other goodies from several of the team's favorite local businesses. They're noticeably excited when you promise an all-day offsite, all-inclusive team retreat after the fifth and final milestone is reached.

Between milestones, you pull the appreciation lever. You focus your efforts on showing appreciation for the hard work of the team as a whole and the contributions of individual team members. Recognizing these contributions publicly, via team email and in-person announcements, seems to motivate not only the specific individuals being recognized but the rest of the team as well. This matches research you read about individual recognition increasing a single team member's performance and also every other member's performance and overall team performance, which the researchers called a recognition "spillover" effect.[5] One technique that has worked well for you over the years is setting reminders in your calendar to recognize a different team member throughout the week. This ensures that you don't forget to perform this important act or leave anyone out. Celebrating team milestones, expressing appreciation, and recognizing individual achievements all serve as motivational fuel critical for your team to forge ahead and persist to the completion of a demanding project. It also helps a team coalesce as a unit by maintaining positive team emotions and strengthening the team's confidence in its ability to deliver a high-quality product on time, even without a vital team member.

One additional way that you facilitate team morale is by managing team conflict. Fortunately, this team typically gets along quite well, and conflict is rather rare. But the current setting isn't typical. Team members are working intensely for extended hours every day. Exhaustion is likely to set in. Combine this exhaustion with potential confusion about a new way of collaborating, and the situation is ripe for conflict.

And that's exactly what happens. You overhear two of your teammates, Jeremy and Robert, raising their voices at one another as they argue about who should be approving a specific campaign piece. This, of course, is easily resolved by referring to the revised plan. It turns out that Robert is correct, but when he points this out, Jeremy responds with an angry retort, which in turn angers Robert—a minor spat but one that could escalate into a full-blown argument. You pull Jeremy aside. "Is everything all right?"

"Yes," he replies, head down, staring at the floor. "I'm just tired, and I got a little chippy. I let my emotions get the best of me. Won't happen again."

You determine that Jeremy was probably just embarrassed about his mistake, and because he was so depleted, he didn't have the self-control to filter his response. You encourage him to take a break and get outside for a short walk. When he returns, he seems refreshed and ready to get back to work. "Thanks," he says. "I needed that."

Teamwork

Although managing morale is all about the activities that keep the team moving forward as a cohesive unit—motivating, building confidence, maintaining positive emotions, and managing conflict—teamwork consists of activities that are directly related to goal attainment. This includes coordinating, monitoring, and backing one another up as needed.[6] Coordinating may be the most challenging in the current team environment. Remember the teamwork roadmap from chapter 4? Well, you've spent the past two years building and fine-tuning that map, only to have it break down two weeks before the biggest deadline of your (and your team's) career. Emily was the one person on this map that tied everyone else together. Without her, the map falls apart. This is why immediately after hearing the news, you called for an all-hands sensemaking and strategy meeting. The purpose was to work together to design a new roadmap for the next two weeks. Knowing Emily's work ethic, you estimate that she probably would have worked around 120 hours total during that period, and so everyone on the team (including you) would need to step in to absorb her responsibilities and make up for those lost hours. In your opinion, your team did a fantastic job of reworking the roadmap—a testament to all the work they've put into building up their capacity to improvise.

Now that you have this new roadmap in place, your job is to help the team navigate it. In other words, you take it upon yourself to help them coordinate their activities in this strange new environment. You begin by designing a visual of the revised roadmap, which you send to everyone on the team and also hang on the wall for easy reference. This visual looks somewhat like a flowchart that illustrates how products and communications will move throughout the team. It also highlights who is responsible for what, with bold and colored font for all duties that are new to a given individual.

Another way you facilitate coordination is by scheduling daily fifteen-minute huddles. Your team is already overworked, so there's no time for long meetings. But eliminating meetings altogether would be risky given the new terrain. In these huddles (which usually don't take the full fifteen minutes), team members share any questions they may have about what they're to do and how they're to do it. They also raise issues (and potential future issues) regarding the new roadmap. Thanks to the psychological safety team members have been building up over the past couple of years, nobody is shy about speaking up, even when the issues being raised are somewhat uncomfortable. Where inefficiencies or unforeseen roadblocks are identified, the roadmap is modified. These huddles are quick and informative, and importantly, they offer continued support for the team's coordination efforts.

These huddles also serve two other important functions. They provide dedicated time and space for team communication, which is essential to coordination. And they facilitate the other two teamwork activities: monitoring and backing one another up. Daily huddles are great opportunities to check the team's pulse. You regularly encourage your team to monitor three categories of information. You ask them to always be vigilant to the team's progress toward its goals, to team systems, and to the team itself. Goal progress checks involve status updates on where we stand relative to our milestones (each of which has a deadline). Team members update one another on where a given deliverable stands and when it's expected to move to the next stage of production.

System checks encourage team members to be on the lookout for changes to the systems that enable team functioning. These include team resources (e.g., equipment, supplies), conditions related to internal workflows (e.g., ineffective communication channels, production bottlenecks), and conditions external to the team that impact team workflows (e.g., new or changing client requests, vendor delays).

Finally, team checks give members a safe space either to admit that they're struggling or to express concerns that one of their teammates could be overwhelmed and, as a result, might slow down the process. This monitoring of teammates makes backing one another up possible. In each meeting, you actively solicit the team to speak up if members need help or think someone else needs help. By making this a norm of each meeting, you reduce the stigma often associated with such an admission. On multiple occasions in these huddles, team members do speak up, either for themselves or on behalf of a teammate. This allows the team to rebalance the workload in a way that unclogs the pipeline. "Who can help out here?" you ask. Typically, someone on the team jumps in to offer a hand. And when it makes sense to do so, you take on some of the extra work yourself. Without these huddles or the psychologically safe environment, it's likely that team members would simply continue to struggle, negatively affecting both their personal well-being and the overall production process.

You find team monitoring and backing up to be so important on your team that you implement an additional mechanism to facilitate these activities. You adopt a buddy system in which each team member is assigned to an accountability partner. The buddy system has only two rules. The first rule is that all team members must check in with their partner at least once a day and ask the same exact question: "Are you OK?" The second rule is that the person being asked must answer honestly. Any information gleaned from this check-in should then be brought to the team during the next huddle (or to you immediately, if it's urgent). Although you believe you've created a psychologically safe environment in which everyone feels comfortable speaking up when they have concerns, this adds a second layer of comfort for anyone that may prefer to acknowledge a struggle with a single team member rather than to the entire team.

The two weeks fly by rather quickly for you and your team. It's not always smooth sailing, and you encounter a few setbacks. But your daily huddles and accountability system bring them to light quickly, allowing your team to resolve them before they escalate. All throughout, you continue to focus your efforts on team morale by encouraging and supporting, expressing appreciation, and celebrating team and individual achievements. And you make yourself available to pitch in when needed.

The team achieves milestone after milestone, and when the final deliverable is sent to the client with more than three hours to spare, your team breaks out in collective applause. A smile forms on your face, and you exit your office to congratulate everyone.

MENDING AFTER ADVERSITY

Before you send everyone home for the weekend, there's one more thing for you to do. You invite everyone to take a fifteen-minute break before joining you in the conference room for a team debrief.

After everyone files in, you begin.

"First of all, let me just say one more time how much I appreciate everything you all accomplished over the last couple of weeks. Working extra hours, picking up additional responsibilities, reimagining our communication and production channels, and ultimately meeting our client's deadline, even without our project manager. You've proved that you're a resilient team, and I'm proud of you. And you should be proud of yourselves.

"I also want to thank you all for bearing with me for just a little longer today. I know you're all exhausted, and the last thing you want to do is sit through another meeting. But debriefing is a critical step in the resilience process. It ensures that we're even more prepared and even more resilient when the next crisis emerges. Ultimately, the purpose of debriefs like this one is to determine what good can come out of this difficult situation. How can we grow stronger as a result of the challenges we've faced and overcome? Rather than wait until next week to do this, I wanted to knock it out now while the experience is still fresh in our minds.

"The evidence tells us that performance improves pretty dramatically when teams take the time to learn together. And one of the best ways to learn is by doing a thoughtful debrief immediately after a meaningful event. In fact, these debriefs typically give teams a 25 percent performance boost! But for this to be effective, I need everyone's input. So, let's all pitch in here, have a good, thoughtful discussion about the last couple of weeks, and then head home for a well-deserved rest. Sound good?"[7]

The team nods in unison, and you jump straight into it.

"What I'd like to do is discuss two aspects of our experiences: successes—the things we did well, and failures—the mistakes we made or the things that went wrong. For simplicity's sake, I'll just refer to successes and failures as 'roses and thorns,' respectively."[8]

You walk over to the whiteboard and write "Roses" and "Thorns" across the top.

"Our roses are easy—and fun—to talk about. So, I'd like to save those for last. Let's focus first on our thorns. What are some things that went wrong in our team? Who has something that didn't go well, or who has the courage to admit you made a mistake at some point in the last couple of weeks?"

Just in case the room fell silent, you were prepared to kick off this discussion by opening up about some areas where you fell short, including a bad decision you made that created more work for the team, a time when you behaved more like a micromanager than a leader, and a time you should've noticed that a team member was struggling but didn't.

But the room didn't fall silent. Jeremy jumped right in: "I messed up late last week. I misunderstood the new roadmap and thought Robert was responsible for a particular task. I was feeling a bit burned out at the time, and so my temper was short. When I saw that Robert hadn't performed the task, I let my emotions get the best of me, and I snapped at him. He pointed out that it was actually my responsibility and showed me the roadmap. He was right, but instead of me owning up to my mistake, I got embarrassed and lashed out at him again. I feel bad about that. He didn't deserve the way I treated him."

"Thank you, Jeremy. I really appreciate your courage in sharing this story. There are several thorns to unpack from your experience. I'm going to write 'confusion with new roadmap,' 'burnout,' and 'team conflict' on the board. Who else has a thorn to share?"

Jeremy's admission sets off a flurry of additional thorns raised by other teammates. The team continues to share information until you have a healthy list on the board. The list includes a variety of errors made by individual team members and also a few team decisions and activities that didn't go as well as planned. Most of the team-level concerns are related to the revised roadmap and the realization that expectations did not always match reality.

"Thank you all. This is a great list of issues we can learn from. But before we do so, we're going to shift over to the fun part of our debrief. Let's discuss our successes. Who has a rose to share? This could be something you yourself accomplished that you're proud of or something that one of your teammates did to help you or the team out. It could also be something the team as a whole accomplished collectively."

"I'll start. For my rose, take a look at this long list of thorns. Despite all these challenges we faced—despite all the things that went wrong, we still found a way to achieve our goal and deliver an amazing campaign before our client's deadline. Words can't explain just how impressive that accomplishment is. Let's give everyone a round of applause for their efforts."

After the room quiets, you turn it over to the team: "Who else has a rose to share?"

The team isn't shy about celebrating their successes. And while there are few self-celebrations, most are comments recognizing a teammate who went above and beyond. The buddy system appears to have been a big hit, as many of the roses were about accountability partners who jumped in to assist one another when they were facing a challenge. By the end of this discussion, the list of roses is more than twice as long as the list of thorns.

"A huge thank you to each one of you for participating in this discussion, but more importantly, for engaging in all these wonderful acts to help your teammates and the team as a whole."

You find the roses-and-thorns exercise to be a simple yet powerful technique that can aid a team in reflecting on an adverse experience. This reflection then transitions into a learning process in which the team identifies changes they can implement so they're better equipped in the future. You begin this discussion in much the same way that you began the initial all-hands sensemaking and strategy meeting right two weeks ago.

"I know you're tired and ready to get out of here. But if you'll hang with me for just a little longer, I have one more ask of you before we wrap up. I'd like to discuss what we can learn from this experience that can make life better for us in the future. Let's identify some specific changes we would make if we were to do it all over again—changes that will better prepare us for confronting future adversities. In other words, let's craft a plan that will allow for more roses and fewer thorns the next time we're in a tough spot. Let's go one by one down the list of thorns and brainstorm some ways we would do each item differently if we were in this position again. Pat, will you please do me a favor and take some good notes on this discussion, so we can keep a record of our action plan?"

Despite the team's level of exhaustion, the conversation is energetic. Many of the thorns were actually addressed in real time as they were encountered, such as unforeseen problems associated with the new roadmap. So the only need for these items, assuming the adjustments worked well, is to write down the changes that were made. The team has some great ideas for overcoming the remaining thorns in the future, and of course, you inject your thoughts and opinions where appropriate.

When all is said and done, your team has created what you believe to be a solid recap of the struggles and successes from the previous two weeks, as well as a plan to better prepare for adversity, sure to arise in the future. Carving out time to discuss trials and triumphs resulted in a humbling yet uplifting opportunity for the team to heal after a grueling two weeks. Generating a plan to reduce future challenges ensured an even stronger and more resilient team because the members shared the experience together.

As your team stands up and exits, you can't help but notice a strange feeling in the room, a feeling you haven't had in quite some time. Relief! Your team is smiling and laughing as they walk out. As the room empties, relief turns to excitement as you begin thinking of fun ideas for the team retreat.

CHAPTER 8

BUILDING TEAM RESILIENCE IN REMOTE AND HYBRID TEAMS

Imagine you are an advertising executive working in the account management department of a medium-sized agency in San Francisco. You are currently on a team developing an ad campaign for a piece of wearable technology that can monitor heart rate, oxygen levels, physical activity, and sleep patterns. You report to two different managers in the agency, including the account management department supervisor and a project team leader for this particular product, who is a vice president of client services. You have been working around the clock for about eight months to develop a cohesive multimedia campaign for the technology, with your focus being on social media presence and engaging with influencers. Your team consists of six members, including you, your agency's creative director, an art director, two copywriters, and a social media director.

Typically, your team members work in the office, averaging about fifty to sixty hours per week during the development of an ad campaign. When the client's needs shift and deadlines get tight, you and your team members often are at the office late into the evenings to get everything done. Your work environment is open concept, which the company believes helps team members be more innovative and engage in impromptu bursts of creativity (your company calls these serendipity moments, a term that always makes you laugh). You acknowledge that, although the work is often hard and requires long hours, there is a sense of true camaraderie and a palpable team spirit. Your work is obviously very fast paced and demanding, but you still find time to socialize with your team members at the office, as well as at your favorite coffee spot and, later in the evening, a pub just down the street. All in all, you love working so closely with a bunch of "work hard, play hard" colleagues, and you have no trouble jumping out of bed each morning and getting to the office prepared to tackle any challenge that might arise.

And then the world changes. You'd been hearing about a potentially troubling virus outbreak overseas for about a month or so, but it seemed so far away from your daily life. However, things had started to feel more serious and foreboding in the news lately. A couple of weeks later, you receive word that your company's New York office is mandating that all employees work from home for the foreseeable future. It isn't long before your senior management team calls an all-hands meeting for your office on a Monday morning to make an important announcement: starting the following week, in preparation for a widespread shutdown across the country, everyone will work from home indefinitely instead of coming into the office. Your heart sinks as you think about how your team will develop an ad campaign while working remotely from home. You know that face-to-face work is associated with greater creativity and innovation; you read several articles on this a few years ago while finishing your MBA. You begin to tune out the rest of your management's discussion, as you feel a bit panicky trying to picture how all this will work logistically and how you will deal with not being around your fellow team members, many of whom you consider good friends.

A couple of days later, your team leaders call a meeting in the office. The project team leader, Sarah, speaks first. She says that nobody asked for this situation, obviously, and that it will be a strain for everyone. She points out many of the things that already occurred to you, including that traditional ad campaign work is normally done in the office, face-to-face, where all the "cool tools" are located. She then says something that raises your spirits: "Although we are now facing tremendous adversity, I have complete confidence in this team to make the transition to remote work. Based on your track record, you should all feel very confident in what you're capable of doing, no matter where or when you work." When Sarah finishes speaking, you notice your team members sitting a little more upright in their chairs and exchanging knowing glances, despite their trepidation.

Your account manager, Brian, jumps in next. "Sarah's right," he says, "You have created many award-winning ad campaigns for this company. Remember all of us celebrating in Cannes, France, last year? Although none of us has any idea when we'll be able to do that again, this team has not even begun to tap its full potential, in my opinion. There are so many great things you are going to accomplish in the near future, starting with the current campaign. I'm proud of you, and I'm counting on this team to deliver what we know it can. And although we'll be physically separated, nobody will be alone. You'll have one another, and you'll have us. Sarah and I will be with you every step of the way."

Despite having some doubts about the details, you and the rest of your team are actually feeling pretty confident about delivering a blockbuster campaign for your client. Sarah and Brian also lead a discussion outlining each team member's roles and responsibilities in the current ad campaign. Because you will all work from home, several adjustments are needed in the workflow. Sarah and Brian assign not only roles but also backups for each role, just in case anyone contracts the virus and can't work for a period of time. They carefully lay out the revised plan and answer the many questions you and your team have. By the time the meeting wrapped up, you and your team had a very good understanding of the teamwork roadmap just discussed. In other words, everyone appeared to be on the same page regarding what they're supposed to do, how they'll do it, and the timelines for each stage of completing the campaign. There shouldn't be any ambiguity when inevitable setbacks arise.

Over the next several weeks, this roadmap is put to the test, as team members do have a variety of issues crop up from time to time, mostly due to increased family responsibilities, such as children home from school and caring for sick relatives. However, the teamwork roadmap ensures that you don't waste time huddling up in virtual meetings to discuss how to handle a missing team member's responsibilities. You simply pivot to your backup plan. This plan was created in the initial team meeting, and Sarah and Brian have been very good about reinforcing it so that nothing falls through the "virtual cracks."

Sarah and Brian hold periodic virtual team meetings over the next few months to "check in" with your team to make sure team confidence levels remain high. You appreciate their consistent efforts because you have seen leaders show great initiative at the beginning of a crisis but then lose steam over time. Especially since your team members are not together physically, the check-ins with Sarah and Brian are critical to keeping your team's spirits up. You were afraid that working from home might start chipping away at team confidence. You and your teammates have always considered yourselves a high-performing team, but at the onset of the pandemic, you worried whether this would hold in the new remote world. And admittedly, there have been days when your team's confidence waned. But that always seems to happen at about the time that Sarah and Brian rally everyone together again. You and your team members always leave the meetings feeling energized and confident.

A few months into the pandemic, things on the whole seem to be going quite well. Everyone has established new routines, and the team is more or less used to the "new normal." However, at 2:30 in the afternoon, you and your team receive an email from Sarah with an urgent request. A major issue was just brought to her attention. She didn't go into details but said she needed everyone in a virtual meeting in thirty minutes and that she would explain everything at that time. The gravity of the situation was made clear by the solemn tone of the email, a tone quite uncharacteristic of Sarah. Everyone was so anxious to find out what happened that they all logged into the meeting ten minutes early—everyone, that is, except for one, who arrived a few minutes late due to his toddler's meltdown over receiving the wrong-colored drink cup (he wanted the red cup, not the green one).

Sarah logged in right at 3:00 p.m. and cut straight to the chase. She said that although the client was hoping that the wearable technology could perform four functions—measuring heart rate, oxygen levels, physical activity, and sleep patterns—they had informed Sarah that the lab testing for the oxygen level assessments was inconsistent. In fact, the results were so unreliable that the company had decided to drop this particular aspect of the device, with the possibility of introducing it at a later time. However, the client felt that the device was still marketable even without the oxygen sensor. This came as a shock and personal disappointment because you had recently thought of a great tagline based on the device's ability to measure oxygen levels that would be featured in all aspects of the campaign. You had even shot a prototype social media ad featuring a runner using the technology with the line "Just Breathe" as a way to instill confidence in the viability of the device. Now, Sarah is telling you that your team needs to start over and eliminate anything from the ad materials that involve measuring oxygen. You use the "Just Breathe" mantra at that very moment yourself to get your own head back in the game.

Normally when things like this happen at work, which they inevitably do, everyone gathers in the conference room and starts throwing out ideas and someone captures them on the whiteboard. How are you supposed to improvise a new ad campaign if you aren't physically present with your team members? Fortunately, Brian reminded the team that your company had invested in a suite of tools that could simulate an in-office face-to-face meeting. He suggests that you all brush up on this new set of tools and meet the next day to start rethinking at least some parts of the ad campaign. Your team members do their homework by generating their own creative ideas individually, and then you assemble virtually the next day. Based on the conversations in your group chat from yesterday and this morning, it's safe to say that your team is experiencing a bit of apprehension. And yet it's clear that everyone is still confident you can pull this off.

Your meeting begins, and your team immediately jumps into brainstorming new ideas for the campaign. You find that the new virtual collaboration tools are pretty good for this type of creative session, with a virtual whiteboard available to share across all team members. You also notice that, because only one person can be heard at a time during the meeting, people do more listening than talking, and ideas can be captured more accurately rather than lost in the multitude of side conversations that typically take place in person. In fact, as your team moves closer to a revised ad campaign with a new tagline that everyone likes, you actually start to think that your team's improvisation skills might have gotten better with the remote meeting technology.

The next day, you and your team present your preliminary ideas to Sarah and Brian. Although Brian is initially enthusiastic, Sarah has reservations and starts to explain why. One team member gently pushes back on some of Sarah's concerns. Other team members, including you, chime in with additional thoughts, which spark a lively discussion. Brian pipes up and encourages each team member to say more about how they're feeling about the idea at the center of the discussion. Everyone obliges. In fact, the team has so many opinions to share that you smile from the realization that this feels just like it did in the old conference room.

But there's one noticeable difference in today's virtual meeting. The most impressive and influential comments are coming from Matt, the quietest team member—the one who rarely gets a word in because the louder voices always seem to overpower him. But today is different—he's saying a lot. He's making great suggestions, and he's building on the suggestions of others. This is something you've never seen him do in the past. And what's fascinating is that he's not using his voice to speak up; he's using the chat window. Each time he types out a new comment, someone on the team reads it aloud. And he's not the only person using this communication channel. Another team member, Heather, is also leaning heavily on the chat window to make her points. Although you wouldn't consider her as quiet as Matt, she's always been more reserved than everyone else. But today, because of the chat window, Matt and Heather are far more "vocal" than the rest of the team. It suddenly dawns on you that these two have probably always had a lot to contribute to your team discussions, but perhaps they didn't feel comfortable doing so in person. This makes even more sense when you realize that, while most of your work friends call you on the phone, Matt and Heather always send text messages. They must feel more comfortable communicating this way. And in the virtual meeting, with the chat option, they feel psychologically safe speaking their mind, even when doing so means going against the grain.

With feedback from Sarah and Brian, your team pushes forward with a slightly revised version of your original idea. Flash-forward four months, and your company is able to launch a successful ad campaign for this new wearable technology. It's a good thing, too, because sales skyrocketed during the pandemic when people started working out at home and needed a personal device to track their progress and health. In the end, you realize that your success was due to your team remaining confident, having a roadmap that all team members could follow, being able to improvise and to be creative even when working virtually, and feeling psychologically safe enough to speak up, disagree, and take interpersonal risks when needed, even when your bosses were in the meeting. Although you felt your team waver from time to time during this unprecedented event, the end results showed that your team was, ultimately, *unbreakable*.

Today's teams, more so than ever before, have members who work remotely at different locations, including their home work spaces. While remote teams have been around for decades, they have traditionally represented a very small percentage of work teams. As our ad campaign example shows, the COVID-19 global pandemic represented the first time in the history of business that most teams functioned completely virtually, and there were a lot of hard lessons learned. Although this was certainly a challenging pivot, after the initial shock wore off, leaders began to realize that their teams can in fact produce high-quality work outside of the physical workplace. This realization has really opened the door for the future of work to involve significantly more virtual arrangements, with some teams working 100 percent remote and others working in a hybrid format—at any given moment, some team members are in the office and others are working from home or elsewhere. In this brave new world, we will never return completely to how things were, and there inevitably will be other shocks that upend things. However, the future of work was always destined to be significantly more remote, even without the pandemic. Indeed, COVID-19 didn't create the remote trend; it simply accelerated it—dramatically.

In this chapter, we address several key questions. For example, how do leaders build team resilience for their remote and hybrid teams? Do the four resources vital to resilience in face-to-face teams apply to these types of teams as well? Are there any specific actions leaders should take to make sure their remote and hybrid teams are resilient?

As demonstrated in the previous ad campaign example, the same four resources used to build resilience in face-to-face teams are also used to build resilience in remote and hybrid teams. Again, those resources are team confidence, teamwork roadmaps, capacity to improvise, and psychological safety. In fact, these four team resources are critical for any type of team to be resilient. With that said, there are a couple of key points to consider for building resilience in remote and hybrid teams, and these points warrant a separate discussion of resilience. First, in some ways, the four resources are even more important for remote and hybrid teams (especially teamwork roadmaps, team capacity to improvise, and team psychological safety), as the challenge associated with collaborating and communicating virtually is itself a form of adversity. The bad news is that, along with the added importance of building resilience in these teams, there is additional time, effort, and energy required of leaders to do so. But the good news is that leaders can take steps to make sure they're ready and able to tackle this complex challenge. And that brings us to the second point. The specific actions leaders need to take to increase team resilience in remote and hybrid teams are oftentimes different from the ones needed for enhancing team resilience when team members are working together in person.

For all four team resilience resources, remote and hybrid leaders must work diligently to ensure healthy interactions among members. Such interactions will help build up the four resources and leverage them so that teams have enough resilience to handle adversity when it strikes. In remote and hybrid teams, this is a tall order because members are naturally less likely to interact informally and have far fewer opportunities for spur-of-the-moment, organic exchanges (of course, there is not as much room for "serendipity" in these situations). Because chance encounters are far less likely in virtual teams, leaders will have to be more intentional in actively promoting these exchanges.

We next discuss each of the four resilient team resources in turn and provide hands-on, actionable advice for leaders to build them up in remote and hybrid teams. Note that we do not focus on all the actions discussed in previous chapters, only those that require specific adaptation for remote and hybrid teams. If a leader action is not mentioned in this chapter, you can follow the advice we provided in earlier chapters for building up the four team resilience resources.

TEAM CONFIDENCE

Of the ways that we've already discussed that leaders can build up their team's confidence, four stand out as needing adapting for remote and hybrid teams, including establishing clarity about goals and processes, using empowering leadership, using transformational leadership, and offering hypothetical but realistic training and practice sessions. We summarize examples of these approaches in table 8.1.

Goal and Process Clarity

Having clear goals and processes is important for all types of teams to be successful. However, in remote and hybrid environments, it is often easy for team members to lose sight of exactly what they're trying to accomplish and the means by which they're supposed to do so. The old saying "out of sight, out mind" certainly applies in this instance. Members can start to fail to understand how their work goals and strategies link to their overall team's goals and strategies, and there is evidence that members of remote teams are more likely to have diverse assumptions about team goals and objectives.[1] On the contrary, in face-to-face environments, team members are physically present and can be constant sources of reinforcement for clearly seeing and understanding team goals and processes. All in-person members need to do is hold impromptu meetings with all (or a subset) of team members to make sure everyone is on track. Doing so in remote and hybrid environments is not impossible, but it is more challenging. Thus, leaders have to work much harder to reinforce linking each individual team member's roles and goals to their team's.

One strategy for making sure there is goal and process clarity for remote and hybrid teams is to have regular virtual meetings in which leaders explicitly discuss each member's goals and processes and how they contribute to overall team success. This is also the case for face-to-face teams, but leaders will simply have to have more of them for remote and hybrid teams. There really is no substitute for having all team members interact with one another to reinforce

TABLE 8.1. Four Ways Leaders Build Team Confidence for Remote and Hybrid Teams

Behaviors	Examples
1. Make sure team goals and processes are crystal clear	a. Have regular team meetings with all team members together to discuss team goals and processes; make them brief and focused; alternate between camera-on and camera-off formats.
	b. For globally dispersed teams, rotate the start times for the meetings so that the same people are not inconvenienced every time
	c. Increase the number of one-on-one check-ins with individual team members to reinforce how each individual team member's goals and processes link up with the team
2. Empower your teams	a. Purposely schedule one-on-one coaching sessions with individual team members, otherwise they will not happen by chance encounters like when in the office
	b. As remote team members will often feel out of the loop because they are not privy to "on the fly" encounters in the office, make a special effort to share important and strategic information with team members (make them feel like insiders, even though they are physically outsiders when working remotely)
	c. Take advantage of remote team meetings to make sure team members know you "have their back" by displaying a high level of concern and caring for the overall team
3. Be a transformational leader	a. Constantly reinforce organizational vision in remote team meetings and make sure it is simple, feasible, tangible, memorable, and translates easily into behavior
	b. Consistently challenge remote team members to think differently about their work and the problems they encounter; help them navigate the perceived risks of being innovative
	c. Use the "buddy system" to pair up remote team members to carry out special projects or assignments in a way that invites innovative solutions and spreads the risk
	d. Display a high level of concern and care for teams and do so in meetings with your entire team present
4. Offer hypothetical and/or sequenced mastery experiences	Conduct synchronous virtual rehearsal sessions and team building to build up team confidence toward facing adversity

clear goals and processes. Such meetings do not have to be lengthy, and there is nothing wrong with brief team check-ins from time to time to make sure everyone is on the same page (recall our discussion in chapter 5—and an example in chapter 7—of the brief daily stand-up meetings common in teams using Agile project approaches). Again, although there is still no substitute for face-to-face, organic interactions, leaders should emphasize the importance of video, which enhances the richness of communication, increases engagement, and facilitates interpersonal connections that are so critical to effective teamwork. And yet despite these benefits, meetings using video can also have a negative impact on teams, as research has shown that being on camera for extended periods of time during remote or hybrid meetings can leave people feeling exhausted, a phenomenon commonly referred to as "Zoom fatigue." Indeed, one study conducted in the early phases of the pandemic found that when cameras in meetings were always on, versus off, people reported greater daily fatigue, which resulted in less speaking up and lower engagement in meetings.[2]

Importantly, these negative effects were stronger for women than men and for employees who were newer to their companies. Reasons for gender effects included greater pressure in the male-dominated corporate environment for women to maintain a "professional" appearance and women being more likely to experience family-related interruptions during meetings (because women tend to be responsible for childcare and other caregiving responsibilities even when their spouses or partners are at home). Newer employees are in the process of building up their image and status in their organization, whereas more established employees have assigned status. Moreover, newer employees likely have less latitude in expressing themselves than longer-tenured employees, and thus they will feel more pressure to make sure they are perceived appropriately when on camera.[3] Given the mixed effects of camera use, we recommend creating a camera schedule that alternates formats, with some meetings designated "camera on" (for highly interactive discussions) and others "camera off" (for more one-way information dissemination). This ensures that your team enjoys the best of both worlds, and it also eliminates the pressure and stress associated with giving your team the option ("Should I turn my camera on? I don't want to be the only one who has it off").

Of course, with time zones and language barriers often a challenge in remote and hybrid teams with members who are globally dispersed, such meetings can be tricky to schedule. One rule of thumb to ensure fairness is to rotate the start times for the meetings across time zones so that the same people are not inconvenienced every time. We've seen companies make the mistake of scheduling all video meetings on "headquarters" time, and this can quickly lead to members feeling disrespected, which then results in them becoming disconnected.

Leaders also need to increase the number of one-on-one check-ins with members of their remote and hybrid teams. Yes, overall team meetings are effective, but each individual member has unique needs and issues, and oftentimes will be reluctant to discuss these in full team meetings. So, goal and process clarity can also be enhanced by having one-on-one meetings with remote and hybrid team members. And of course, we hear you—all these meetings and reinforcing of goals and processes will take so much time! Yes, it will. That's why we stated earlier that building up resilience in remote and hybrid teams simply takes more effort and is very time-consuming. But the payoff from investing now (remember the adage "pay now or pay much more later") will be worth it. The key when scheduling meetings is that they are all intentional and have a meaningful purpose. Forcing your team to meet regularly without a clear objective or agenda is a recipe for burnout. So, yes, schedule those meetings, but make sure that they're well-planned and not a waste of your team's (and your!) time.

Empowering Leadership

The second key approach leaders need to adopt when building up their remote and hybrid teams' confidence is to use the five empowering leader behaviors we touched on in chapter 3 to promote team confidence. The goal of empowering leadership is to instill a sense of ownership and self-determination in teams. Importantly, team confidence is only one of the four dimensions of team empowerment. The others are meaningfulness (do members of your team believe that the work they are doing is intrinsically motivating?), autonomy (do team members have some degree of discretion and control about how they carry out their work?), and impact (can members clearly see how their work has significant benefits for other teams, customers, their company?). All four dimensions add up to create a team's overall experience of team empowerment.

Autonomy is arguably more critical for remote and hybrid teams than for in-person teams. Remember that communication in virtual teams is usually delayed because members can't just pop in the leader's office and ask a question anytime they want. Imagine how frustrating it would be to depend on a leader for every little decision if you had to wait for them to reply to your email, chat, or phone call. All leaders, but especially remote and hybrid leaders, must learn to trust their team to take ownership of their tasks and make their own decisions.

A team's perceived impact is enhanced when its leader shares stories about how their efforts have helped the company achieve its goals, or shares testimonials from other employees or customers who have directly or indirectly benefited from the team's efforts. Again, chance encounters with others are rare in remote and hybrid teams, and so we recommend that team leaders orchestrate occasional guest visits in team meetings so that the team can meet and interact with those who they impact (for example, senior leaders or leaders of other teams who may want to take five minutes to extend their gratitude for the team's hard work).

Instilling meaning in a team is partially achieved through the aforementioned techniques: giving the team control over important decisions and helping them see the impact of their work. But it also comes from ensuring they have opportunities to build strong relationships with one another; that is, we're far more motivated when we enjoy the people with whom we work. Again, this comes from leaders being intentional about creating virtual (and if possible in person) social encounters that can boost meaningfulness. But ultimately, intrinsic motivation is a function of need fulfillment, and we all have different needs. This is why those one-on-one meetings with team members are so critical, especially in a virtual world. This is the best (and often the only) way to uncover each person's needs so that you can help them craft a job that is intrinsically meaningful. McKinsey reports that when employees experience their work as meaningful, their performance improves by 33 percent, they are 75 percent more committed to their organization, and they are 49 percent less likely to leave. The problem, though, is that only 50 percent of employees find meaning in their work.[4]

Leaders can also empower their teams by simply keeping them "in the know." Sharing strategic information with teams not only helps them visualize the big picture and how their specific roles fit into that picture; it also sends a powerful signal that the leader values and trusts them with important information. Again, this is made more complicated in remote and hybrid settings, as a lot of this informal knowledge is often exchanged "on the fly" in chance encounters. In our work with the high-tech travel reservations company Sabre, we found that remote team members reported feeling "out of the loop" when it came to knowing what was happening with their company, fellow team members, or other teams.[5] And they lost confidence as a result because they couldn't clearly see how their team's work fit into the overall big picture. Leaders at Sabre overcame this by being good knowledge-sharing role models in team meetings and using one-on-one check-ins. Ultimately, they made their team members feel like insiders.

Although in our work with many teams and companies we have found that team empowerment helps all teams to be more successful, we discovered that team empowerment is actually more important for teams whose members work more remotely than for those that work more in person. For example, with Sabre, we found that the more members in a team worked remotely, the more that team benefited from empowerment, which in turn led to more successful completion of knowledge- and learning-oriented tasks (which are, of course, critically important for team resilience).[6] Similarly, in a study of remote procurement teams in a major multinational company, researchers found that empowering leadership had a stronger effect on remote team collaboration and performance, to the extent that members were more, rather than less, dispersed (in terms of physical or spatial distance, number of different countries members work in, and number of different work sites represented on the team).[7] So, our advice here is that if you lead a team, you should always try to empower it. But if you lead a remote or a hybrid team, you simply *must* empower it for team members to succeed.

Transformational Leadership

In addition to empowering leadership, evidence has shown that transformational leadership consistently promotes positive remote team functioning.[8] Similar to research examining empowering leadership, studies have shown that the effects of transformational leadership on team performance are stronger for remote teams than for face-to-face teams.[9] A key element of transformational leadership is that leaders need to communicate a clear and compelling vision for where the team is headed. Again, remote and hybrid work can get in the way of leaders establishing and maintaining such a vision. As a result, leaders should consistently reinforce their company's vision and specifically communicate how their team's vision fits into the bigger picture. Without such a vision, a team's members can feel lost and consequently lose confidence in where their team fits in. Visions should be simple, feasible, tangible, memorable, and translate easily into behavior. We were fortunate enough a few years ago to hear Dr. Nicholas La Russo, professor of gastroenterology and hepatology in the Department of Internal Medicine at the Mayo Clinic in Rochester, Minnesota, speak at a leadership conference about the importance of vision for organizations. He told the audience that everyone at the Mayo Clinic, from the CEO all the way down the organization, can recite by heart the clinic's vision statement: "Transforming medicine to connect and cure as the global authority in the care of serious or complex disease." They also know exactly how their specific job fits into and supports that statement. Now that is an effective vision.

Another aspect of transformational leadership that is key to building team confidence in remote and hybrid teams is challenging team members to think differently about their work by pushing back on more tried-and-true approaches that the team may have used in the past. As transformational leadership is all about changing the status quo, remote and hybrid team leaders can work to build up team confidence by offering teams a degree of latitude in coming up with new and innovative approaches to their work. Such work will be risky, as team members may challenge very popular or well-supported ways of getting things done in their company (a.k.a. sacred cows). However, nothing builds up team confidence faster than a leader pushing members to think creatively about how to accomplish their tasks and then actually using their ideas going forward. In remote and hybrid settings, however, it is more challenging to get team members to work together to develop new approaches, as there just aren't as many opportunities to do so as there are in face-to-face settings. One approach that we discussed in chapter 7 is to use the buddy system in which leaders pair up members of remote or hybrid teams to carry out special projects or assignments in a manner that invites innovative solutions.

Finally, transformational leaders must also display a high level of concern and care for teams, which again presents a challenge in remote working environments. However, this shouldn't stop leaders from learning as much as they can about the specific obstacles and barriers that could prevent their teams from doing their best work. Remote and hybrid team members, because they typically see and interact with their leaders less, can start to lose sight of the fact that those leaders do have their best interests at heart and are looking out for them. Although one-on-one check-ins can be helpful here, the target of the leader's care and concern we're discussing here is the overall team. Thus, leaders would be advised to use their team meetings to show that they care about their whole team's welfare. A team's members will want to know that their leader "has their back." If they do, their team's confidence will soar. Questions can go a long way toward showing your team you care about its members' welfare, such as "What is the biggest challenge you all are facing this week?" "Is there anything I can do to help make your working from home easier?" and "What is your energy level right now?"

Hypothetical and/or Sequenced Practice Sessions

We noted earlier that engaging in practice and rehearsals is critical for building up a team's confidence to handle any type of adversity. Again, this is why fire-fighters spend so much time training together in preparation for uncertainty and adversity. But what about remote and hybrid teams? How do members who never, or rarely, see one another prepare for and rehearse their responses to unforeseen events? Although not as common as face-to-face team building, remote and hybrid teams can also engage in virtual rehearsal sessions and team building to build up their confidence. There's simply no substitute for teams practicing and conquering difficult challenges together.

TEAMWORK ROADMAPS

A teamwork roadmap is used to make sure that everyone on a team knows his or her own roles, responsibilities, and job requirements and is also familiar with every other team member's roles, responsibilities, and job requirements. It is also used so that all members fully understand one another's knowledge, skills, attitudes, strengths, and weaknesses. Although a teamwork roadmap is important for any type of team to be resilient, its importance is magnified in remote and hybrid teams. As we've suggested, it is very easy for remote and hybrid team members to lose sight of their role in their team, feel disconnected from fellow team members, and experience uncertainty about how their ac-tions tie into their overall team's purpose and objectives. Having a teamwork roadmap helps provide guidance on all of these and keeps members focused on what they are supposed to be doing at any given time. In short, teamwork roadmaps provide clarity about work to battle against the ambiguity and uncer-tainty that often accompany remote and hybrid work. We cannot overstate the importance of having a teamwork roadmap to help build up a team's resilience. There are two key elements we recommend for enhancing teamwork roadmaps that have to be adjusted in remote and hybrid teams: using team charters and shared leadership. We summarize examples of these elements in table 8.2.

Team Charters

We spent some time in chapter 6, on psychological safety, discussing the im-portance of team charters, and such charters can also be helpful for enhancing teamwork roadmaps (after all, a charter is a type of roadmap). Recall that a team charter is a written agreement regarding how a team will make decisions and share accountability for producing and delivering high-quality outputs that

TABLE 8.2. Two Ways Leaders Build Teamwork Roadmaps for Remote and Hybrid Teams

Behaviors	Examples
1. Use team charters	a. Have members complete a written document outlining their own individual values, goals, preferences, and work habits; they should then rank order the values they think are most important when working in a team; they should answer questions such as, What are their expectations of themselves and their team, how will they hold themselves accountable, and how will they celebrate their and their team's success?
	b. Facilitate a meeting in which all team members share their individual portions of the team charter; remote team members can post their responses in a shared repository so that members can view everyone else's document before the meeting; help team members to reach agreement on the most important team attributes (e.g., shared goals, objectives, values, norms)
2. Use shared leadership	a. Do not assume that remote teams are just "more difficult" face-to-face teams and that what works well face-to-face will work in remote teams
	b. Accept the reality that remote team members are often leaders themselves in their specific areas, and they should be respected and valued as sources of leadership
	c. Do not sit back and wait for shared leadership to emerge; rather, proactively encourage members to take leadership roles in their team; create a climate of shared leadership
	d. Avoid the "responsibility trap" of avoiding shared leadership because it makes you feel more vulnerable; do not simply pay lip service to shared leadership, make it happen
	e. Work to become a team member yourself by participating in shared leadership to support team task accomplishments

satisfy customer needs in a timely and cost-efficient manner. As we've noted, it is very easy for team members in remote and hybrid teams to lose their way. They just don't have the type of constant reinforcement about goals, roles, processes, and decision making that teams with more face-to-face contact do. The situation becomes even more problematic if remote or hybrid teams are composed of members from different countries or cultures. Because those members bring various cultural values and business practices to their teams, members could have different ideas about the meaning of team elements such as deadlines, quality, or trustworthiness. Team charters are designed to clear up any confusion associated with these "loose" concepts while also reinforcing members' roles and how they all fit together.

For a team charter to be effective, remote and hybrid team leaders should co-construct it with their team rather than imposing one upon them. The best team charter creation occurs in two phases. First, team members individually complete a written document outlining their own values, goals, preferences, and work habits. They may be asked to rank order the values they think are most important when working in a team. They are also asked to think about preferred norms in their teams, such as how work gets distributed and assigned, characteristics of effective remote team meetings, rules guiding team member behavior, and best practices for remote team processes like information sharing, decision making, communication, problem solving, and conflict management. They need to reflect on issues such as their expectations of themselves in the team, how they will hold themselves accountable, and how they will celebrate their and their team's successes. Because all this information is derived from individual team members, remote and hybrid team leaders can provide a document that members complete on their own and have ready by a certain date.

The second step is that the team leader facilitates a meeting of all team members in which they begin to share their individual portions of the team charter. One good idea used by some companies we work with is to have team members post their responses in a shared repository so members can view one another's answers prior to a team meeting. Team leaders can keep all documents "hidden" and reveal them simultaneously at a particular time so that no member's individual responses are influenced by anyone else's. During the team portion of the charter process, leaders will need to facilitate agreement across the members on important team attributes. For example, agreement needs to be reached on a team's shared goals and objectives, values, and norms. Team members also need to hammer out the particulars of how their team will operate, such as how work gets distributed and assigned, how meetings are managed, and other team processes. Decisions will also have to be made regarding how teams will celebrate success and, maybe more important, how they will deal with violations of team rules. As we suggest next, these important tasks cannot be left up to a single formal leader.

Shared Leadership

We frequently tell leaders of remote and hybrid teams this: If you think you are going to provide all of the leadership your team needs to be effective, you are setting yourself up to fail. In other words, micromanagers, control freaks, and dictators need not apply to lead remote or hybrid teams. Much more so than in face-to-face teams, there is too much volatility, uncertainty, complexity, and ambiguity facing remote and hybrid teams for one leader to tackle. That is why teamwork roadmaps are essential to promoting effective remote and hybrid team functioning. An advantage to using shared leadership in these types of teams is that by delegating some of the leadership responsibilities to members of your team, you can accomplish two important things. One, not "doing it all" frees you up to focus on the very things you are supposed to be focused on as a leader in your company: the bigger picture, more strategic, vision-oriented dimensions of your role. Two, by sharing leadership, you will build up the leadership capabilities of your team members so they can go on to be successful leaders of remote and hybrid teams in the future. Empowering your remote or hybrid team members using shared leadership will motivate them to persevere and reduce their dependency on you when adversity strikes.

We mentioned previously how essential it is to provide autonomy to remote and hybrid teams. Again, this is because it is significantly more difficult (and frustrating) to depend on a leader for every little decision when that leader is in a different building, town, time zone, or even country. Implementing shared leadership is one great way to provide autonomy to teams. It allows remote and hybrid team members to take the actions they feel are best to solve problems and satisfy clients. And yet despite the enhanced importance of shared leadership in remote and hybrid teams, our research shows that leaders of these teams are significantly more reluctant to share their leadership with team members.[10] It's almost as if they cannot let themselves grant others control when they can't physically see what they're doing.

In fact, one study examining almost one hundred remote software development project teams in thirty-six different companies found that leaders are often hesitant to share responsibility and authority with team members for various reasons.[11] These included having a traditional, top-down view of leadership; being overly confident in their ability to "do it all"; and feeling afraid that they could become dispensable or obsolete. The researchers also identified five best practices for enabling remote team leaders to use shared leadership. One, leaders cannot assume that remote or hybrid teams are just "more difficult" face-to-face teams; they are indeed a unique form of teaming. Thus, leaders cannot assume that what works face-to-face will work in remote or hybrid teams. Specifically, leaders will have to accept that they cannot be aware of everything going on in their team, and so out of necessity, they need to rely on their team members more.

Two, they need to accept the reality that their remote and hybrid team members are often leaders themselves in their specific areas, and thus they should be respected and valued as sources of leadership. Remote and hybrid teams frequently have a number of subject matter experts who are already making key decisions in various ways. These individuals should be tapped for their unique knowledge and expertise and encouraged to lead when appropriate.

Three, rather than sit back and wait for shared leadership to emerge, remote and hybrid team leaders should proactively encourage team members to take leadership roles in their team. Some members, particularly those in countries where status and hierarchy are very important (i.e., workers typically just do whatever the boss says), could be reluctant to get out there and take a leadership role for fear of showing up the formal team leader or risking any type of embarrassment as a result. Leaders have to make sure there is a climate for shared leadership; otherwise, it often won't happen.

Four, because leaders are often held responsible for the outcomes of their team, they may feel more vulnerable when using shared leadership, falling into what researchers call the responsibility trap. Thus, some leaders might engage in shared leadership in name only and give lip service to passing leadership responsibility on to team members (while still making all the key decisions themselves). Don't let this happen to you, as team members will see right through it.

Finally, leaders should work to become team members themselves by participating in shared leadership to support team task accomplishments. To be sure, shared leadership is not easy for many leaders, and there is already evidence that some leaders actually try to retain even more control when their team is a remote one.[12] However, teamwork roadmaps will never be built if team leaders fail to share leadership responsibilities with their team members.

TEAM CAPACITY TO IMPROVISE

A team's capacity to improvise is the ability to make something new and novel out of previous experiences, practices, and knowledge. There are two key levers that need to be adapted for use in remote and hybrid teams: enhance team transactive memory and bolster team creativity. We summarize key examples of these approaches in table 8.3.

Transactive Memory

Transactive memory refers to the extent to which all team members are aware of who knows what in their team. In other words, it's an understanding of how expertise is distributed throughout the team. This is important for a team's ca-

TABLE 8.3. Two Ways Leaders Build Team Capacity to Improvise for Remote and Hybrid Teams

Behaviors	Examples
1. Enhance transactive memory	a. Use collaboration tools, such as knowledge repositories and shared work spaces, where team members can access information to help their teams perform well
	b. Have members create profile pages with detailed information about education, experience, certification, badges, and other accomplishments
	c. Facilitate remote team meetings in which members are encouraged to share information about their knowledge, expertise, experiences, and talents because richer communication tools, such as videoconferencing, have been shown to be more effective in building up transactive memory compared to leaner tools like email and chat
	d. Make sure to have several meetings of this type early on in the creation of a remote team to create a shared identity
2. Enhance team creativity	a. Do not let team members block one another's ideas when meeting remotely ("Don't judge my ideas, just generate them" is the mantra); meetings should be used more for idea sharing than for idea generation (which can occur offline)
	b. Create a climate of remote team creativity by making sure members do not feel any pressure to conform in their teams; members will feel less pressure to do so in remote team meetings compared to face-to-face
	c. Ask team members to individually generate creative ideas before a remote team meeting occurs, thereby reducing conformity pressures; use whiteboards or other shared spaces to "blind" team members to the sources of ideas (i.e., remove authorship and make ideas anonymous)
	d. Push members to focus on the big picture when engaging in creative idea generation or problem solving, which should be easier to do remotely than face-to-face
	e. Encourage team members with diverse perspectives and mindsets to interact by, for example, sending people to breakout rooms that do not have the same thought worlds
	f. Make sure to record or archive remote team meetings so that members can modify existing work to adapt it to new problems and provide a digital roadmap of a team's creative processes

pacity to improvise, because when adversity strikes, team members need to know who to go to for specific types of information and resources. After all, you cannot collectively improvise with others if you are not aware of their talents, strengths, and tendencies. For remote and hybrid teams, this knowledge of who knows what can be particularly challenging because members are not in the same location and thus cannot benefit from informal interactions in which they get to know one another well and become aware of each team member's capabilities and skills. Some research has shown that the extent to which teams become more remote, they actually struggle more with developing transactive memory systems.[13] Thus, remote and hybrid team leaders have to be purposeful in building this memory.

An established remedy for offsetting the negative effects of a high degree of remoteness on shared understanding and developing transactive memory is the use of collaboration tools.[14] One set of tools available to remote teams is knowledge repositories, or shared work spaces where team members can access information to help their teams perform well. These repositories have to be updated constantly so that information availability is maximized.[15] One practice that could help with transactive memory is to make sure each team member has a profile page with detailed information about education, experience, certifications, badges, and other accomplishments; then team members can reference it and learn quickly and effectively about the team member's strengths and experiences. Because most remote teams will have members who do not interact frequently and have diverse expertise and backgrounds that may not be familiar to fellow members, this type of information sharing is critical. When adversity strikes in a remote or hybrid team, members will not have time to try to get up to speed on who knows what in order to get improvisation processes going. Leaders should reinforce the importance of teammates getting to know one another well, including the use of profile pages in knowledge repositories.

In addition to knowledge repositories, team leaders should also facilitate remote and hybrid team meetings in which members are encouraged to share information about their knowledge, expertise, experience, and talents. In fact, there is evidence that face-to-face interactions, either in person or through videoconferencing, help build up transactive memory, while communication tools like email or phone are much less effective.[16] Other studies echo these findings and show that when members reported using "richer" communication media like videoconferencing (compared to "leaner" media like chat or email, which do not convey information like body language or tone of voice), they were more effective at building their transactive memory systems, and this was particularly true for smaller teams.[17] Such meetings are especially important early on in a team's life span to get members up to speed quickly about who knows what. Research has shown that as transactive memory systems develop over time in a remote team, team members do not have to communicate as much as they did prior to developing such systems because they already have the critical information they need.[18] Remote and hybrid team meetings can also be used to develop shared team identity and shared context, both of which should improve transactive memory in remote and hybrid teams.[19] Shared identity means that all team members buy into their membership on their remote or hybrid team, and a shared context means that members have access to similar information, tools, work processes, and work cultures.

Team Creativity

We have already discussed the key ingredients teams in general need to be more creative, including composing teams comfortable with perspective taking (i.e., understanding the thoughts, motivations, and emotions of fellow members), encouraging pro-diversity beliefs, setting superordinate goals, establishing team identities, and following fundamental brainstorming rules. Well, there is also some really good news for leaders attempting to promote creativity in their remote and hybrid teams.

Although conventional wisdom might suggest that remote and hybrid teams would struggle more with being creative than face-to-face teams (indeed, conventional wisdom and earlier research did conclude that successful creativity and innovation mainly occur face-to-face), accumulating evidence suggests that it actually can be the opposite. Remote and hybrid teams, with the proper resourcing and leadership, could find it easier to be creative and generate more, rather than fewer, innovative ideas.[20] For example, despite the belief that teams are generally more creative than individuals, research shows that levels of creativity (per person) actually decrease in teams, especially as the teams grow larger.[21] This is because team dynamics can work against creativity, as some members might shut down while others may dominate the discussion. This could seem like an argument against remote or hybrid team creativity, but remember how most discussions on videoconferences take place these days.

For many technologies, only one person can be heard at a time, meaning that people have to actually listen to one another and consider everyone's ideas and suggestions one at a time. In that sense, remote and hybrid team meetings could actually be superior to face-to-face ones in terms of harnessing individual creativity and turning it into team creativity.[22] Also, constraints at work often enhance team creativity because they motivate members to develop solutions in ways that are different from situations where there are not any limitations. Again, compared to face-to-face meetings, virtual meetings place such constraints on members due to fewer nonverbal cues, equalizing status (there is no "head of the table"), strict time constraints for meeting start and end times, and so on.[23]

So, what should remote and hybrid team leaders do to get the most creativity they can from their teams and ensure they are leveraging the creativity advantages offered by them? Evidence suggests six such actions.[24] First, don't let members engage in blocking others' ideas when meeting remotely. "Don't judge any ideas, just generate them" should be the mantra. The good news here is that in virtual meetings, members do not have to constantly communicate and interact (again, one person at a time, please!), so they will likely have more time to generate creative ideas and less time judging them. Members can even be assigned "creative time" away from video meetings, rejoining calls for idea sharing rather than idea generation.[25]

Second, remote and hybrid team leaders should do everything they can to protect team members from pressure to conform with the rest of the team and to create an overarching climate of team creativity.[26] After all, team conformity is the enemy of team creativity. Research has shown that, compared to in-person meetings, people in virtual meetings are less likely to worry about what others think or whether others like them.[27] There is something about the digital world that leads people to feel less pressure to please others by agreeing with them or repeating only what is already known. This is great news for leaders looking to harness remote or hybrid team creativity, as virtual meetings have this "pressure releasing" quality built into them.

Third, remote and hybrid team leaders can ask team members to individually generate creative ideas before a virtual meeting occurs, thereby reducing the risk associated with offering up "off the wall" ideas during a meeting. Typical brainstorming sessions that occur in person often make team members feel uncomfortable because they experience a form of judgment from other members through body language and other visual cues when they offer up their ideas. Virtual meetings can minimize those cues, and leaders can "blind" team members to the source of ideas by using virtual whiteboards or other shared spaces. Removal of authorship and making ideas anonymous means that members can offer up very creative ideas without fear and also support or challenge any ideas without regard to status or other social cues.

Fourth, pushing remote and hybrid team members to focus on the big picture when engaging in creative idea generation or problem solving can help stimulate more and better ideas than when members get down into the weeds. Interestingly, one study showed that bigger-picture, more abstract thinking can actually be stimulated when people understand that they are communicating with people at a greater physical distance than in face-to-face interactions.[28] Fortunately, virtual meetings have that feature hardwired in, so leaders should emphasize this before kicking off a virtual brainstorming session.

Fifth, we have already suggested that team leaders need to compose teams with a great deal of thought diversity and encourage pro-diversity beliefs if they expect their teams to achieve high levels of team creativity. In contrast to face-to-face meetings in which people are likely to sit by their friends and have sidebar conversations with like-minded others, leaders can leverage the impossibility of doing so in their virtual meetings to encourage people with diverse mindsets to interact. When sending team members to breakout rooms, for example, leaders should make sure to separate those who are likely to have similar styles of thinking so that they can build in thought diversity using electronic meeting tools. Forcing people to interact with those who they do not know well and who have ideas different from their own should allow remote teams to generate more creative thoughts and solutions.

Finally, another downside of the face-to-face world is that meeting minutes are often taken but they do not capture creativity in any meaningful way. In contrast, virtual meetings can have digital traces, ranging from simply recording video meetings and saving chat content for archiving and later viewing to capturing the content of electronic whiteboards and other tools. This could allow companies to reuse or modify existing work to apply to new problems and provide a digital roadmap of a team's creative processes.[29] So remote and hybrid team leaders need to make sure they take advantage of these attributes of virtual meetings to maximize team creativity.

As the above steps should suggest, simply expecting less team creativity in remote or hybrid versus face-to-face teams is a fallacy. There is plenty of research that supports the superiority of virtual interaction for harnessing team creativity. Remote and hybrid team leaders just need to make sure they actually take advantage of these creativity-generating attributes of virtual meetings and not expect them to work in the same way that face-to-face meetings do.

TEAM PSYCHOLOGICAL SAFETY

Psychological safety is the extent to which team members feel safe to take interpersonal risks in their team. Although team psychological safety is typically built up and reinforced through a great deal of personal interactions and time spent together, that is not as likely to happen in remote or hybrid teams.[30] In fact, a common challenge facing remote and hybrid team members as they try to create psychological safety is that day-to-day team processes simply take more time when at least some members are working virtually.[31] Virtual team members often try to solve all problems on their own because they're afraid that their fellow team members could doubt their capabilities if they asked for help or because trying to explain their situation just takes way more time using email, virtual meetings, or phone calls than dropping into someone's office for a quick chat. So, they often just hunker down and try to do everything themselves, which does nothing for creating team psychological safety.

Another challenge of building psychological safety in remote and hybrid teams is the tendency for team members to develop closer, more trusting bonds with a subset of their fellow remote team members instead of the team as a whole.[32] This happens especially in hybrid teams, in which some members are located in the same physical space and others are remote. In a way, that can create unhealthy in- and out-groups, making some members feel excluded. That means that the entire team will not be able to develop a healthy level of psychological safety. With these challenges, leaders have to be prepared to take a different set of steps and actions to build psychological safety in their remote and hybrid teams. There are three critical ways that have been recommended to enhance remote and hybrid team psychological safety,[33] and there are strategies for creating psychologically safe virtual team meetings as well. We summarize key examples of these approaches in table 8.4.

First, leaders need to explicitly help their teams identify the challenges associated with working as a team in a remote or hybrid fashion.[34] This means accepting the fact that members cannot operate in the same way they do in their face-to-face teams and acknowledging the reality that remote and hybrid teams are different. In addition, getting to know fellow team members simply takes more time and effort. However, if leaders help members accept that reaching a level of comfort and safety with their teams will require particular steps, remote team members will be more ready and able to take those steps. Being open and honest about how to accomplish work remotely and how responsibility will be divided among members is paramount. Part of this honesty is being realistic about balancing flexibility of work-from-home policies with clear expectations that remote employees do not have to be "on" and available 24/7. Leaders need to set the tone by limiting communication after hours to avoid burnout, as research has shown that people actually worked significantly more hours in the early phases of the pandemic than they did before they pivoted to

TABLE 8.4. Two Ways Leaders Build Psychological Safety for Remote and Hybrid Teams

Behaviors	Examples
1. Set clear expectations for remote team working	a. Help team members identify the unique challenges associated with the ability to work well as a team remotely; acknowledge that remote teams are different from face-to-face teams; be open and honest about how to accomplish work remotely and how responsibility will be divided among members b. Help team members connect on a personal level, rather than sitting back and waiting for it to happen organically; encourage members to develop genuine interest in one another; have them ask questions that go beyond the work environment (e.g., family issues, child care, comfort level with face-to-face meetings); encourage members to share (appropriate) personal information with fellow members; encourage them to swap stories of personal triumphs and setbacks, at work and in personal lives, to get to know the "whole person" rather than just the work version; encourage virtual team building and happy hours c. Make sure that members develop and fully accept and embrace how the team wants to work together remotely (i.e., establish the "rules of the game"); set expectations and make them clear (e.g., how long is too long to respond to an email, are we going to have a "camera on" policy when we have video meetings and what are the rules for this, or who is responsible for capturing what information in meetings?)
2. Hold effective remote team meetings	a. For particularly sensitive subjects or times when members might hold back, use anonymous polls rather than the hand-raise or yes-no features in videoconferencing b. Use breakout rooms instead of the chat feature because chat attaches authorship to opinions and can get overwhelming with the sheer number of messages; breakout rooms can be used for brainstorming and idea sharing and members will be more confident when all team members get back together because they will have "road tested" their ideas with a smaller subset of members c. Have members hide their own video window when speaking to avoid watching themselves and becoming distracted or self-conscious d. Consider the use of a meeting facilitator to help with member participation e. Check-in after the meeting with quieter members to help them feel more heard and safer f. Rely on team charters to capture the norms and rules for safe remote team meetings, which will also enhance role clarity

bring very different expectations about teamwork to the table. Questions can arise, such as the appropriate time for responding to emails, whether there is a camera-on policy or other rules for virtual meetings, and who is responsible for capturing specific types of information in meetings. All these team norms will have to be more explicitly discussed so that psychological safety can be built quickly and effectively as members agree about how and what they are supposed to do.

There are also some best practices that leaders can use to build psychological safety in their remote and hybrid teams when holding virtual meetings.[42] For example, for particularly sensitive subjects or times when certain members might hold back, rather than using the hand-raise feature when members want to be called on or the yes-no tool (a green checkmark for yes and a red X for no), anonymous polls are likely the better choice. Team members can express their honest opinions without fear of being ostracized or singled out. In addition, rather than using the chat feature, which also attaches authorship to opinions and in many meetings can get overwhelming, try breakout rooms, so a remote team meeting with many members can be broken down into smaller meetings for brainstorming and idea sharing. We do the same thing for case discussions in our MBA classes because students often feel more confident and safer offering their opinions to the entire class if they have first "vetted" them with smaller groups. And although we have argued for using video to get the benefits of nonverbal cues, it is recommended that when team members are speaking, they hide their own video window to avoid watching themselves. Research from Stanford University's Virtual Human Interaction Lab has shown that watching yourself on camera can be very distracting and cause people to hold back their true thoughts because they are more critical of themselves.[43] It's as if someone came into one of our classrooms and followed us around with a giant mirror while we taught. No thanks. Finally, leaders might want to consider the use of a meeting facilitator, which could even be a member of the team to assist with member participation. And of course, checking in after the meeting with quieter team members can help them feel more heard and psychologically safe.

We have already noted that hybrid meetings are different from 100 percent remote ones because there can be a tendency for the members who are physically present in the office to dominate the conversation and trade inside gossip and information. As a result, remote team members can feel isolated and left out. And unlike remote meetings using virtual collaboration technology in which everyone is visible and can clearly be heard, hybrid meetings can be more challenging for the remote members, as they might not be able to see everyone's facial expressions and body language. Technology companies have worked to enhance the ability of the communication tools to create a more even playing field between physically present and remote members.[44] However, there are some best practices that apply more exclusively to hybrid meetings so all members feel more included and the overall level of team psychological safety is enhanced.[45]

For example, to foster feelings of inclusion, make sure you notify everyone on your team about your objectives for the meeting, particularly those that are remote. Be consistent about posting decisions and information on your hybrid team's messaging board so that nothing falls through the cracks for remote members. Remote team members can also use this space to post any questions they have that can be answered asynchronously. Share important goals in advance so that all members will be ready to contribute and feel safe to do so. Record all team meetings so that those that cannot attend can get up to speed and still feel in the know. For members who are physically present, try arranging them into a semicircle facing the (hopefully larger-than-a-laptop) screen to foster feelings of inclusion and safety with remote members. Make sure you don't overcompensate for remote team members by ignoring those who are physically present, being sure to allow for them to speak up (one at a time, for the sake of the remote members who won't be able to decipher side-bars or other chatter). Rotate various meeting roles among members who are physically present and remote to fairly share workloads and create safety by ensuring everyone gets to participate in a variety of roles. Consider assigning someone the role of producer or facilitator of the meeting to make sure all members—present or remote—have a chance to offer their thoughts and feel psychologically safe regardless of location.

Another tool that we already discussed for creating teamwork roadmaps is a team charter. Some of the norms and rules just discussed for psychological safety can be captured in this more formal document. Team charters can effectively head off mismatched expectations hybrid team members are likely to bring to their teams, which will work to increase psychological safety. Team charters also serve the purpose of enhancing role clarity, which also has been linked to stronger psychological safety in teams.[46]

All in all, building up the four team resilience resources in remote and hybrid teams is different from doing so in face-to-face teams and more challenging and time-consuming. However, the concrete actions we describe above can help you focus your efforts on building remote and hybrid teams that, when faced with adversity, will be *unbreakable.*

HELPFUL RESILIENCE MEASURES TO ASSESS YOUR TEAMS

We hope after reading through this book, you have a very clear understanding of what team resilience is and how to enhance the four team resources—team confidence, teamwork roadmaps, team capacity to improvise, and team psychological safety—so critical to building resilience in your teams and making them virtually *unbreakable*. Because business environments continue to increase in volatility, uncertainty, complexity, and ambiguity, the need for team resilience has never been greater. The lessons you can take away from this book should arm you with the tools you need to start building resilient teams right away.

In chapter 3, we discussed the importance of a team having a healthy level (not too little, not too much) of team confidence to give teams the motivational fuel to persist in the face of adversity. We used the example of the Miracle on Ice, when the US men's hockey team defeated the Soviet team in the 1980 Olympics, to reinforce how important team confidence really is for team resilience. We also explained the five actions leaders should take to build their team's confidence: (1) establishing clarity around team goals and processes so team members can agree and be clear on what they are supposed to accomplish and how they should go about doing so; (2) using the five empowering leadership behaviors so team members can accomplish their tasks with greater responsibility and authority; (3) using transformational leadership to constantly challenge teams to think differently about how they approach their tasks; (4) behaving ethically at all times so that team members have confidence in their leaders and team; and (5) engaging in repeated hypothetical simulations and practice sessions to rehearse the actions members should take if adversity strikes.

In chapter 4, we argued that teams also need teamwork roadmaps to assist with coalescing, promoting coordination, and preventing team activities from deteriorating into chaos when adversity strikes. We drew from the example of the Miracle on the Hudson, when Captain Sully Sullenberger and his team landed a plane on the Hudson River after both engines failed midair on a cold January afternoon in 2009. We also discussed key ways that team leaders can build effective and informative teamwork roadmaps for their teams: holding regular briefings and meetings so that all team members understand the contextual information they need to be resilient in unfamiliar territory; conducting team interaction training, which should help members to learn continuously how to work better as a team; using shared leadership so that members develop capabilities to take on more leadership tasks in their teams, which will allow them to better understand the various roles and responsibilities of their fellow team members; leading with a growth mindset to promote learning and the development of an accurate and shared understanding of what everyone on the team does and how it all fits together; and simulating hypothetical adversities so team members can get comfortable in uncomfortable situations.

In chapter 5, we discussed the critical role of improvisation in making sense of an adverse situation and responding effectively. We relied on the miraculous story of the rescue of the Wild Boars soccer team in Thailand in 2018 to powerfully demonstrate how a capacity to improvise can offer teams the flexibility to maneuver in various creative ways and bounce back from novel adversity. We discussed two ways that leaders can help develop their team's capacity to improvise, including building up their team's transactive memory, or knowledge of who knows what in a team, by ensuring that team members possess a variety of skills, expertise, and experiences, by training members together as a unit, and by helping them accurately identify who on the team has what specific knowledge, skills, and abilities, and increasing their team's ability to be creative by ensuring they have adequate thought diversity, promoting the discussion of unique (rather than common) information, encouraging perspective taking, building up a strong superordinate identity, and leading productive creative-problem-solving sessions by leveraging evidence-backed brainstorming rules.

In chapter 6, we argued that psychological safety could very well be the single most essential ingredient in building resilient teams, as it is most strongly and directly related to all three resilient actions: sensemaking, coalescing, and persisting. We drew upon the research that Google conducted showing that psychological safety was the number one predictor of team performance in the company. We also shared the story of Dharmendra Modha, an IBM fellow and lead researcher of the Cognitive Computing group at the IBM Research–Almaden, who used a variety of techniques to make sure that all team members felt safe speaking up and offering their ideas. We discussed a variety of leader behaviors critical to enhancing team psychological safety: being inclusive, being accessible and asking for input early and often (and showing appreciation when team members take you up on this request!), leading by example in terms of discussing one's own mistakes constructively and revealing lessons learned, leveraging transformational leadership, encouraging perspective taking, and making sure your team members fully trust you as a leader. We also highlighted a number of structural actions that leaders can take to promote psychological safety in teams, including creating and using team charters, enhancing role clarity, making sure teams have a high level of peer-to-peer support, and ensuring that team members know that they have a high level of support from their company.

In chapter 7, we highlighted the various steps leaders should take while leading teams through a crisis, including steps to minimize adversity before and immediately after it strikes, manage adversity in a way that enables the team to coalesce and persist, and mend after adversity subsides so the team grows stronger and more resilient as a result of lessons learned. Leaders can minimize the severity of an adverse event by proactively preparing teams and developing the four resilient resources, by engaging in simulated hypothetical adversities, and by encouraging everyone to be vigilant to the changing environment and to report any observed irregularities immediately. When adversity presents itself, team leaders should facilitate a team sensemaking discussion in which they work with their team to create a strategy for addressing the adversity. Following this discussion, leaders should shift into action mode, in which they assist their team with managing the adversity. The two key areas of focus during this phase are team morale and teamwork.

Team morale includes important team dynamics, such as motivation, confidence building, maintaining positive emotions, and managing conflict. Morale can be enhanced by setting milestones, celebrating each time a milestone is achieved, promoting a shared purpose, expressing appreciation for team member effort and accomplishments, and managing any conflicts that may arise.

Teamwork includes activities that contribute to team goals include coordinating, monitoring, and backing one another up. Teamwork can be enhanced by ensuring that everyone has access to and clearly understands the new action plan, holding brief but frequent team huddles, implementing a buddy system, and pitching in where appropriate.

Finally, leaders can help their teams mend after an adverse episode by facilitating a debrief in which the team reflects on the experience by identifying roses (successes) and thorns (struggles) and learns from these experiences by determining precisely what they'll do differently the next time adversity emerges.

In chapter 8, we provided a set of actions for leaders to take with their remote and hybrid teams. Teams that work more remotely present a set of challenges that are distinct from ones that work more face-to-face, and leaders should attend to these differences when trying to build team resilience. All four team resources are important for any type of team to enhance team resilience, but three of the team resilience resources—teamwork roadmaps, capacity to improvise, and psychological safety—are actually more important for those leaders charged with building resilience in remote and hybrid teams. Then, we provided a set of actions specifically tailored for enhancing remote and hybrid team resilience.

At this point, you may be wondering how you can determine whether your team is actually resilient. How strong are the four resilient resources on your team? Is there a way to measure these attributes so you'll know how much work you have cut out for you? Fortunately, yes, there are established measures for everything we have discussed so far in this book. In the next section, we provide a set of assessment tools you can put into practice right away to ensure that you have or can create *unbreakable* teams.

TOOLS TO ASSESS TEAM RESILIENCE AND
THE RESOURCES NEEDED TO BUILD IT

One of the most important things leaders can do to build team resilience is to assess where their teams currently are on team resilience and the four team resilience resources. This will help them get a baseline read on existing levels of these team attributes and determine how much is needed to get their teams to higher levels.

Below we include a variety of measures that are important for determining where your teams are currently and how far they are from where you want them to be. We believe that the best data for all these measures comes from multi-rater assessment systems. It would be ideal if you could compare your own ratings on all of these attributes to those generated by team members themselves and possibly by the teams' clients or customers as well. Getting a complete picture of team resilience is critical, and multi-rater approaches are ideal for revealing any lurking problematic gaps in perception. For example, a team's members might believe that their team is highly resilient, but customers might disagree. This is important information to have when helping your teams to realize that they're "not there yet" when it comes to team resilience. To increase variability in responses, we recommend that you assess all measures using a 7-point agreement-disagreement scale, where 1 = *strongly disagree*, 2 = *somewhat disagree*, 3 = *slightly disagree*, 4 = *neither agree nor disagree*, 5 = *slightly agree*, 6 = *somewhat agree*, and 7 = *strongly agree*.

Team Resilience (from Our Own Work)

When adversity reduces my team's performance . . .

1. We can continue to work well together.
2. We can recover quickly as a team.
3. We can focus our collective efforts on achieving our goals.
4. We can overcome the situation together.
5. We can persevere together.
6. We can stay focused on the task.
7. We can persist through the most difficult moments.
8. We can return to our pre-adversity level of performance.

Team Confidence (Guzzo et al., 1993)[1]

1. This team has confidence in itself.
2. This team believes it can be unusually good at producing high-quality work.
3. This team expects to be known as a high-performing team.
4. This team feels it can solve any problem it encounters.
5. This team believes it can be very productive.
6. This team can get a lot done when it works hard.
7. No task is too tough for this team.
8. This team expects to have a lot of influence around here.

Teamwork Roadmaps (from Our Own Work)

Similarity

1. Members of the team agree on how the roles and responsibilities are divided across the team.
2. Members of the team share a common understanding of how each person fits into the overarching purpose of the team.
3. Members of the team have similar views about how to work together as a team.
4. Team members agree on teamwork practices we should follow.

Accuracy

1. Members of the team have an accurate understanding of how the roles and responsibilities are divided throughout the team.
2. Members of the team have an accurate understanding of how each person fits into the overarching purpose of the team.
3. Members of the team have an accurate understanding of what teamwork approaches work best in this team.
4. Members of this team know exactly which aspects of teamwork are best suited for high performance.

Team Capacity to Improvise (Vera and Crossan, 2005)[2]

1. The team deals with unanticipated events on the spot.
2. Team members think on their feet when carrying out actions.
3. The team responds in the moment to unexpected problems.
4. The team tries new approaches to problems.
5. The team identifies opportunities for new work processes.
6. The team takes risks in terms of producing new ideas in doing its job.
7. The team demonstrates originality in its work.

Team Psychological Safety (Edmondson, 1999)[3]

1. If team members make a mistake on this team, it is often held against them (reverse-scored item).
2. Members of this team are able to bring up problems and tough issues with other team members.
3. People in this team sometimes reject others for being different or having a different point of view (reverse-scored item).

4. Members of my team make each other feel valued.
5. It is difficult to ask other members of this team for help (reverse-scored item).
6. No one on this team would deliberately act in a way that would undermine anyone else's work.
7. The unique skills and talents of members of this team are valued and utilized by other members.

CREATING A TEAM CHARTER

Throughout this book, we've discussed the importance of having a team charter to ensure that team members understand roles, responsibilities, norms, and expectations on the team. By laying out in writing what is expected of everyone, team charters give members a sense of confidence, create an established teamwork roadmap, allow for improvisation in the face of adversity, and allow members to feel psychologically safe. Here, we provide a guide to creating a team charter that we use with both our MBA and client teams. This is only an example, and you should feel free to modify it as you see fit. The charter is split into two parts. First, we give an example of the individual portion of the charter. This is the section that members complete individually before they get together to share their information with fellow team members. Second, we give an example of the team portion of the charter. This is the section that members complete together as a team using consensus and commitment.

Team Charter Instructions

For teams to be effective and resilient, positive synergy must be achieved and sustained. This involves recognizing that team members bring different cultures, personalities, experiences, skills, abilities, and motivations to the team. It also involves knowing how to use this diversity fully so that the team is more than the sum of its parts. For a team to succeed, team members also need to know what is expected of them so they can organize themselves to best accomplish their goals. The following guide to creating a charter asks your team to consider a series of important issues that new teams should discuss before getting down to work and that existing teams should reassess periodically. Such questions include the following:

- What are the team's goals and objectives?
- What values and norms will guide the team?
- How will labor be distributed and responsibilities assigned?

- How and when will the team communicate and meet?
- How will decisions be made, information shared, and conflicts resolved?
- How will the team handle leadership as well as contingencies such as late arrivals, missing meetings, and arriving unprepared?

Individual Portion

Goals and Objectives

Goals and objectives are typically the tasks assigned to a team and cover what team members need to accomplish during their tenure together. General, large goals are fine. However, at some point you need to break them down. Also, remember the characteristics of good goals: specific, challenging, achievable, and accepted.

Think about your role in your organization. What are your personal goals and objectives? Write down four or five.

Values

Although values, which are core beliefs or desires that guide or motivate attitudes and actions, may appear to be the "softest" elements of team performance, they are often the primary determinant of whether a team will accomplish its goals and perform at the highest levels. Values provide a set of guiding principles. If members abide by them, trust—a key ingredient of high-performing, resilient teams—ensues. It is sometimes hard to have a "values" discussion in a team. A good way to start the process is for each team member to individually identify the top ten values that should guide the team. See the list of values in table 9.1. Before meeting with your team, mark the top ten for you. Rank them from first to last if you wish to indicate which values are the most important to you.

Norms

Norms, or rules of behavior, follow naturally from values and address which behaviors are expected from team members. If norms do not reflect team values, or if a member violates team norms, then the team is not "walking the talk" and mistrust and discord arise. This leads to teams crumbling in the face of adversity. Please answer the following questions:

- How would you like your team to distribute work and assign responsibilities?

TABLE 9.1. Dream Team Values

Accountability	Having fun
Added value	Helping each other; cooperation
Agreed-on priorities	Honesty
Balanced task and process focus	Joy of work
Balanced workload among members	Making the most of limited resources
Being open minded	Measurable results
Building of friendships	Mutual development of mission/vision
Celebration of success	Open and candid feedback
Clear ambitious goals	Positive attitude
Coaching	Positive stress
Commitment	Productivity
Common goals	Recognition
Complementary skills	Respect
Continuous improvement	Role clarity
Coordination	Setting clear expectations
Courage	Sharing expertise and experience
Creativity	Striving for excellence
Demonstrating empathy and support	Success; accomplishments
Each person empowered to do tasks	Team rewards
Enthusiasm	Time pressure
Fairness	Tolerance of diversity
Flexibility	Trust
Focused discipline	Well-trained people
Good communication	Working hard
Good planning	OTHERS? (Add any you want)

- Which characteristics would you like your team meetings to have (e.g., timing, place, formal or informal, efficient or inefficient)?
- Which rules of behavior (explicit or implicit) would you like to guide your team for the attendance, preparation, information sharing and communication, decision making and problem solving, conflict management, others)?

Other Individual Questions to Answer
- What type of leader do I want to show up as in this team?
- What type of participant do I want to show up as in this team?
- Why is it important to me to lead/participate in this way?
- How will I know if I am living up to my own personal expectations?
- How will I hold myself accountable to being the leader or team member I aspire to be?
- How will I personally celebrate my success on this team?

Team Portion

Goals and Objectives
- What are our shared goals and objectives?
- Share your individual goals and objectives list. Consolidate and reach consensus on shared goals and objectives.

Values
Here is a suggested approach to consolidating individual preparation:
- Create a team list by asking each team member to read out their list of top ten values. Make sure to note any that were added to the list.
- Did any values receive a unanimous vote? If so, they are your first "wins."
- Circle the values that received the highest number of votes.
- Work through this list, asking if there could be unanimous or consensus agreement on any of these values.
- Discuss areas of strong disagreement. Look for areas of compromise.

Note that some values are so strongly held that a particular team member is unwilling to compromise. These are the most difficult and important discrepancies to resolve. It is much better to understand the value biases of your team and work them out in the beginning than to experience conflict, frustration, and perhaps disappointment down the road.

Starting to Work Together as a Team
Share your individual answers to these questions. Try to reach consensus on how your team will function on these attributes.
- How will we distribute work and assign responsibilities? How will we divide up our tasks? How will we integrate our outputs?
- How will we manage meetings? How frequently and where will we meet?

TABLE 9.2. Consolidated Values List

How will we manage our meeting time? Who will manage our meeting time? What is our meeting attendance policy?

- What other rules of behavior (norms) would we like to see operating in our team on the following (attendance, preparation, information sharing/ communication, decision making/problem solving, conflict management, others)?
- How will the team celebrate successes and deal with violations of rules of

behavior? This is always an interesting and useful discussion to have. If team members are made to focus on the consequences of behavior (positive and negative), the team spends less time improvising responses to nonroutine or unexpected adverse events.

Names and Signature of All Team Members
- Members should sign and date the team contract to enhance commitment to what has been decided.

NOTES

CHAPTER 1

1. Norman Maclean, *Young Men and Fire* (Chicago: University of Chicago Press, 1992).

2. Adam C. Stoverink, Bradley L. Kirkman, Sal Mistry, and Benson Rosen, "Bouncing Back Together: Toward a New Theoretical Model of Work Team Resilience," *Academy of Management Review* 45 (2020): 395–422.

3. Rick Edgeman, "Routinizing Peak Performance and Impacts via Virtuous Cycles," *Measuring Business Excellence* 21 (2017): 261–71.

4. Karl E. Weick, "The Collapse of Sensemaking in Organizations: The Mann Gulch Disaster," *Administrative Science Quarterly* 38 (1993): 628–52.

5. James E. Driskell, Eduardo Salas, and Joan Johnson, "Does Stress Lead to a Loss of Team Perspective?," *Group Dynamics: Theory, Research, and Practice* 3 (1999): 291–302; Alexander P. J. Ellis, "System Breakdown: The Role of Mental Models and Transactive Memory in the Relationship between Acute Stress and Team Performance," *Academy of Management Journal* 49 (2006): 576–89.

6. Maclean, *Young Men and Fire.*

CHAPTER 2

1. Patrick Conroy, "Everest '96—The First Casualty," *ENCA*, May 9, 2016, https://www.enca.com/life/travel/everest-96-the-first-casualty.

2. Jon Krakauer, "When You Reach the Summit of Everest, You Are Only Halfway There," *Medium*, May 24, 2016, https://medium.com/galleys/into-thin-air-e5a2756a87c1.

3. Bryn Davies, "The True Story of Everest 1996: One of Mountaineering's Worst Tragedies," *Wired for Adventure*, April 29, 2020, https://www.wiredforadventure.com/tragedies-on-the-mountain-everest-1996/.

4. Marina Manoukian, "The Tragic Story of the 1996 Mount Everest Disaster," *Grunge*, May 20, 2021, https://www.grunge.com/416820/the-tragic-story-of-the-1996-mount-everest-disaster/?utm_campaign=clip.

5. Norman Maclean, *Young Men and Fire* (Chicago: University of Chicago Press, 1992).

6. Sheri Fink, "The Deadly Choices at Memorial," *New York Times Magazine*, August 25, 2009, https://www.nytimes.com/2009/08/30/magazine/30doctors. html#:~:text=By%20the%20time%20Katrina%20began,of%20rocks%20from%20 nearby%20rooftops.

7. Jason Berry, "Harrowing Questions, and Ethics, During Katrina," *New York Times*, September 3, 2013, https://www.nytimes.com/2013/09/04/books/five-days-at-memo-rial-by-sheri-fink.html.

8. Sheri Fink, *Five Days at Memorial: Life and Death in a Storm-Ravaged Hospital* (New York: Crown Publishers, 2013); Daniel Schorn, "Was It Murder?," *60 Minutes*, August 15, 2007, https://www.cbsnews.com/news/was-it-murder/.

9. Fink, *Five Days at Memorial*.

10. Sheri Fink, "The Deadly Choices at Memorial," *ProPublica*, August 27, 2009, https://biotech.law.lsu.edu/katrina/reports/deadly-choices.htm.

11. Daniel Gigone and Reid Hastie, "The Common Knowledge Effect: Information Sharing and Group Judgment," *Journal of Personality and Social Psychology* 11 (1993): 959–74.

12. Irving L. Janis, "Groupthink," *Psychology Today* (November 1971): 84–90.

13. Russell Hotten, "Volkswagen: The Scandal Explained," *BBC News*, December 10, 2015, https://www.bbc.com/news/business-34324772.

CHAPTER 3

1. Richard A. Guzzo, Paul R. Yost, Richard J. Campbell, and Gregory P. Shea, "Potency in Groups: Articulating a Construct," *British Journal of Social Psychology* 32 (1993): 87–106.

2. Deanna M. Kennedy, Lauren B. Landon, and Travis M. Maynard, "Extending the Conversation: Employee Resilience at the Team Level," *Industrial and Organizational Psychology* 2 (2016): 466–75, 472.

3. Joey T. Cheng, Elizabeth R. Tenney, Don A. Moore, and Jennifer M. Logg, "Overconfidence Is Contagious," *Harvard Business Review*, November 17, 2020, https://hbr.org/2020/11/overconfidence-is-contagious?utm_medium=email&utm_ source=newsletter_weekly&utm_campaign=weeklyhotlist_activesubs&utm_content=s igninnudge&deliveryName=DM106942.

4. Joey T. Cheng, Cameron Anderson, Elizabeth R. Tenney, Sebastien Brion, Don A. Moore, and Jennifer M. Logg, "The Social Transmission of Overconfidence," *Journal of Experimental Psychology: General* 150 (2021): 157–86.

5. Cheng et al., "Social Transmission."

6. Deborah L. Feltz and Cathy D. Lirgg, "Perceived Team and Player Efficacy in Hockey," *Journal of Applied Psychology* 83 (1998): 557–64.

7. Craig L. Pearce, Cynthia A. Gallagher, and Michael D. Ensley, "Confidence at the Group Level of Analysis: A Longitudinal Investigation of the Relationship between

Potency and Team Effectiveness," *Journal of Occupational and Organizational Psychology* 75 (2002): 115–19.

8. Stanley M. Gully, Kara A. Incalaterra, Aparna Joshi, and J. Matthew Beaubien, "A Meta-Analysis of Team Efficacy, Potency, and Performance: Interdependence and Level of Analysis as Moderators of Observed Relationships," *Journal of Applied Psychology* 87 (2002): 819–32; Alexander D. Stajkovic, Dongseop Lee, and Anthony J. Nyberg, "Collective Efficacy, Group Potency, and Group Performance: Meta-Analyses of Their Relationships, and Test of a Mediation Model," *Journal of Applied Psychology* 94 (2009): 814–28.

9. Ed Graney, "Miracle on Ice Coach Herb Brooks Was Miserable but Brilliant," *Las Vegas Review-Journal*, February 18, 2020, https://www.reviewjournal.com/sports/goldenknights/miracle-on-ice-coach-herb-brooks-was-miserable-but-brilliant-1960089/.

10. "Snapped: The Moment that Proved Miracles Do Happen," *Olympics.com*, February 22, 2019, https://olympics.com/en/news/snapped-the-moment-that-proved-miracles-do-happen

11. "Miracle on Ice," *Wikipedia*, https://en.wikipedia.org/wiki/Miracle_on_Ice#Olympic_group_play, last modified June 29, 2021.

12. Jia Hu and Robert C. Liden, "Antecedents of Team Potency and Team Effectiveness: An Examination of Goal and Process Clarity and Servant Leadership," *Journal of Applied Psychology* 96 (2011): 851–62.

13. Mary Holland, "Meet the Black Mambas, South Africa's Fierce Female Anti-Poaching Unit," *Conde Nast Traveler*, May 3, 2018, https://www.cntraveler.com/story/meet-the-black-mamba-south-africas-fierce-female-anti-poaching-unit.

14. Payal Sharma and Bradley L. Kirkman, "Leveraging Leaders: A Literature Review and Future Lines of Inquiry for Empowering Leadership Research," *Group & Organization Management* 40 (2015): 193–237.

15. Allen Lee, Sara Willis, and Amy W. Tan, "Empowering Leadership: A Meta-Analytic Examination of Incremental Contribution, Mediation, and Moderation," *Journal of Organizational Behavior* 39 (2018): 306–25.

16. Ali E. Akgun, Halit Keskin, John Byrne, and Salih Z. Imamoglu, "Antecedents and Consequences of Team Potency in Software Development Teams," *Information & Management* 44 (2007): 646–56.

17. Soo Youn, "America's Workers Are Exhausted and Burned Out—And Some Employers Are Taking Notice," *Washington Post*, June 29, 2021, https://www.washingtonpost.com/business/2021/06/28/employee-burnout-corporate-america/.

18. Oscar Raymundo, "Richard Branson: Companies Should Put Employees First," *Inc. Magazine*, October 28, 2014, https://www.inc.com/oscar-raymundo/richard-branson-companies-should-put-employees-first.html.

19. "Jim Valvano: 'Cutting Down the Nets'—Million Dollar Round Table Meeting—1987," *Speakola*, https://speakola.com/sports/jim-valvano-cutting-down-the-nets-1987.

20. Linda Dishman, "How Extreme Transparency Can Make Your Team Its Most

Productive," *FastCompany*, March 11, 2013, https://www.fastcompany.com/3006798/how-extreme-transparency-can-make-your-team-its-most-productive.

21. John Schaubroeck, Simon S. K. Lam, and Sandra E. Cha, "Embracing Transformational Leadership: Team Values and the Impact of Leader Behavior on Team Performance," *Journal of Applied Psychology* 92 (2007): 1020–30.

22. David Gelles, "Marc Benioff of Salesforce: 'Are We Not All Connected?,'" *New York Times*, June 15, 2018, https://www.nytimes.com/2018/06/15/business/marc-benioff-salesforce-corner-office.html

23. John M. Antonakis, Marika Fenley, and Sue Liechti, "Learning Charisma: Transform Yourself into the Person Others Want to Follow," *Harvard Business Review* 90 (2012): 127–47.

24. Nathan Wiita and Orla Leonard, "How the Most Successful Teams Bridge the Strategy-Execution Gap," *Harvard Business Review*, November 23, 2017, https://hbr.org/2017/11/how-the-most-successful-teams-bridge-the-strategy-execution-gap.

25. Pascale M. Le Blanc, Vicente Gonzalez-Roma, and Hai-Jiang Wang, "Charismatic Leadership and Work Team Innovative Behavior: The Role of Team Task Interdependence and Team Potency," *Journal of Business and Psychology* 36 (2021): 333–46.

26. Jillian D'Onfro, "The Truth about Google's Famous '20% Time' Policy," *Business Insider Australia*, April 18, 2015, https://www.businessinsider.com.au/google-20-percent-time-policy-2015-4.

27. Jane M. Howell and Christine M. Shea, "Effects of Champion Behavior, Team Potency, and External Communication Activities on Predicting Team Performance," *Group & Organization Management* 31 (2006): 180–211.

28. G. A. Yukl, *Leadership in Organizations* (9th ed.) (Boston: Pearson, 2020).

29. "Business of Business Is People: Herb Kelleher," YouTube video, posted by HSMAmericas, October 14, 2008, https://www.youtube.com/watch?v=oxTFA1kh1m8.

30. Deanne N. Den Hartog, "Ethical Leadership," *Annual Review of Organizational Psychology and Organizational Behavior* 2 (2015): 409–34.

31. Michael E. Brown, Linda K. Trevino, and David Harrison, "Ethical Leadership: A Social Learning Perspective for Construct Development and Testing," *Organizational Behavior and Human Decision Processes* 97 (2005): 117–34.

32. Akanksha Bedi, Can M. Alpaslan, and Sandy Green, "A Meta-Analytic Review of Ethical Leadership Outcomes and Moderators," *Journal of Business Ethics* 139 (2016): 517–36.

33. Anne Doris, "Ethical Leaders: Holding Teams Together in Adversity," *UVA Darden Ideas to Action*, February 11, 2021, https://ideas.darden.virginia.edu/ethical-leaders-holding-teams-together.

34. João Medeiros, "McLaren Learned to Treat Its Pit Crew Like Athletes," *Wired*, October 17, 2018, https://www.wired.com/story/book-excerpt-mclaren-f1-pit-crew/.

CHAPTER 4

1. American Nurses Association, "ANA Responds to the Joint Commission Sentinel Event Alert on Physical and Verbal Violence against Health Care Workers," April 18,

2018, https://nursingworld.org/news/news-releases/2018/ana-responds-to-the-joint-commission-sentinel-event-alert-on-physical-and-verbal-violence-against-health-care-workers.

2. US Occupational Safety and Health Administration, *Guidelines for Preventing Workplace Violence for Healthcare and Social Service Workers*, 2016, https://osha.gov/Publications/osha3148.pdf; Jennifer M. Zicko, Rebecca A. Schroeder, William S. Byers, Adam M. Taylor, and Dennis L. Spence, "Behavioral Emergency Response Team: Implementation Improves Patient Safety, Staff Safety, and Staff Collaboration," *Worldviews Evidence Based Nursing* 14 (2017): 377–84.

3. Michael J. Burtscher and Tanja Manser, "Team Mental Models and Their Potential to Improve Teamwork and Safety: A Review and Implications for Future Research in Healthcare," *Safety Science* 50 (2012): 1344–54; Janice Langan-Fox, Jeromy Anglim, and John R. Wilson, "Mental Models, Team Mental Models, and Performance: Process, Development, and Future Directions," *Human Factors and Ergonomics in Manufacturing & Service Industries* 14: 331–52.

4. Beng-Chong Lim and Katherine J. Klein, "Team Mental Models and Team Performance: A Field Study of the Effects of Team Mental Model Similarity and Accuracy," *Journal of Organizational Behavior* 27 (2006): 403–18.

5. John E. Mathieu, Tonia S. Heffner, Gerald F. Goodwin, Eduardo Salas, and Janis A. Cannon-Bowers, "The Influence of Shared Mental Models on Team Process and Performance," *Journal of Applied Psychology* 85 (2000): 273–83.

6. Heidi K. Westli, Bjorn Helge Johnsen, Jarle Eid, Ingvil Rasten, and Guttorm Brattebo, "Teamwork Skills, Shared Mental Models, and Performance in Simulated Trauma Teams: An Independent Group Design," *Scandinavian Journal of Trauma, Resuscitation, and Emergency Medicine* 18 (2010): 1–8.

7. Lorelei Lingard, Sherry Espin, S. Whyte, Glenn Regehr, G. Ross Baker, Richard Reznick, J. Bohnen, B. Orser, D. Doran, and E. Grober, "Communication Failures in the Operating Room: An Observational Classification of Recurrent Types and Effects." *Quality and Safety in Health Care* 13 (2004): 330–34.

8. Leslie A. DeChurch and Jessica R. Mesmer-Magnus, "The Cognitive Underpinnings of Effective Teamwork: A Meta-Analysis," *Journal of Applied Psychology* 95 (2010): 32–53.

9. "US Airways Flight 1549," *Wikipedia*, https://en.wikipedia.org/wiki/US_Airways_Flight_1549, last updated May 5, 2021.

10. Leigh Buchanan, "10 Years after the 'Miracle on the Hudson,' Sully Sullenberger Talks Incredible Mental Discipline and How to Handle Pressure," *Inc. Magazine*, March 6, 2019, https://www.inc.com/leigh-buchanan/sully-sullenberger-leadership-lessons.html

11. Buchanan, "10 Years after the 'Miracle on the Hudson.'"

12. Buchanan, "10 Years after the 'Miracle on the Hudson.'"

13. Janis A. Cannon-Bowers and Eduardo Salas, "Reflections on Team Cognition," *Journal of Organizational Behavior* 22 (2001): 195–202, 196.

14. Michelle A. Marks, Stephen J. Zaccaro, and John E. Mathieu, "Performance

Implications of Leader Briefings and Team-Interaction Training for Team Adaptation to Novel Environments," *Journal of Applied Psychology* 85 (2000): 971–86.

15. Edwin A. Fleishman, Michael D. Mumford, Stephen J. Zaccaro, Kerry Y. Levin, Arthur L. Korotkin, and Michael Hein, "Taxonomic Efforts in the Description of Leader Behavior: A Synthesis and Functional Interpretation," *Leadership Quarterly* 2 (1991): 245–87.

16. Andrea Gurtner, Franziska Tschan, Norbert K. Semmer, and Christof Nagele, "Getting Groups to Develop Good Strategies: Effects of Reflexivity Interventions on Team Process, Team Performance, and Shared Mental Models," *Organizational Behavior and Human Decision Processes* 102 (2007): 127–42.

17. Rebecca Knight, "How to Talk to Your Team When the Future Is Uncertain," *Harvard Business Review*, April 20, 2020, https://hbr.org/2020/04/how-to-talk-to-your-team-when-the-future-is-uncertain.

18. Scott I. Tannenbaum and Christopher P. Cerasoli, "Do Team and Individual Debriefs Enhance Performance? A Meta-Analysis," *Human Factors* 55 (2013): 231–45.

19. Nathanael L. Keiser and Winfred Arthur Jr., "A Meta-Analysis of the Effectiveness of the After-Action Review (or Debrief) and Factors that Influence its Effectiveness," *Journal of Applied Psychology* 106 (2021): 1007–32.

20. Scott L. Zuckerman, Daniel J. France, Cain Green, Susie Leming-Lee, Shilo Anders, and J. Mocco, "Surgical Debriefing: A Reliable Roadmap to Completing the Patient Safety Cycle," *Neurosurgery Focus* 33 (2012): 1–8.

21. "Crisis Management Planning—A Hypothetical Scenario," *American Bar Association*, April 20, 2016, https://www.americanbar.org/groups/business_law/publications/blt/2016/04/08_evans/.

22. Michelle A. Marks, Mark J. Sabella, C. Shawn Burke, and Stephen J. Zaccaro, "The Impact of Cross-Training on Team Effectiveness," *Journal of Applied Psychology* 87 (2002): 3–13.

23. Morten T. Hansen, "IDEO CEO Tim Brown: T-Shaped Stars: The Backbone of IDEO's Collaborative Culture," *Chief Executive*, January 21, 2010, https://chiefexecutive.net/ideo-ceo-tim-brown-t-shaped-stars-the-backbone-of-ideoaes-collaborative-culture__trashed/.

24. Maria Rogers, "Is Being a 'T-Shaped' Person Still Enough?," *Medium*, November 16, 2017, https://medium.com/re-write/is-being-a-t-shaped-person-still-enough-2d0b43073285.

25. Heather H. McIntyre and Roseanne Foti, "The Impact of Shared Leadership on Teamwork Mental Models and Performance in Self-Directed Teams," *Group Processes & Intergroup Relations* 16 (2013): 46–57. See also Andrew Hanna, Troy A. Smith, Bradley L. Kirkman, and Ricky Griffin, "The Emergence of Emergent Leadership: A Comprehensive Framework and Directions for Future Research," *Journal of Management* 47 (2021): 76–104.

26. Andres Salas-Vallina, Yasin Rofcanin, and Mireia Las Heras, "Building Resilience and Performance in Turbulent Times: The Influence of Shared Leadership and Passion at Work across Levels," *Business Research Quarterly* 25 (2022): 8–27.

27. Melissa Sanfilippo, "Shared Leadership: How Modern Businesses Run Themselves," *Business News Daily*, December 1, 2021, https://www.businessnewsdaily.com/135-shared-leadership-social-media-fuel-business-growth.html.

28. Charles C. Manz, Frank M. Shipper, and Greg L. Stewart, "Everyone a Team Leader: Shared Influence at W. L. Gore and Associates," *Organizational Dynamics* 38 (2009): 239–44.

29. Carol Dweck, *Mindset: The New Psychology of Success* (New York: Random House, 2006).

30. "History Up Close: Kennedy Podium," Space Center Houston, https://spacecenter.org/exhibits-and-experiences/starship-gallery/kennedy-podium/.

31. Kyle M. Brykman and Danielle D. King, "A Resource Model of Team Resilience Capacity and Learning," *Group & Organization Management* 46 (2021): 737–72.

32. Amy McCaig, "Leaders Who Embrace On-Job Learning and Listen to Employees Have More Resilient Teams," Rice University, June 10, 2021, https://news.rice.edu/2021/06/10/leaders-who-embrace-on-job-learning-and-listen-to-employees-have-more-resilient-teams-research-shows/.

33. "MARS-500," *Wikipedia*, https://en.wikipedia.org/wiki/MARS-500, last modified July 29, 2021.

34. Joan R. Rentsch and Richard J. Klimoski, "Why Do 'Great Minds' Think Alike? Antecedents of Team Member Schema Agreement," *Journal of Organizational Behavior* 22 (2011): 107–20.

35. Sarah Wise, Christine Duffield, Margaret Fr, and Michael Roche, "A Team Mental Model Approach to Understanding Team Effectiveness in an Emergency Department: A Qualitative Study," *Journal of Health Services Research & Policy* 27 (2002): 14–21.

CHAPTER 5

1. Dusya Vera and Mary Crossan, "Improvisation and Innovative Performance in Teams," *Organization Science* 16 (2005): 203–24.

2. Massimo Magni and Likoebe M. Maruping, "Sink or Swim: Empowering Leadership and Overload in Teams' Ability to Deal with the Unexpected," *Human Resource Management* 52 (2013): 715–39.

3. Antonio Cunha Meneses Abrantes, Ana Margarida Passos, Miguel Pina e Cunha, and Catarina Marques Santos, "Bringing Team Improvisation to Team Adaptation: The Combined Role of Shared Temporal Cognitions and Team Learning Behaviors Fostering Team Performance," *Journal of Business Research* 84 (2018): 59–71.

4. Ali E. Akgun, John C. Byrne, Gary S. Lynn, and Halit Keskin, "New Product Development in Turbulent Environments: Impact of Improvisation and Unlearning on New Product Performance," *Journal of Engineering and Technology Management* 24 (2007): 203–30.

5. Massimo Magni, Likoebe M. Maruping, Martin Hoegl, and Luigi Proserpio, "Managing the Unexpected across Space: Improvisation, Dispersion, and Performance in NPD Teams," *Journal of Product Innovation Management* 30 (2013): 1009–26.

6. Edivandro Carlos Conforto, Eric Rebentisch, and Daniel Amaral, "Learning the Art of Business Improvisation," *MIT Sloan Management Review* 57 (2016): 8–10.

7. "The Full Story of Thailand's Extraordinary Cave Rescue," *BBC News*, July 14, 2018, https://www.bbc.com/news/world-asia-44791998.

8. Daniel G. Bachrach, Kyle Lewis, Youngsang Kim, Pankaj C. Patel, Michael C. Campion, and Sherry M. B. Thatcher, "Transactive Memory Systems in Context: A Meta-Analytic Examination of Contextual Factors in Transactive Memory Systems Development and Team Performance," *Journal of Applied Psychology* 104 (2019): 464–93.

9. Ali E. Akgun and Gary S. Lynn, "New Product Development Team Improvisation and Speed-to-Market: An Extended Model," *European Journal of Innovation Management* 5 (2002): 117–29; Kyle Lewis, Donald Lange, and Lynette Gillis, "Transactive Memory Systems, Learning, and Learning Transfer," *Organization Science* 16 (2005): 581–98; Yanfeng Zheng and Yiyuan Mai, "A Contextualized Transactive Memory System View on How Founding Teams Respond to Surprises: Evidence from China," *Strategic Entrepreneurship Journal* 7 (2013): 197–213.

10. Suy Young Choi, Heeseok Lee, and Youngjin Yoo, "The Impact of Information Technology and Transactive Memory Systems on Knowledge Sharing, Application, and Team Performance: A Field Study," *MIS Quarterly* 34 (2010): 855–70.

11. "Interview with Wynton Marsalis Musical Director, Trumpet," *PBS Live from Lincoln Center*, July 1, 1998, https://wyntonmarsalis.org/news/entry/interview-with-wynton-marsalis-musical-director-trumpet.

12. John R. Austin, "Transactive Memory in Organizational Groups: The Effects of Content, Consensus, Specialization, and Accuracy on Group Performance," *Journal of Applied Psychology* 88 (2003): 866–78.

13. Amanda Van Nuys, "New LinkedIn Research: Upskill Your Employees with the Skills Companies Need Most in 2020," *LinkedIn Learning Blog*, December 28, 2019, https://www.linkedin.com/business/learning/blog/learning-and-development/most-in-demand-skills-2020.

14. Sun Young Sung and Jin Nam Choi, "Effects of Team Knowledge Management on the Creativity and Financial Performance of Organizational Teams," *Organizational Behavior and Human Decision Processes* 118 (2012): 4–13; Laurence G. Weinzimmer, Eric J. Michel, and Jennifer L. Franczak, "Creativity and Firm-Level Performance: The Mediating Effects of Action Orientation," *Journal of Managerial Issues* 23 (2011): 62–82; Seung-Bum Yang and Sang Ok Choi, "Employee Empowerment and Team Performance: Autonomy, Responsibility, Information, and Creativity," *Team Performance Management* 15 (2009): 289–301; Seung Won Yoon, Ji Hoon Song, Doo Hun Lim, and Baek-Kyoo Joo, "Structural Determinants of Team Performance: The Mutual Influences of Learning Culture, Creativity, and Knowledge," *Human Resource Development International* 13 (2010): 249–64.

15. Astrid C. Homan, Claudia Buengeler, Robert A. Eckhoff, Wendy P. van Ginkel, and Sven C. Voelpel, "The Interplay of Diversity Training and Diversity Beliefs on Team Creativity in Nationality Diverse Teams," *Journal of Applied Psychology* 100 (2015): 1456–67; Holly K. Osborn and Michael D. Mumford, "Creativity and Planning: Training

Interventions to Develop Creative Problem-Solving Skills," *Creativity Research Journal* 18 (2006): 173–90; Ginamarie Scott, Lyle E. Lerizt, and Michael D. Mumford, "The Effectiveness of Creativity Training: A Quantitative Review," *Creativity Research Journal* 16 (2004): 361–88.

16. Yingjie Yuan and Daan van Knippenberg, "From Member Creativity to Team Creativity? Team Information Elaboration as Moderator of the Additive and Disjunctive Models," *PLOS One* 15 (2020): 2.

17. Gwen M. Wittenbaum, Anne P. Hubbell, and Cynthia Zuckerman, "Mutual Enhancement: Toward an Understanding of the Collective Preference for Shared Information," *Journal of Personality and Social Psychology* 77 (1999): 967–78.

18. Julia Lee Cunningham, Francesca Gino, Daniel Cable, and Bradley Staats, "Seeing Oneself as a Valued Contributor: Social Worth Affirmation Improves Team Information Sharing," *Academy of Management Journal* 64 (2021): 1816–41.

19. Jia Li, Meir Shemla, and Jurgen Wegge, "The Preventative Benefit of Group Diversification on Group Performance Decline: An Investigation with Latent Growth Models," *Journal of Organizational Behavior* 42 (2020): 332–48.

20. Inga J. Hoever, Daan van Knippenberg, Wendy P. van Ginkel, and Harry G. Barkema, "Fostering Team Creativity: Perspective Taking as Key to Unlocking Diversity's Potential," *Journal of Applied Psychology* 97 (2012): 982–96.

21. Hoever et al., "Fostering Team Creativity."

22. Sharon K. Parker and Carolyn M. Axtell, "Seeing Another Viewpoint: Antecedents and Outcomes of Employee Perspective Taking," *Academy of Management Journal* 44 (2001): 1085–1100.

23. Astrid C. Homan, Daan van Knippenberg, Gerben A. Can Kleef, and Carsten K. W. De Dreu, "Bridging Faultlines by Valuing Diversity: Diversity Beliefs, Information Elaboration, and Performance in Diverse Work Groups," *Journal of Applied Psychology* 92 (2007): 1189–99.

24. Daan van Knippenberg, S. Alexander Haslam, and Michael J. Platow, "Unity through Diversity: Value-in-Diversity Beliefs as Moderator of the Relationship between Work Group Diversity and Group Identification" (paper presented at the nineteenth annual conference of the Society for Industrial and Organizational Psychology, Chicago, 2004).

25. Roger Mayer, Richard S. Warr, and Jing Zhao, "Do Pro-Diversity Policies Improve Corporate Innovation?," *Financial Management* 47 (2018): 617–50.

26. Jennifer Liu, "These Are the Best CEOs for Diversity, According to Employee Reviews," *CNBC*, July 20, 2020, https://www.cnbc.com/2020/07/20/the-best-ceos-for-diversity-according-to-comparably-employee-reviews.html.

27. Astrid C. Homan, John R. Hollenbeck, Stephen E. Humphrey, Daan van Knippenberg, Daniel R. Ilgen, and Gerben A. Van Kleef, "Facing Differences with an Open Mind: Openness to Experience, Salience of Intragroup Differences, and Performance of Diverse Work Groups," *Academy of Management Journal* 51 (2008): 1204–22.

28. Jacquelyn S. DeMatteo, Lillian T. Eby, and Eric Sundstrom, "Team-Based Rewards: Current Empirical Evidence," *Research in Organizational Behavior* 20 (1998): 141–83.

29. Anne Field, "Are You Rewarding Solo Performance at the Team's Expense?," *Harvard Management Update*, August 1, 2006, https://hbsp.harvard.edu/product/U0608A-PDF-ENG; Steven Kerr, "On the Folly of Rewarding A, While Hoping for B," *Academy of Management Journal* 18 (1975): 769–83.

30. Alex F. Osborn, *Applied Imagination*, 2nd ed. (New York: Scribner, 1957); Robert I. Sutton and Andrew Hargadon, "Brainstorming Groups in Context: Effectiveness in a Product Design Firm," *Administrative Science Quarterly* 41 (1996): 685–718.

31. "7 Simple Rules of Brainstorming," *IDEO Blog*, https://www.ideou.com/blogs/inspiration/7-simple-rules-of-brainstorming.

32. "7 Simple Rules of Brainstorming," *IDEO U* (blog), https://www.ideou.com/blogs/inspiration/7-simple-rules-of-brainstorming.

33. Kris Byron, "Creative Reflections on Brainstorming," *London Review of Education* 10 (2012): 201–13; Donald Taylor, Paul C. Berry, and Clifford H. Block, "Does Group Participation When Using Brainstorming Facilitator Inhibit Creative Thinking?," *Administrative Science Quarterly* 6 (1958): 22–47.

34. Brian J. Lucas and Loran F. Nordgren, "People Underestimate the Value of Persistence for Creative Performance," *Journal of Personality and Social Psychology* 109 (2015): 232–43.

35. Loran F. Nordgren and Brian J. Lucas, "Your Best Ideas Are Often Your Last Ideas," *Harvard Business Review*, January 26, 2021, https://hbr.org/2021/01/your-best-ideas-are-often-your-last-ideas.

36. Mary J. Waller, "The Timing of Adaptive Group Responses to Nonroutine Events," *Academy of Management Journal* 42 (1999): 127–37.

37. Daniel Isenberg and Alessandro Di Fiore, "You Don't Have to Pivot in a Crisis," *Harvard Business Review*, September 21, 2020, https://hbr.org/2020/09/you-dont-have-to-pivot-in-a-crisis.

38. Adam C. Stoverink, Cody Bradley, Michael Johnson, Bradley L. Kirkman, and Travis M. Maynard, "Bouncing Back by Pushing Forward: Balanced Reflexivity and Team Persistence in the Face of Adversity" (paper presented at the eightieth annual meeting of the Academy of Management, August 2020).

CHAPTER 6

1. Amy Edmondson, "Psychological Safety and Learning Behavior in Teams," *Administrative Science Quarterly* 44 (1999): 350–83.

2. Cody Bradley, Adam C. Stoverink, Bradley L. Kirkman, and Marilla Kingsley, "Building Resilience through Vulnerability: The Effects of Team Disclosure and Team Cohesion on Resilient Team Performance" (working paper).

3. Nancy L. Collins and Lynn C. Miller, "Self-Disclosure and Liking: A Meta-Analytic Review," *Psychological Bulletin* 116 (1994): 457–75.

4. James E. Driskell, Eduardo Salas, and Joan Jolinnston, "Does Stress Lead to a Loss of Team Perspective?," *Group Dynamics: Theory, Research, and Practice* 3 (1999): 291–302; Alexander P. J. Ellis, "System Breakdown: The Role of Mental Models and

Transactive Memory in the Relationship between Acute Stress and Team Performance," *Academy of Management Journal* 49 (2006): 576–89.

5. Edmondson, "Psychological Safety and Learning Behavior in Teams."

6. Bret H. Bradley, Bennett E. Postlethwaite, Anthony C. Klotz, Maria R. Hamdani, and Kenneth G. Brown, "Reaping the Benefits of Task Conflict in Teams: The Critical Role of Team Psychological Safety Climate," *Journal of Applied Psychology* 97 (2012): 151–58.

7. Cristina B. Gibson and Jennifer L. Gibbs, "Unpacking the Concept of Virtuality: The Effects of Geographic Dispersion, Electronic Dependence, Dynamic Structure, and Nationality Diversity on Team Innovation," *Administrative Science Quarterly* 51 (2006): 451–95.

8. M. Lance Frazier, Stav Fainschmidt, Ryan L. Klinger, Amir Pezeshkan, and Vaselina Vracheva, "Psychological Safety: A Meta-Analytic Review and Extension," *Personnel Psychology* 70 (2017): 113–65.

9. Barbara L. Fredrickson, "Positive Emotions Broaden and Build," *Advances in Experimental Social Psychology* 47 (2013): 1–53; Barbara L. Fredrickson, "The Role of Positive Emotions in Positive Psychology: The Broaden-and-Build Theory of Positive Emotions," *American Psychologist* 56 (2001): 218–26.

10. Laura Delizonna, "High-Performing Teams Need Psychological Safety. Here's How to Create It," *Harvard Business Review*, August 24, 2017, https://hbr.org/2017/08/high-performing-teams-need-psychological-safety-heres-how-to-create-it.

11. Charles Duhigg, "What Google Learned from Its Quest to Build the Perfect Team," *New York Times Magazine*, February 25, 2016, https://www.nytimes.com/2016/02/28/magazine/what-google-learned-from-its-quest-to-build-the-perfect-team.html.

12. Jennifer Alsever, Jessi Hempel, Alex Taylor III, and Daniel Roberts, "6 Great Teams That Take Care of Business," *Fortune*, April 10, 2014, https://fortune.com/2014/04/10/6-great-teams-that-take-care-of-business/amp/.

13. Kutsko Consulting, "What We Can Learn about Psychological Safety from Pixar," 2022, https://www.kutskoconsulting.com/blog/what-we-can-learn-about-psychological-safety-from-pixar.

14. Amy C. Edmondson, *The Fearless Organization: Creating Psychological Safety in the Workplace for Learning, Innovative, and Growth* (San Francisco: Jossey-Bass, 2018).

15. Kutsko Consulting, "What We Can Learn about Psychological Safety from Pixar," 2022, https://www.kutskoconsulting.com/blog/what-we-can-learn-about-psychological-safety-from-pixar.

16. Aaron De Smet, Kim Rubenstein, Gunnar Schrah, Mike Vierow, and Amy Edmondson, "Psychological Safety and the Critical Role of Leadership Development," *McKinsey & Company*, February 11, 2021, https://www.mckinsey.com/business-functions/organization/our-insights/psychological-safety-and-the-critical-role-of-leadership-development.

17. Jason Nazar, "20 Leadership Lessons with ZipRecruiter Co-Founder and CEO Ian Siegel," *Entrepreneur*, May 10, 2021, https://www.entrepreneur.com/article/369331.

18. Amy C. Edmondson, "Strategies for Learning from Failure," *Harvard Business Review*, April 2011; Sim B. Sitkin, "Learning through Failure: The Strategy of Small Losses," *Research in Organizational Behavior* 14 (1992): 231–66.

19. Amy C. Edmondson and Per Hugander, "4 Steps to Boost Psychological Safety at Your Workplace," *Harvard Business Review*, June 22, 2021, https://hbr.org/2021/06/4-steps-to-boost-psychological-safety-at-your-workplace.

20. Frazier et al., "Psychological Safety."

21. Byung-Jik Kim, Sungjin Park, and Tae-Hyun Kim, "The Effect of Transformational Leadership on Team Creativity: Sequential Mediating Effect of Employee's Psychological Safety and Creativity," *Asian Journal of Technology Innovation* 27 (2019): 90–107.

22. Stephen K. Kumako and Maxwell A. Asumeng, "Transformational Leadership as a Moderator of the Relationship between Psychological Safety and Learning Behaviour in Work Teams in Ghana," *South African Journal of Industrial Psychology* 39 (2013): 1–9.

23. Elizabeth Raes, Stefan Decuyper, Bart Lismont, Piet Van den Bossche, Eva Kyndt, Sybille Demeyere, and Filip Dochy, "Facilitating Team Learning through Transformational Leadership," *Instructional Science* 41 (2013): 287–305.

24. Jon Krakauer, *Into Thin Air: A Personal Account of the Mount Everest Disaster* (New York: Anchor Books, 1997).

25. Krakauer, "Into Thin Air."

26. Katie Burke, "Great Leaders Do These 3 Things to Foster Psychological Safety," *Inc. Magazine*, February 27, 2021, https://www.inc.com/katie-burke/great-leaders-do-these-3-things-to-foster-psychological-safety.html.

27. Brené Brown, *Daring Greatly: How the Courage to Be Vulnerable Transforms the Way We Live, Love, Parent, and Lead* (New York: Avery Publishing, 2012).

28. John E. Mathieu and Tammy L. Rapp, "Laying the Foundation for Successful Team Performance Trajectories: The Roles of Team Charters and Performance Strategies," *Journal of Applied Psychology* 94 (2009): 90–103.

29. Nancy L. Wilkinson and John W. Moran, "Team Charter," *TQM Magazine* 10 (1998): 355–61.

30. Mike Carlin, "How Do You Talk about Culture, Diversity, and Inclusion with a Global Team: Five Questions with Abhijit Dasgupta," LinkedIn, September 10, 2020, https://www.linkedin.com/pulse/how-do-you-talk-culture-diversity-inclusion-global-team-mike-carlin/.

31. Kim Scott, *Radical Candor: How to Get What You Want by Saying What You Mean* (London: Pan Books, 2019).

32. Josh Vaisman, "Building Psychological Safety," American Animal Hospital Association, August 6, 2020, https://www.aaha.org/publications/newstat/articles/2020-08/Building-psychological-safety/.

33. Lauren Joseph, "Is Your Team in 'Psychological Danger'?," *Forbes*, April 12, 2016, https://www.forbes.com/sites/worldeconomicforum/2016/04/12/is-your-team-in-psychological-danger/?sh=249b67735569.

34. Shane Snow, "How Psychological Safety Actually Works," *Forbes*, May 4, 2020,

https://www.forbes.com/sites/shanesnow/2020/05/04/how-psychological-safety-actually-works/?sh=466d3cf9f864.

35. Frazier et al., "Psychological Safety."

36. James N. Kurtessis, Robert Eisenberger, Michael T. Ford, Louis C. Buffardi, Kathleen A. Stewart, and Cory S. Adis, "Perceived Organizational Support: A Meta-Analytic Evaluation of Organizational Support Theory," *Journal of Management* 43 (2017): 1854–84.

37. De Smet et al., "Psychological Safety and the Critical Role of Leadership Development."

CHAPTER 7

1. Amy C. Edmondson and Tomas Chamorro-Premuzic, "Today's Leaders Need Vulnerability, Not Bravado," *Harvard Business Review*, October 19, 2020, https://hbr.org/2020/10/todays-leaders-need-vulnerability-not-bravado.

2. Mary J. Waller, "The Timing of Adaptive Group Responses to Nonroutine Events," *Academy of Management Journal* 42 (1999): 127–37.

3. Cindi Pearce, "Definition of 'Team Morale'" *Career Trend*, October 11, 2019, https://careertrend.com/about-6682854-definition—team-morale-.html

4. Patricia L. Costa, Ana M. Passos, and Arnold B. Bakker, "Team Work Engagement: A Model of Emergence," *Journal of Occupational and Organizational Psychology* 87 (2014): 414–36; Stanley M. Gully, Kara A. Incalcaterra, Aparna Joshi, and J. Matthew Beaubien, "A Meta-Analysis of Team-Efficacy, Potency, and Performance: Interdependence and Level of Analysis as Moderators of Observed Relationships," *Journal of Applied Psychology* 87 (2002): 819–32.

5. Bradley L. Kirkman, Ning Li, Xiaoming Zheng, T. Brad Harrs, and Xin Liu, "Teamwork Works Best When Top Performers Are Rewarded," *Harvard Business Review*, March 14, 2016, https://hbr.org/2016/03/teamwork-works-best-when-top-performers-are-rewarded.

6. Michelle A. Marks, John E. Mathieu, and Stephen J. Zaccaro, "A Temporally Based Framework and Taxonomy of Team Processes," *Academy of Management Review* 26 (2001): 356–76.

7. On taking time to learn together, see Christopher W. Wiese, C. Shawn Burke, Yichen Tang, Claudia Hernandez, and Ryan Howell, "Team Learning Behaviors and Performance: A Meta-Analysis of Direct Effects and Moderators," *Group & Organization Management* 47 (2022): 571–611. On debriefing, see Shmuel Ellis and Inbar Davidi, "After-Event Reviews: Drawing Lessons from Successful and Failed Experience," *Journal of Applied Psychology* 90 (2005): 857–71; Scott I. Tannenbaum and Christopher P. Cerasoli, "Do Team and Individual Debriefs Enhance Performance? A Meta-Analysis." *Human Factors* 55 (2013): 231–45.

8. Bob Frisch and Cary Greene, "Don't End a Meeting Without Doing These 3 Things," *Harvard Business Review*, April 26, 2016, https://hbr.org/2016/04/dont-end-a-meeting-without-doing-these-3-things.

CHAPTER 8

1. Virginia Brandt, William England, and Susan Ward, "Virtual Teams," *Research Technology Management* 54 (2011): 62–63.

2. Kristen M. Shockley, Allison S. Gabriel, Daron Robertson, Christopher C. Rosen, Nitya Chawla, Mahira L. Ganster, and Maira E. Ezerins. "The Fatiguing Effects of Camera Use in Virtual Meetings: A Within-Person Field Experiment," *Journal of Applied Psychology* 106 (2021): 1137–55.

3. Shockley et al., "Fatiguing Effects."

4. Timothy Bromley, Taylor Lauricella, and Bill Schaninger, "Making Work Meaningful from the C-Suite to the Frontline," McKinsey & Company, June 28, 2021, https://www.mckinsey.com/business-functions/organization/our-insights/the-organization-blog/making-work-meaningful-from-the-c-suite-to-the-frontline.

5. Bradley L. Kirkman, Benson Rosen, Cristina B. Gibson, Paul E. Tesluk, and Simon O. McPherson, "Five Challenges to Virtual Team Success: Lessons from Sabre, Inc.," *Academy of Management Executive* 16 (2002): 67–79.

6. Bradley L. Kirkman, Benson Rosen, Paul E. Tesluk, and Cristina B. Gibson, "The Impact of Team Empowerment on Virtual Team Performance: The Moderating Role of Face-to Face Interaction," *Academy of Management Journal* 47 (2004): 175–92.

7. N. Sharon Hill and Kathryn M. Bartol, "Empowering Leadership and Effective Collaboration in Geographically Dispersed Teams," *Personnel Psychology* 69 (2016): 159–98.

8. Stefano Ruggieri, "Leadership in Virtual Teams: A Comparison of Transformational and Transactional Leaders," *Social Behavior and Personality* 37 (2009): 1017–22.

9. Radostina K. Purvanova and Joyce E. Bono, "Transformational Leadership in Context: Face-to-Face and Virtual Teams," *Leadership Quarterly* 20 (2009): 343–57.

10. Payal Sharma, Lauren D'Innocenzo, and Bradley L. Kirkman, "Why Leaders Resist Empowering Virtual Teams," *Sloan Management Review* 63 (2021): 78–84.

11. Martin Hoegl and Miriam Müthel, "Enabling Shared Leadership in Virtual Project Teams: A Practitioner's Guide," *Project Management Journal* 47 (2016): 7–12; Miriam S. Müthel, S. Gehrlein, and Martin Hoegl, "Socio-Demographic Factors and Shared Leadership Behaviors in Dispersed Teams: Implications for Human Resource Management," *Human Resource Management* 51 (2012): 525–48.

12. Sharma et al., "Why Leaders Resist Empowering Virtual Teams."

13. Terry L. Griffith and Margaret A. Neale, "Information Processing in Traditional, Hybrid, and Virtual Teams: From Nascent Knowledge to Transactive Memory," *Research in Organizational Behavior* 23 (2001): 379–421.

14. Terry L. Griffith, John E. Sawyer, and Margaret A. Neale, "Virtualness and Knowledge: Managing the Love Triangle of Organizations, Individuals, and Information Technology," *MIS Quarterly* 27 (2003): 265–87; Ann Majchrzak, Ronald E. Rice, Nelson King, Arvind Malhotra, and Sulin Ba, "Computer-Mediated Inter-Organizational Knowledge-Sharing: Insights from a Virtual Team Innovating Using a Collaborative Tool," *Information Resources Management Journal* 13 (2000): 44–53.

15. Margaret Luciano, "4 Ways Managers Can Increase Flexibility without Losing Productivity," *Harvard Business Review*, February 1, 2022, https://hbr.org/2022/01/how-companies-are-using-tech-to-give-employees-more autonomy.

16. Kyle Lewis, "Knowledge and Performance in Knowledge-Worker Teams: A Longitudinal Study of Transactive Memory Systems," *Management Science* 50 (2004): 1519–33.

17. Bettina C. Riedl, Julia V. Gallenkamp, Arnold Picot, and Isabell M. Welpe, "Antecedents of Transactive Memory Systems in Virtual Teams—The Role of Communication, Culture, and Team Size" (Proceedings of the 45th Hawaii International Conference on System Sciences, 2012).

18. Youngjin Yoo and Prasert Kanawattanachai, "Developments of Transactive Memory Systems and Collective Mind in Virtual Teams," *International Journal of Organizational Analysis* 9 (2001): 187–208.

19. Yide Shen, "Transactive Memory System Development in Virtual Teams: The Potential Role of Shared Identity and Shared Context" (Proceedings of the 2007 SIGMIS Computers and People Research Conference, April, St. Louis, MO, 2007).

20. Leigh Thompson, *Creative Conspiracy: The New Rules of Breakthrough Collaboration* (Boston: Harvard Business Review Press, 2013).

21. Wolfgang Stroebe and Michael Diehl, "Why Groups Are Less Effective Than Their Members: On Productivity Losses in Idea-Generating Groups," *European Review of Social Psychology* 5 (1994): 271–303.

22. Leigh Thompson, "Virtual Collaboration Won't Be the Death of Creativity," *MIT Sloan Management Review* 62 (2021): 42–46.

23. Thompson, "Virtual Collaboration."

24. Thompson, "Virtual Collaboration."

25. Jill Nemiro, "The Building Blocks for Creativity in Virtual Teams," in *Higher Creativity for Virtual Teams: Developing Platforms for Co-Creation*, ed. Steven P. Macgregor and Teresa Torres-Coronas, 98–121 (Hershey, NY: Information Science Reference, 2007).

26. Nemiro, "Building Blocks."

27. John Suler, "The Online Disinhibition Effect," *CyberPsychology and Behavior* 7 (2004): 321–26.

28. Lile Jia, Edward R. Hirt, and Samuel C. Karpen. "Lessons from a Faraway Land: The Effect of Spatial Distance on Creative Cognition," *Journal of Experimental Social Psychology* 45 (2009): 1127–31.

29. Jill E. Nemiro, "The Creative Process in Virtual Teams," *Creativity Research Journal* 14 (2002): 69–83.

30. Alexandra Lechner and Jutta Tobias Mortlock, "How to Create Psychological Safety in Virtual Teams," *Organizational Dynamics* 50 (2021).

31. Lechner and Mortlock, "How to Create Psychological Safety."

32. Lechner and Mortlock, "How to Create Psychological Safety."

33. Lechner and Mortlock, "How to Create Psychological Safety."

34. Amy C. Edmondson and Mark Mortensen. "What Psychological Safety Looks Like in a Hybrid Workplace," *Harvard Business Review*, April 19, 2021, https://hbr.org/2021/04/what-psychological-safety-looks-like-in-a-hybrid-workplace.

35. Bobbi Thomason and Jennifer Franczak, "3 Tensions Leaders Need to

Manage in the Hybrid Workplace," *Harvard Business Review*, February 3, 2022, https://hbr.org/2022/02/3-tensions-leaders-need-to-manage-in-the-hybrid-workplace.

36. Lindsey Trimble O'Connor and Erin A. Cech, "Not Just a Mother's Problem: The Consequences of Perceived Workplace Flexibility Bias for All Workers," *Sociological Perspectives* 61 (2018): 808–29.

37. Lechner and Mortlock, "How to Create Psychological Safety"; Nemiro, "Creative Process in Virtual Teams."

38. Edmondsen and Mortensen, "What Psychological Safety Looks Like in a Hybrid Workplace."

39. Thomason and Franczak, "3 Tensions Leaders Need."

40. Adam Smiley Poswolsky, "How Leaders Can Build Connection in a Disconnected Workplace," *Harvard Business Review*, January 21, 2022, https://hbr.org/2022/01/how-leaders-can-build-connection-in-a-disconnected-workplace.

41. Lechner and Mortlock, "How to Create Psychological Safety."

42. Amy C. Edmondson and Gene Daley. "How to Foster Psychological Safety in Virtual Meetings," *Harvard Business Review*, August 25, 2020, https://hbr.org/2020/08/how-to-foster-psychological-safety-in-virtual-meetings.

43. Jeremy N. Bailenson, "Nonverbal Overload: A Theoretical Argument for the Causes of Zoom Fatigue," *Technology, Mind, and Behavior* 2 (2021): https://doi.org/10.1037/tmb0000030.

44. Jim Keane and Todd Heiser. "4 Strategies for Building a Hybrid Workplace that Works," *Harvard Business Review*, July 22, 2021, https://hbr.org/2021/07/4-strategies-for-building-a-hybrid-workplace-that-works.

45. Antonia Bowring, "Four Tips for Successful Hybrid Meetings," *Forbes*, November 8, 2021, https://www.forbes.com/sites/forbescoachescouncil/2021/11/08/four-tips-for-successful-hybrid-meetings; Bob Frisch and Cary Greene, "What It Takes to Run a Great Hybrid Meeting," *Harvard Business Review*, June 3, 2021, https://hbr.org/2021/06/what-it-takes-to-run-a-great-hybrid-meeting; Michael Peachey, "9 Tips and Tools for Effectively Managing Your Hybrid Meetings," *Fast Company*, July 30, 2021, https://www.fastcompany.com/90660340/9-tips-and-tools-for-effectively-managing-your-hybrid-meetings.

46. M. Lance Frazier, Stav Fainschmidt, Ryan L. Klinger, Amir Pezeshkan, and Vaselina Vracheva, "Psychological Safety: A Meta-Analytic Review and Extension," *Personnel Psychology* 70 (2017): 113–65.

CONCLUSION

1. Richard A. Guzzo, Paul R. Yost, Richard J. Campbell, and Gregory P. Shea, "Potency in Groups: Articulating a Construct," *British Journal of Social Psychology* 32 (1993): 87–106.

2. Dusya Vera and Mary Crossan, "Improvisation and Innovative Performance in Teams," *Organization Science* 16 (2005): 203–24.

3. Amy Edmondson, "Psychological Safety and Learning Behavior in Teams," *Administrative Science Quarterly* 44 (1999): 350–83.

INDEX